CW00739402

THREE TUDOR SURVEYS

THREE TUDOR SURVEYS

THE DORSET MANORS OF SIR THOMAS KITSON:
OKEFORD FITZPAINE, DURWESTON CUM KNIGHTON
AND LYTCHETT MINSTER,

1584 – 1585

Edited by
JUNE PALMER

Foreword by
J.H. BETTEY

June Palmer

DORSET RECORD SOCIETY
VOLUME 18

© Dorset Record Society 2015

Published 2015 by Dorset Record Society
Dorset History Centre, Bridport Road, Dorchester, Dorset DT1 1RP

General Editor Dr Mark Forrest

All rights reserved. No part of this publication may be reproduced, in any form or by
any means, without permission from the publishers.

Typeset in ITC New Baskerville by John Chandler,
and printed by Henry Ling Ltd., The Dorset Press, Dorchester, Dorset
on Chromomat 100 gsm.
Cover case bound in Wibalin over 3mm boards

British Library Cataloguing in Publication Data:
A catalogue record for this book is available from the British Library.

ISBN 978-0-900339-21-9

CONTENTS

ACKNOWLEDGEMENTS

I came to live in Lytchett Minster in Dorset in 2003 after spending the previous forty years in Cornwall where I became involved in the study of local history. My particular interest was in the structure and development of towns and other communities from c 1600- c 1850 and in the people who lived in them, a process which my tutor and friend, Veronica Chesher, described as a process of 'putting people into place'. I was therefore pleased to find, from the catalogue in the Dorset History Centre to the documents which the Lees family had kindly given to the Dorset History Centre, a reference to a survey of 1584 for Lytchett Minster which appeared could be a useful starting point for my own parish.

This document is in abbreviated Latin and, as I had previously worked mostly with documents later than this and I had not used the Latin I learnt at school in the 1940s for many years. I therefore required assistance.. I was fortunate to receive expert help and encouragement from Dr Mark Forrest of the Dorset History Centre, who has given up many hours of his time to this project, including the laborious jobs of reordering the many maps so that they could be used clearly in the text. The staff of the Dorset History Centre too have always been very kind and helpful to an aged researcher as myself. I would also like to thank the staff at the Suffolk and Hertfordshire Record Offices and Mrs Christine Hiskey, archivist to the Holkham Estate.

When the possibility of publication of the survey was suggested it was thought that more than one manor should be included. We discovered that there were not only other contemporary documents for Lytchett Minster in the Suffolk archives at Bury St Edmunds, but also documents referring to two other manors in Dorset: Durweston cum Knighton and Okeford Fitzpaine, owned by Sir Thomas Kitson of Hengrave Hall in Suffolk, who was also the lord of the manor of Bere cum Lytchett Minster in 1584. Among these was another survey, with the same date of 1584, for Okeford Fitzpaine, and a map for Durweston from the same period. Several trips have had to be made, mostly by Mark, to bring back for use in Dorset copies of as many of these documents as possible from Suffolk as well as from the archives at Holkham Hall where a third survey, that of Durweston cum Knighton, was discovered, and also to Hertfordshire and to the National Archives for other vital documents. The help of the staff of the above Record Offices is greatly appreciated and in particular that of the West Suffolk Record Office who have been required to produce a large number of documents for photographing. The Hengrave archive at the West Suffolk Record Office is very large and complex and therefore I am not certain that everything relevant has been uncovered. Some of the most important documents, which initially did not appear to refer to Dorset, and have necessitated the rewriting of much of the text in order to answer the basic question of why the surveys were written. I must emphasise that this is a study of three Dorset manors; it is not a study of all the many manors owned by the Kitson family which would be a large undertaking. It would be of great interest if someone undertook this, and of especial interest to me if a study of Ipplepen and Torbryan in Devon were made.

I am grateful for the help received from my U3A Lytchett Minster History Group especially in correcting mistakes I have made as a newcomer. The help of one of their members, June King, (neé Palmer), the author of the popular book *Memoirs of a Dorset Parish. Bygone Lytchett Minster* has been very much welcome. I would like to thank my neighbour, Brian Cooper for all the help he has given my family for many years, both practical and with information.

Due to my lack of transport and difficulty in exploring the countryside, I am grateful to my sons, Colin and Gerald when they visit Dorset, for driving me to Okeford Fitzpaine and Durweston and taking photographs to help my later recognition of the buildings. I have been to these two villages, in which I am so interested, much less frequently than should be necessary which I regret greatly. The maps and documents in the Pitt-Rivers collection at the Dorset History Centre have also been invaluable and great thanks should be given to the members of that family who have transferred so many documents to the Centre.

I appreciate the help of Dr. Oliver Padel with a query over any special meaning of some Latin text and also my daughter in law, Susan Palmer, archivist at the Sir John Soane museum, for help on other text. I appreciate too the observations of Dr Joanna Mattingly and other friends and colleagues in Cornwall, in particular Veronica Chesher, for their help and interest over the years. I am grateful to Mrs Ryall of Durweston for her help with the history of that parish.

I would like to reiterate my thanks to Mark and express the pleasure I have had in the long discussions that I have much enjoyed with him over the long period that this book has come to fruition.

June Palmer

FOREWORD

by J. H. Bettey

This volume is based on surveys of the manors of Okeford Fitzpaine, Durweston cum Knighton and Lytchett Minster which were produced during 1584-5. Manorial surveys are a rewarding source for many aspects of local history. They not only provide detailed accounts of tenements, tenants and land tenure which was their main purpose, but also contain a wealth of genealogical information, early forms of place and field names, details of houses, farming practice, landscape and inclosure. Dorset was dominated by great estates, many with non-resident landowners, including the three manors which are the subject of this volume. Manorial control over tenant farmers remained strong and landowners were dependent upon reliable stewards for the efficient management of the affairs of each manor through the manorial courts. The manors discussed in this volume were bought during the 16th century by the Suffolk merchant and landowner, Sir Thomas Kitson. Like many others, the Kitson family acquired their Dorset lands in the great land sales which followed the dissolution of the monasteries. Since so much of the land in Dorset had formerly been monastic, the dissolution brought a large influx of new landowning families.

For landowners occasional surveys were essential for maintaining their knowledge of the tenants and tenements on each manor. By far the most common tenure throughout Dorset was copyhold whereby tenants held their land during the lives generally of three named persons, holding successively. The evidence of their title was a copy of the entry in the court book or roll. Copyhold tenants paid a low or nominal rent, and a large fine at entry or when a new name was added. The main part of the landlord's income from each manor depended on noting the death of tenants, and on large estates, such as those in Dorset, where the steward was responsible for the oversight of several manors, he depended on the evidence given by the jury at the manorial court. An important feature of the tenure was that it was subject to the customary law of each manor, and since these customs often varied from one manor to another, there was great variety in the rights and obligations of copyholders. From the mid-16th century manorial surveys became increasingly valuable since a new breed of professional surveyors emerged, with improved methods and newly-developed equipment. The three surveys in this volume were made by Thomas Wright who was an experienced surveyor. He would have based his work mainly on previous manorial records and the information he extracted from the tenants' copies of court rolls together with the evidence given under oath by a jury of the most trustworthy tenants. As John Norden, a leading surveyor of the period expressed it 'The Lords records and the Tennants information are the pillars of a survey'.

The task which confronted the Editor, June Palmer, in producing a full translation and transcript of these surveys was formidable. Apart from their length, they were written in the heavily abbreviated Latin of the Tudor period while the handwriting presented an additional difficulty. Her achievement is evident from the illustrations of some of the original pages which are reproduced in this volume. The originals are in different places which has added to the problems. In addition she has written an informative Introduction with a careful analysis of the contents of these surveys and has incorporated evidence drawn from other sources. It is a measure of the detail contained in the surveys that she has been able to produce perambulations of each manor, showing the layout of the settlements, with details of tenants, streets, roads, fields and grazing land. A feature of the surveys which emerges from the analysis is that the two manors of Okeford Fitzpaine and Durweston cum Knighton are different in many ways from Lytchett Minster. The first two have their lands stretching from the meadows by the Stour up to the high downland in the traditional 'sheep and corn' situation of the central Dorset chalkland, while the third manor, Lychett Minster, lies on much poorer soil with more than half being heath producing only poor grazing or peat and furze.

At Okeford Fitzpaine and Durweston settlement was concentrated in nuclear villages, although the situation at Durweston was complicated by the fact that it had been amalgamated with the manor of Knighton in 1381. The contrast with Lychett Minster is shown most clearly in the extent of inclosure. This was to be a major feature of the chalkland area during the 17th century and had already been completed at Okeford Fitzpaine where no common arable fields remained in 1584. This inclosure had been accomplished by a carefully-planned process of agreement between tenants and the manorial steward. Each tenement had the arable land inclosed into discrete fields with deliberately arranged access to each, while the downland grazing for the sheep flocks was to remain open for many decades. Durweston cum Knighton still had many of its strip fields in 1585, but these were rapidly being replaced by inclosures. At Lytchett Minster, however, inclosure was not carried out until the 19th century. The Introduction shows the way in which the chalkland inclosures were carried out and the profound effect which this had on the landscape.

Sheep were an essential feature of chalkland farming since the dung provided by the sheepfold was essential for producing viable crops of wheat and barley on the thin chalk soils. Very large numbers of sheep were kept on other chalkland manors, although there is no evidence of specified limits for sheep grazing on the downland in these surveys. There is, however, a detailed grazing calendar for the sheep flocks at Durweston. The Durweston survey also provides evidence of the importance of the manorial mill where tenants would have been obliged to have their corn ground. Evidence is given of the high entry fine and rental for the mill and of the high cost of its maintenance. A few tenants were still obliged to render labour services on the demesne farm, and the Durweston survey shows that seven tenants each remained liable to provide three days work a year, while at Knighton the tenants claimed the right to a dinner provided by the lord at Christmas. The surveys provide invaluable evidence of the trend which was to be repeated across the Dorset chalklands of inclosure and the amalgamation of holdings. They illustrate the overwhelming importance of agriculture in the economy of all three manors, and give little indication of work outside farming, although no doubt some tenants had by-employment as craftsmen or day labourers. Particularly impressive is the evidence of careful and precise measurement of inclosures and meadow land, while at Durweston even common grazing land is carefully measured. The collection of so much information, the examination of documents, taking evidence given under oath by tenants and all the necessary measurement must have been time-consuming and expensive, but such surveys were meant to last and be used by stewards and manorial officials for many years.

In some ways copyhold tenants were in a favourable position in relation to their landlord. They had low annual rents and while any of the persons named in their tenancy agreements remained alive they had security of tenure. Writing in 1630 the eminent judge and former attorney-general, Sir Edward Coke, in his book The Complete Copyholder could declare that as long as the copyholder fulfilled the terms of his tenure 'then let the Lord frown, the Copyholder cares not, knowing himself safe, and not within any danger …… Time hath dealt very favourably with Copyholders in divers respects'. A different impression of the life of tenant farmers such as those listed in these surveys is obtained when the number of tenements held by widows is considered. Manorial custom on most Dorset manors allowed the widow to retain full possession of the estate held by her late husband as long as she remained unmarried and chaste. The large number of widows appearing in these surveys is evidence of how many men died young. The hard life and harsh conditions endured by men farming on Dorset manors, exposed to all weathers and without adequate waterproof clothing or footwear meant that many succumbed to disease at an early age.

This is an impressive volume, the result of painstaking research and scholarly analysis. It is well-illustrated with clearly-drawn maps and examples of the original surveys. The Editor is to be warmly congratulated on her achievement which is a worthy and welcome addition to the Dorset Record Society series.

Joe Bettey
Former Reader in Local History
University of Bristol

ABBREVIATIONS, FREQUENTLY CITED SOURCES AND BIBLIOGRAPHICAL NOTES

Dorset History Centre (DHC)

D-LEE/C/5/1   Survey of Lytchett Minster cum Bere, 1584

D-PIT/P/28   Map of Okeford Fitzpaine, 1782

D-2301/M/1   Survey of Lytchett Minster, 1798

D-PIT/Acc 9202 Box 3 item 4   Particulars Okeford Fitzpaine, 19th century

T/DUR   Map of Durweston, reused as tithe map, 1801

D-CRL/B11/3/1   Survey of Lytchett Minster, 1825

PC-LMA/2/1   Inclosure map of Lytchett Matravers and Lytchett Minster, 1825

T/LMR   Tithe map Lytchett Minster, 1838-1841

T/OFP   Tithe map Okeford Fitzpaine, 1839-1840

Hertfordshire Record Office (Herts RO)

Gorhambury Collection XI/4   Surveys of Durweston cum Knighton, Lytchett Minster and Okeford Fitzpaine, *c.*1587

Holkham Hall Muniments

Survey of Durweston cum Knighton, 1585

The National Archives (TNA)

PROB 11   Various wills proved in the Prerogative Court of Canterbury.

Suffolk Record Office, Bury St Edmunds Branch (SRO)

HA/528/24   Accounts of Edward Golding, *c.*1564

449/3/26   Valuation of Lytchett Minster, 1565

HA/528/27   Notes of Thomas Golding, 1582

449/1/E3/15.53/1.1   Extracts of manor court rolls, 1569-1583

449/1/E3/155.53/3.2   Extracts court rolls, *c.*1570-1593

449/8/4   Map of Durweston cum Knighton, late 16th century

HA/528/28   Survey of Okeford Fitzpaine, 1584

HA/528/86   Rentals, various manors, 1590

449/1/E3/15.102/2.1   Survey of Durweston cum Knighton, *c.*1593

Printed Works

Hutchins. J. *The History and Antiquities of the County of Dorset* 3rd Edition, W.Shipp and J.W. Hodson, Westminster, 1874.

Mills A.D. *The Place-Names of Dorset*, vols. I-III, English Place-Name Society 1977-89

National Heritage List for England (NHLE): including listed buildings and other scheduled sites, www.historicengland.org.uk

Proceedings of the Dorset Natural History and Archaeological Society (*Proc. DNHAS*).

Taylor C., *The Making of the English Landscape: Dorset* (Wimborne, 2004).

Thorn C. and Thorn F. (eds.) *Domesday Book: Dorset* (Chichester 1983).

Bibliographical Notes

The history of the manors of Okeford Fitzpaine, Lytchett Minster and Durweston has led to widespread dispersal of the documents that record their history.

The majority are held in the Suffolk Record Office at Bury St Edmunds in the Hengrave Collection. This includes most of the steward's papers produced in the sixteenth century as well as the 1584 survey of Okeford Fitzpaine and the map of Durweston. This collection also puts the Dorset manors into a broader context and allows their management to be contrasted with that of the other parts of the estate across the country.

The Dorset History Centre holds the archives of the Lees family of Lytchett Minster which contain the 1584 survey and numerous associated title deeds. Complementary deeds have been deposited by Druce and Atlee Solicitors. The tithe maps, nineteenth century inclosure maps and estate maps for all three manors are also available.

Many Durweston documents were transferred to the National Archives after the sale of the Portman estate in 1961 and are to be found under the heading CRES for the Crown Estate Documents. Others, including the 1584 survey, are at Holkham Hall, Norfolk, in the archive of the Earl of Leicester.

A small collection of surveys and title deeds may also be found in the Hertfordshire Record Office in the Gorhambury Collection.

Mrs Palmer has deposited her research notes at the Dorset History Centre. These contain a significant amount of further detail on the sixteenth century, including copies of documents from the other repositories, and relating these documents to later maps, censuses, surveys and building records.

INTRODUCTION

The Manuscripts

This book contains transcripts of three manuscript surveys of the Dorset manors owned by Sir Thomas Kitson: Lytchett Minster cum Bere , Okeford Fitzpaine and Durweston cum Knighton.

These three documents are all written in an abbreviated Latin with occasional English annotations. The surveys of Lytchett Minster cum Bere (Dorset History Centre, D-LEE/C5/1) and Okeford Fitzpaine (Suffolk Record Office, HA/528/28) are both written on parchment, perhaps by the same scribe, in 1584. That for Durweston cum Knighton (Holkham Hall muniments) is on paper and was compiled by a different scribe the following year. The contents of each volume are discussed in their sections of the introduction. Examples of the different hands may be found on the plates in the centre of this book.

Editorial policy

The Latin text has been translated in a slightly abbreviated form, which omits some common forms and insignificant verbiage. The English sections have been transcribed retaining their original word order and spelling. As far as possible the format of the manuscripts' paragraphs, lists and headings have been retained.

Christian names have been standardised with modern spellings. Surnames have been transcribed with their original spellings. Place names have been transcribed with their original spellings with the exception of parish names which have been modernised.

Square brackets have been used to supply additional information such as modern dates, changes in the language of the manuscript, modern place names and obvious scribal errors.

Sums of money and other figures have been standardised as arabic numerals with £ *s. d.* for pounds, shillings and pence.

Areas of land are usually measured in acres, roods and perches

1 acre = 4 roods = 4840 square yards = 0.4 hectares

1 rood = 40 perches = 1210 square yards = 0.1 hectares

1 perch = 5½ square yards = 25.29 square metres

A distinction is clearly intended in all three surveys between '*clausum*', translated as 'close', referring to a piece of land enclosed sometime in the distant past, and '*inclausum*', translated as 'inclosure', referring to a piece of land recently enclosed.

Occasionally other units are used: 'curtillage', 'piece', 'paroke' and 'pightle' are small areas usually adjacent to roads or dwellings. Crofts were enclosed areas which, contrary to modern usage, did not contain dwellings. Tenements were large composite holdings usually including a dwelling, arable and rights to common pasture. The demesne was the area retained in hand by the lord of the manor; sometimes, but not always, including a manor house, arable, pasture, closes, dovecots, outbuildings, woods and waste. By the sixteenth century the demesne was usually leased.

The Kitson Family and their ownership of Okeford Fitzpaine, Lytchett Minster and Durweston cum Knighton

In the sixteenth century the three Dorset manors of Okeford Fitzpaine, Lytchett Minster and Durweston cum Knighton shared a common history after they were bought by the Suffolk merchant and landowner Sir Thomas Kitson. The sixteenth century was a period when there was considerable change in the ownership of land. Extensive reorganisation succeeded the dissolution of the monasteries and increasingly prosperous merchants looked to invest their newly acquired wealth in some safe commodity: and above all else this meant land.

Sir Thomas Kitson, who purchased these manors and many others elsewhere in the country, was born in 1485, the son of a Robert Kitson from Lancashire. He made his fortune as a mercer and Merchant Adventurer with a base in Antwerp and became one of the wealthiest men in England. He was knighted by Henry VIII and was Sheriff of London. He purchased the manor of Hengrave in Suffolk in 1521 where he built a beautiful and prestigious house. Much of the cloth he bought came from the West Country: the accounts for some of these transactions survive.[1] He was therefore well acquainted with the area when he had to make decisions about the purchase of manors. In 1529 he bought the manors of Okeford Fitzpaine and Durweston from Henry, the fourth Earl of Northumberland.[2] The manor of Lytchett Minster cum Bere was purchased in February 1540 from Sir Thomas West, Lord Lawarre for £486.[3] Sir Thomas Kitson died in September of the same year but a son was born posthumously in the October and was named Thomas after his father. This Thomas Kitson was the owner of the Dorset manors at the time of the surveys of 1584. He did not come of age until 1561, the year in which his mother Margaret, who had managed the estate

---

1   J. Hare *A Prospering Society Wiltshire in the later Middle Ages* (Hertfordshire, 2011) p.190. C. J. Brett, 'Thomas Kytson and Somerset clothmen', 1529-1539, *Somerset Archaeology and Natural History,* (1999), vol. 143, pp.29-56. C. J. Brett, 'Thomas Kytson and Wiltshire clothmen', *Wiltshire Archaeological and Natural History Magazine,* (2004) vol. 97, pp. 39-40.
2   SRO, 449/2/664 and 668.
3   DHC, D-LEE/A1/4. Lytchett Minster and Bere had been two separate manors in the early medieval period, but had been united using the Latin '*cum*', with, in the fifteenth century.

for much of his minority, died. By that time her son had married twice: first to Jane Paget when he was only seventeen and, following her death, to Elizabeth, the eldest daughter of Sir Thomas Cornwallis. She had been brought up in the household of the Catholic Duchess of Norfolk and the Kitson family remained Catholic sympathisers. Despite their religious beliefs Hengrave house became one of the central pivots for society in Suffolk: Thomas Kitson and his wife were well known as patrons of music, a large list of the musical instruments was included in the inventory taken on his death in 1602.[4] Thomas was knighted by the Queen when she stayed at Hengrave on her perambulation of Suffolk in 1578.

Thomas Kitson died in 1602 leaving two daughters but no male heir. The Gage family eventually inherited Hengrave, through the marriage of Kitson's grand-daughter, Penelope, to John Gage.[5] Durweston cum Knighton was sold to Sir Edward Coke. This manor remained with that family until the death of Thomas Coke, Earl of Leicester when it was sold in 1753 to Julines Beckford who resold it to H. William Portman in 1774.[6] Sir George Trenchard purchased the manor of Lytchett Minster in 1604 and it remained in the hands of the Trenchard family until the 1820s.[7] The manor of Okeford Fitzpaine was acquired by the Freke family from whom it passed to the Pitt-Rivers estate.[8]

Surveying and estate management in the sixteenth century

During the lives of the two Thomas Kitsons there were many improvements in surveying: books on techniques were published and surveyors became increasingly valuable members of the community, professionals not only in the measurement of land but also in giving advice to landowners on its management. The new techniques required for measuring land were disseminated by books such as that by Rycharde Benese, a canon of Merton Priory which, according to its title 'sheweth the maner of measuringe of all maner of lande newly invented by the author'.[9] A surveyor

---

4   Articles and theses have been written about Thomas Kitson using the national important Hengrave documents, including two very interesting theses on the subject of the music of that period submitted to the University of Birmingham for the degree of Ph.D. Both of these refer to the instruments in the house. 1) Teresa Ann Murray, *Thomas Morley and the Business of Music in Elizabethan England* Internet ref http://etheses.bham.ac/uk/1247/1/Murray10PhD-A1b. 2) Hector Sequera, *House music for recusants in Elizabethan England: performance practice in the music collection of Edward Paston (1550-1630)* See especially Chapter II: 'Music in the Recusant Circle' p.33 Internet ref http://etheses.bham.ac/uk/1028/1/Sequera10PhD1.
5   East Suffolk Record Office SAS/G21/64 Marriage settlement, 1611.
6   Hutchins, vol.I 265.
7   DHC, D-LEE/A1/4. George Trenchard's son George married Penelope the grand-daughter of Thomas Kitson. She later married John Gage.
8   Hutchins, vol.IV p.330.
9   R. Benese, *This Boke Sheweth the Maner of Measurynge of all Maner of Lande, as well as Woodlande,*

needed expertise in many fields as well as the measuring of land, including some mathematical ability not only for simple processes but for the keeping of accounts and making valuations. Sufficient legal knowledge was required for the holding of courts and the interpretation of documents together with an ability to negotiate and deal with people of all classes in society. As Dodd has observed 'there was substantial agreement among the authors of the treatises that the surveyor was to answer the basic question of "what it is? and what it is worth?" and, in answering these questions the art could be divided into legal, judicial and mensurational parts'.[10]

New surveying techniques and equipment spread rapidly in the sixteenth century. An early version of the theodolite had been invented and triangulation came into use. Ravenhill notes that 'in addition to techniques, successful triangulation required appropriate and good angle-measuring instruments' which were at hand in Britain by this time.[11] They would have been available to Christopher Saxton who, by 1577, had completed his maps of England. A further new piece of cartographic equipment, the plane table, may have been used when producing the 1580s map of Durweston.

There are some problems in comparing the measurements used in the surveys with later maps. In the sixteenth century the statute acre was common, but the customary acre was still in use and varied between different regions. The use of the customary acre is found in Okeford Fitzpaine where Yeovil almshouse had been granted 128 acres in 1476. When the trustees measured their land at the beginning of the nineteenth century they found it contained only 102 acres. They imagined some land had been misappropriated, but when they examined a map of 1727 it was found that the boundaries were identical to the land then in possession of the charity. The land itself was intact but the deficiency could be accounted for by the initial use of the customary acre which was smaller by about one sixth part than the statute acre'.[12]

Thomas Wright, surveyor, Edward Golding, steward and attorney, and Thomas Golding, Edward's brother, surveyor and perhaps later a steward were all employed by Kitson.[13] Edward Golding, was Thomas Kitson's principal steward and the person chiefly responsible for starting to restructure the estates in the 1560s.[14] In the three years between 1561, when Thomas Kitson came of age, and 1564 not only had Edward

as of Lande in the Felde, Newly Invented and Compyled by Syr Richarde Benese, Canon of Marton Abbey Besyde [London], edited and prefaced by T. Paynell (Southwark, 1537). The numerous reprints are listed in A.W. Pollard and G.R. Redgrave, (eds.), A Short Title Catalogue of Books Printed in England, Scotland and Ireland, and English Books Printed Abroad, 1475-1640, (London, 2nd ed., 1991), vol. I, A-H, 79.

10 K. M. Dodd The Field Book of Walsham-Le-Willows, Suffolk Record Society (1974) vol. 23.

11 W. Ravenhill Christopher Saxton's 16th Century Maps, (Shrewsbury, 1992) p.22.

12 Report from Commissioners: Charities in England and Wales, 1820, p.718.

13 Thomas Golding was described as a surveyor when working on a manor in Northumberland for Kitson. Cumbria Archives WD D/Acc.950/33. In Suffolk at this time the Golding family was of some importance and mentioned in several documents.

14 The notes in the catalogue for the West Suffolk catalogue suggest that he was Thomas Kitson's attorney living in London. HA 528/13-23.

Golding started the reorganisation of the Dorset manors but also the important Devon manors of Ipplepen and Torbryan. Thomas Golding was responsible for at least some of the preliminary surveys required when inclosures took place and later carried through the process after his brother disappeared from the records.[15] Thomas Golding's early surveys often estimated the areas of land, and were not particularly accurate, so to complete the process it was necessary to employ a professional. Thomas Wright was praised by later surveyors for the surveys he made in 1591 of manors in Suffolk: it was said that Wright's survey 'has this mark of authenticity above all other Common surveys'.[16] His own description in the preamble to the 1580s surveys of the various activities he had to perform describe very well the work of surveyors, focusing upon accuracy of measurement and consultation with the tenants of the manor. Thomas Wright was sent to Dorset to make a survey of each of Kitson's manors in that county. He was in Okeford Ftzpaine by April 1583 and in Lytchett Minster and Durweston in May.

Wright found the three manors were situated in very different landscapes. Taylor points out that 'it is the variety of landscape in Dorset which gives the county its great charm and which has resulted in the equally varied landscape history. Dorset has a greater variety of rock type and scenery than any other part of the country in southern England.'[17] These physical differences meant that each manor had its own character, and settlement pattern, created by the balance of pasture, arable, meadow and woodland that was available.

Okeford Fitzpaine Manor

1. Surveying Okeford Fitzpaine

In 1584 Okeford Fitzpaine was a compact village with many of the inhabitants living in the nucleated settlement even though their land was elsewhere. The village was built on either side of one principal road called in the 1584 survey the Queen's highway from 'Sturmester' [Sturminster Newton] to Blandford'. The cross and the town hall were at the centre of the village near to a turn in this through road, one part of which was called High Street and the other West Street. There was also a White Street in the area close to the church.

A method of dividing the manor into sections had existed before the time of Thomas Wright. This is mentioned in the reeves accounts for 1492 and was probably initiated in the reign of Richard III, although it could have gone back to that of Edward IV.[18] The method consisted of dividing the copyhold tenements into nine areas, the rent due for each area being given as a total. Areas mentioned include Stroud £7 13s., and Southeley and Sugston together £6 18s. 4d., Milleyne £3 8s. 9d.,

---

15 SRO, HA 528/27.
16 SRO, HA 528/40.
17 Taylor *The Making of the English Landscape, Dorset*, pp.21-22.
18 SRO, 449/1/E3/15.103/2.4.

Akeford Fitzpaine 35*s*. 8*d*., 'lovelands' 8*d*., Fittalford £5 12*s*. and three areas around the three streets in the village: Whytstrete £10 9*s*. 11½*d*., Hyghstrete £5 17*s*. 3¾*d*. and Weststrete £8 5*s*. 1¼*d*.[19] The total rent for these tenements of £49 10*s*. 10½*d*. is almost identical to that given for Okeford Fitzpaine at the end of the sixteenth century, that for Fiddleford is identical, but none of the other amounts can be reconciled with the later surveys or rentals. The total amount has been divided differently which suggests a major change in the organisation of the parish during the sixteenth century.[20]

Wright based his survey upon the land occupied by the tenants, and he used the position of their dwellings as the order of many of his entries, working along each street in turn. The sections of the survey consist of the areas of land held by one tenant, the first paragraph usually containing a reference to the area of the house and the following paragraphs to the remaining areas of land. In practice this approach made it easier for a reader to determine the contents of each tenement and to evaluate its worth. It also allowed a direct comparison with the documents that were produced at the meeting in May of 1582 when all tenants demonstrated their rights to the land they held. However, for the modern historian the scattered nature of these lands in different parts of the parish often makes it difficult to pinpoint their whereabouts.

At first an attempt to discover the exact position of the areas as described by Wright seems impossible, although names used for the different areas of Okeford Fitzpaine are of some help, but a map dated almost two hundred years after the survey provides some clues.[21] This map is beautifully and meticulously drawn and coloured by W. Corfield and dated 1782. From Corfield's map it is possible to recognise the majority of the sites as described by Wright using the names and areas involved. Most of the sites on the 1782 map have been given not only a number but also a preceding letter or letters which refer to the then tenants of the land and are abbreviations of their surnames.[22] Many of the tenements had remained more or less intact over the two hundred years after the 1584 survey and therefore the whereabouts of the lands of a substantial proportion of the 1584 inhabitants can be traced and plotted.[23]

The survey starts with John Iles, whose tenement was the first on the southwest side of the High Street, it continues along the street as far as the bend and then transfers to the southeast side. The houses in the central area and around the church are then described followed by the north side of West Street (now Lower Street)

---

19 Mills *Place Names of Dorset*, Part III, pp.182 and 184: Strode 1497 meaning 'marshy ground overgrown with brushwood'; 'Suthgarson' being 1316 'south grass inclosure'; Southley 1497 'south wood or clearing'. Milleyne implies the area around the mill, Akeford Fitzpaine is probably the demesne.

20 SRO, HA/528/86. The rental of Okeford Fitzpaine dated 1590.

21 DHC, D-PIT/P/28 dated 1782.

22 The names of later tenants may be found by consulting the eighteenth century court books, rentals, existing leases and a survey made in the 1800s provides very valuable information on Okeford Fitzpaine for this later period. DHC, D-PIT/ Acc 9202 Box 3 item 4.

23 The reference numbers on the1782 map have been added to the text for each area of land to suggest its whereabouts. Where there is considerable doubt on the accuracy of this suggestion a question mark has been inserted.

and the south side. Apart from those having houses in the village there were a few tenements where the holder lived outside in dispersed settlements. These consisted of the larger integrated farms, small isolated cottages and also that part of Fiddleford lying in Okeford Fitzpaine. Part of Fiddleford which included both the manor and the mill was not in the parish and was owned at that time by Thomas White.[24]

The 1584 survey does not give details of every area of land in the parish: some were part of other manors in 1584. The parish of Okeford Fitzpaine was considerably less than the 3,700 acres it is now as areas from other parishes have been added over the years. Some of the areas not described in the survey are those shown on the map without preceding letters. Lowbrook or Lolbrooke Farm, for example, was not held by Kitson: it became part of the manor of Okeford Fitzpaine towards the end of the eighteenth century when it was the property of the Pitt-Rivers family.[25] Another tenement not in the parish or the manor in 1584, called Darknoll, was mentioned as a boundary to the manor in 1584 and held by George Trenchard of Wolfeton (i.e the same George Trenchard who would purchase the manor of Lytchett Minster in 1604-1606). It is labelled 'B' on the map of 1782 by which time it was also owned by the Pitt-Rivers family. Some of the free land belonging to the manor of Okeford Fitzpaine was held by annual payments listed in the 1590 rental, but Thomas Whyte was the only free tenant mentioned in a separate entry in the 1584 survey; the land he held being labelled 'M' on the 1782 map. In 1584 Henry Ford and John Newton also held free land as did the Yeovil Almshouse.

An area of land in Marnhull parish, Nashcourt, was a free tenement belonging to the manor of Okeford Fitzpaine. It is not mentioned in the survey but is mentioned in contemporary documents including the rental of 1590. It has an interesting history: in 1492 it was referred to as part of the manor of Okeford Fitzpaine but was then named Ashcourte.[26] It was part of the lands forfeited to the crown on the execution of Thomas Arundell by Henry VIII but returned to Thomas Kitson. In 1564 it was confirmed that this free tenement belonged to him and was held by his tenant John Pystor.[27] Shortly afterwards Pystor negotiated to reduce the amount paid to the manor of Okeford Fitzpaine: the steward's accounts for 1566 contain the information that the £8 13s. 4d. previously charged for the tenement was not included because it had been sold to Pystor to hold for ever from the manor of Okeford Fitzpaine subject to a few pence paid annually. In the rental of 1590 Pystor's successor, Richard Henning, paid 8½d. Another person who held land not under the control of Thomas Kitson was

---

24 The Okeford Fitzpaine part of Fiddleford was in the parish of Okeford Fitzpaine in the survey of 1584. At some time before this and possibly after the 1492 document quoted at the beginning of this chapter Fiddleford was split up among six tenants all but one paying a rent of 18s. 8d. for similar but not identical lands. The date might have been before 1527 when a William Stasye would seem to be there paying a rent of 18s. 8d. but this could be a coincidence. (SRO, 449/2/665).

25 DHC, D-PIT/E/129, dated 1784-1791.

26 SRO, 449/1/E3/15.103/2.4.

27 SRO, HA/528/24.

the rector of the parish. His glebe was extensive and is described in the survey: it too appears to be the same in 1782 as it had been in 1584.

At the end of the survey there are two areas belonging to the village including the Towne house elsewhere called the Gildehall.[28] The town also owned 'Grenehay' also known as 'Playing Place': the second part of its name suggesting its function. Thomas Kitson retained in hand the two main areas of woodland, Coniger and the smaller area on 'Le Cliffe'. There was also a smaller area of woodland for the use of his tenants in Hebed. The common lands were of vital importance to the economy of the parish and they are referenced where they were adjacent to the land described in the survey. 'Le Downes' are recorded where they formed a boundary, but its area was not given in 1584. In 1782 the same area was described as 'The Hill' and was about 255 acres. There is also a reference to the common land called Gobson.

2. A walk through Okeford Fitzpaine in 1584

Pevsner considered that Okeford Fitzpaine in the twentieth century was 'unusually coherent, with almost nothing out of scale or in other ways striking a false note' and he described the High Street being 'lined with cottages and long garden walls that maintain the village texture'.[29] From Pevsner this is high praise. Certainly there are many buildings that illustrate the long history of the parish. If Thomas Wright were able to return today he might recognise Okeford Fitzpaine. Although there are few survivals from 1584 there are many houses fairly close to that period of a type he would not have found strange. The arrangement of the survey for Okeford Fitzpaine is for the most part in 'walking order' beginning with the most south westerly house in the High Street where John Iles lived [OF.1.1]. Many of the wealthiest families in the village lived in this street.[30] This house like most others in the village was used as a farmhouse. Most of the tenants had a garden and a yard, John Iles was fortunate in having an acre of land adjacent. The house which stands on the site today still has 'farmhouse' as part of its name.[31] John Iles, who held two tenements, would certainly have been classified as a 'yeoman' and was one of the leading men of the village. The whole of his land remained as one unit until at least 1782 when it was shown as the plots with the prefix 'Fu' on the map.

Nearby, on the same side of the road, were other 'yeomen'. Henry Reynolds [OF.4.1] held forty acres and Edward Howe over ninety acres: he was one of the largest copyholders in the parish and he acted as the reeve for Sir Thomas Kitson. His land consisted of two tenements, one of which later belonged to the Pleydell family, the land is shown prefixed 'Pl' on the 1782 map, and is remembered today in the name of the house on the site of that in which Edward Howe lived in 1584 [OF.5.1]. Richard Prower was another near neighbour [OF.8.1]. He held over forty acres and belonged to the most durable family in the parish for they still held the same land

28 SRO, HA 528/24.
29 J. Newman and N. Pevsner *The Buildings of England. Dorset,* (London, 1999) p.307.
30 The Iles surname is Eyles elsewhere and may have been Hayles in the subsidy of 1525.
31 Rosehill Farmhouse.

in 1782. Another of the most important families in the parish, the Whites, lived near here also, but they had less land. This was perhaps because they did not derive all of their income from farming: John White was known as a 'merchant' [OF.9.1].

John Newton lived in a cottage 'newly built' near to the corner of the road before it turned to the left up Lower Street [OF.10.1]. Nearby was Richard Goby who held the common bakery in a central and convenient position.

Henry Forde held the house on the south west corner of the cross roads now known as Darknoll Farmhouse [OF.11.1]. Altogether he had around 75 acres and his rent according to the 1590 rental amounted to £2 3s. 6½d.. Again all the land remained undivided in 1782 under one owner, shown on the 1782 map prefixed with the letter 'T' which stood for either the Revd Giles Templeman or Mr Twynihoe who had the land before Templeman. Templeman paid a similar rent so in this case, as in many others, the customary rent remained fixed for almost two hundred years. The Forde family themselves were connected with the land until almost half way through the eighteenth century.

Opposite John Iles on the east side of the High Street lived Alice Harris [OF.12.1]. Alice was one of a number of widows in the village: of all the land holders mentioned in 1584 about one third were widows and together they had control over a considerable proportion of the land. By the customs of the manor widows would automatically succeed to their husband's copyhold property and would retain control for their lives unless they re-married. How far they used their position to have influence over village affairs is not known. Emma Russell [OF.15.1] was another widow who lived adjacent to the rectory near cross roads at the centre of the village and where the remains of the old cross still stand.

Most of the properties in the village are described as 'tenements', but there are a few described as 'cottages'. Three of these are to be found to the north of the rectory, with the central one being described as the 'Smythes Forge' [OF.27.15]. Some of the other cottages in this area are described as 'newly built'. Three are mentioned as being in one block: in the rental of 1590 they are given a special section in which they are described as 'New Rents'. They may have been built on part of the demesne and their construction may have been as part of the process of inclosures in the manor to provide housing for those with little or no land.

In 1584 Margery Skott, the wealthiest of all the widows, was the holder of a large part of the old demesne as well as the mill pool and the mill. The survey contains a list of the various areas which she owned. There is also another list slightly different in content written some time earlier.[32] From the two lists some details of the manor might be deduced. The site of the manor house itself was on the area called Court Close [OF.27.3], on which a barn had been built, and where there had once been fishponds.[33] In his survey of Dorset compiled in the 1620s Thomas Gerard found that

---

32 SRO, HA/528/27. This list is given in the Appendix A.
33 SRO, HA/528/27. A close containing one and a half acres is called Courte Close and Fysheponds in 1564.

"the mansion house be now subverted, that scarce the footings remain of it".[34] Next to Court Close was the Culver Close which was not held by Margery Skott but by Joan Osmond [OF.31.2]; within the close was the dove house held by John Pystor. The list of 1564 suggests that he paid one or possibly two doves for this right.[35] It is probable that Culver Close would also have been part of the demesne. In the 1582 list for the Skott family a reference is made to the Great Garden - the area [OF.D] would be the most likely place to suggest the whereabouts of this but it may have included parts of the areas called Bawtry Hawe in the survey but 'Betty Hall' on the map, the name having changed by being mispronounced in the intervening two centuries. The Pound too was in this area in 1584 as well as the stream driving the mill. Margery Skott herself could have occupied the house at the corner of the lane [OF.27.1] which is listed as Downs Cottage and is probably of the seventeenth century.[36]

There are no remains of the manor buildings today but, according to the British Listed Buildings survey, some parts of houses survive in Okeford Fitzpaine from the sixteenth century and a section of one of the most important houses in the parish near to the cross roads is still in existence. This belonged in 1584 to William White but, much later, was in the hands of the St. Lo family. The Whites were the most prominent family in the village but William's relationship to the Thomas White gentleman of Fiddleford is unclear: William White in 1584 held over ninty acres by copyhold, including the large inclosure of fifty-eight acres of Gobson. The earliest part of his house was built with jointed cruck trusses and a wattle and daub infilling and the later sixteenth century part with a wall of course rubble. A sixteenth century fireplace remains. It was enlarged again in 1638 according to the date on the south east wall of that enlargement. This part may have replaced a porch which gave a nickname to the John White le Porche who had taken over from William by the rental of 1590.[37]

Another house which may have survived from this period is that on the site Wr 78 on the 1782 map. In 1584 Edward Williams lived there [OF.29.1].[38]

To the north of William White, lived another widow, Joan Osmond, [OF.31.1] in a house where today's Post Office stands and around the corner were Walter Rose [OF.32.1], Robert Hynde [OF.33.1 and Elizabeth Saye. [OF.34.1]. The latter which appears to be on the site of Sheephayes today is also probably seventeenth century in origin.[39]

---

34 Gerard's text, written in the 1620s, was originally published as *A Survey of Dorsetshire* in 1732 under the name of John Coker. *Coker's Survey of Dorsetshire* (reprint, Milborne Port, 1980) p.102.
35 SRO, E3/15.103/1.1.
36 NHLE, ID: 402285.
37 NHLE, ID: 102617 Listed as St.Lo farmhouse. A plan of the house is given in the *Historic Manuscripts Commission Inventory of Dorset* 1970 vol. 3 205.
38 NHLE, ID: 402283.
39 NHLE, ID: 102611.

William Forde [OF.35.1] held part of the site called 'Bawtry Hawe'. Unfortunately no surviving will exists for the Forde family at this time but there is one for a Walter Forde, who could have been either Henry or William's son, dated 1633.[40] It lists not only some of the contents but also some of the rooms. The principal room was the 'hall' as in the houses of previous generations. In the hall was a fireplace. A son called John was left not only a cupboard, table board, forms, chairs, sideboards and benches which were in the hall, one cupboard board in the chamber within the hall, but also all the glass and doors, windows, window leads, gates, locks, bars and fences about the house and tenement. As the house could scarcely have functioned without these, one assumes that John had no intention of removing these items which today would be regarded as 'fixtures'. There was another chamber on the ground floor but no mention of any chambers above. This house could be the one now listed as Castle Farm Cottage described as '17th century or earlier' [OF 35.1].[41]

After William Forde the survey then continued with the properties along the north side of 'West Street', (Lower Street today). Agnes Whight held a large site of about one acre containing a tenement [OF.36.1] and also another tenement on the corner where the Royal Oak is today [OF.36.2] Walter Roose (called Rose elsewhere) held a piece of land, described as an orchard to the north of this site.

Some of the houses on the north side of the road were also held by widows in 1584: Alice Lynsey in Netherway Farm House [OF.39.1] held an area of land [OF.36.3] which was also called Netherway and was thus the origin of the name of the house. Alice is mentioned in the will of Gilbert Muncke written in 1597.[42] Among his charitable donations one poor child is specially mentioned: 'I give to the poor fatherless child that is at Alice Lynsie's in Ockford Fitzpaine 6s. 8d.'.

On the south side of Lower Street, near the house of Henry Forde are three houses all with possible sixteenth century origins. That of another widow, Joanne Phillips, is described as late sixteenth century, altered in the seventeenth century 'probably of long house origin with a cross passage' [OF.42.1]. It has dormer windows: the sixteenth century was the period when some houses were 'ceiled' (given ceilings) thus allowing the roof space to be used for the bedchambers. To provide light to these areas dormer windows were eventually inserted and it would be interesting to know if the windows openings (not the frames) were part of the original house construction in the sixteenth century.[43]

The left wing of the house called 'Yeatmans' is described as being sixteenth century, if not earlier. The British Listed Buildings site says that 'it is possible that the house originated in a timber framed, jointed cruck open hall with the upper end to the east'. A new wing was added in the seventeenth century. Like Edward Howe's house in High Street, it takes its name from the family who lived there in 1782. The

40 TNA, PROB 11/169, proved 9 November 1635.
41 NHLE, ID: 102612.
42 TNA, PROB 11/91 Gilbert Munke, husbandman 10 March 1598.
43 NHLE, ID: 402274.

Yeatmans were already prominent in the parish at this period. Hugh Keane held it in 1584 [OF.44.1].[44]

Langstone Farmhouse is also of some age and is described as possibly on a 'cross passage plan', a common plan for farmhouses in the sixteenth century, it was held by Agnes Mahewe who also had a tenement in High Street. The plot there, according to the map of 1782, almost joined, at right angles, to the house in West Street and may possibly have done so in the sixteenth century. Like its adjacent houses it has a very long burgage plot [OF.6.13].[45]

The houses on both sides of the street continue up the street as far as the more modern houses of the twentieth century. The survey then describes the few tenements where the house was not in the village.

Richard Foote is the first of five [OF.48.1]. He held almost fifty-two acres of land with about twenty-one acres in one block where his house stood. The letter reference on the 1782 map is 'E' which stood for Etheridge at that time and is still the same today. The house is listed and described as probably of seventeenth century origin with an earlier core which implies that part of this house may have been standing when Richard Foote lived here. The house is mentioned in a copy of a Court Roll of 1582 when it was handed over to Richard by his father William, but the latter retained part of the area and buildings so that he and his wife could continue to live in them once retired.[46] Alice Dallidowne [OF.49.1], John Bythewood [OF.50.1] and Laurence Frampton [51.1] had houses away from the village. The most important occupant of such a house was Edward Phillipes [54.1] who had in total seventy-seven acres of land including Strowde Farm, with one large close of about thirty-nine acres containing many trees. Stroud Farmhouse is a listed building today and described as of seventeenth century origin.[47] Also two cottages are mentioned newly built on the side of the road with only very small areas of land.

There follows a separate section, with its own heading, describing the part of Fiddleford that was in the manor and parish of Okeford Fitzpaine. Six tenants are mentioned all with similar areas of land. It would seem that some care was taken to give each tenant a fair share and all had between three and a half and four acres of good quality land in Fittleford meadow [OF.55-60].

Lytchett Minster cum Bere

1. The origins and structure of Lytchett Minster
When Thomas Wright arrived at Lytchett Minster he discovered that here the structure was more complicated than that of Okeford Fitzpaine. The complications were due to both the geography and history of the parish. Unlike Okeford Fitzpaine it was not

44 NHLE, ID: 402275.
45 NHLE, ID: 402276.
46 SRO, 449/1/E3/15.53/3.2.
47 NHLE, ID: 102605.

mentioned in Domesday; the first reference found to the name of the parish is 1244.[48] This does not mean that the area was empty of inhabitants. Several aspects of the parish were not conducive to early settlement: half of it was heathland, of poor quality, and large parts of the remainder were either marshy or well wooded. There was, however, some good quality land. The notes to the 1983 edition of Domesday suggest that it may have been settled by the inhabitants of the manors of Canford, Lytchett Matravers or of Sturminster Marshall.[49] It is more probable, due to the number of manors involved, that Lytchett Minster was settled by inhabitants from all of these manors with that of Sturminster Marshall being the most important: the church of Lytchett Minster was regarded as no more than a chapel under Sturminster Marshall, a position which continued until the nineteenth century. Christopher Taylor writes 'It can be established that Sturminster Marshall, a relatively small parish, little larger than those around it, was once much larger'.[50] In a sale of property to the Trenchard family in 1565 South Lytchett is described as 'within the parish of Sturminster Marshall'.[51]

Notes are to be found at the end of the 1584 survey with the names of people owing allegiance to other manors. Also included is a reference to meadow which was part of the manor of Bere in Spetisbury parish on the river Stour. There are also interesting notes which refer to the right of several of the Lytchett Minster tenants (and possibly those with the earliest tenements) to what is called a 'foreshare' in the meadow of Sturminster Marshall which was next to the river Stour (and south of the White Mill). The 'foreshare' was the right to the first cut of hay after which the tenants of Sturminster Marshall held the 'after' share to the meadow. Tenants of the manor of Lytchett Matravers, the neighbouring parish to that of Lytchett Minster, also had this right. It is therefore also of interest that the reference to Lytchett Matravers in Domesday mentions the existence of water meadows. This is queried in the notes to Domesday because water meadows seem very unlikely in a parish of mostly higher ground and 'the only likely places for water meadows being on the Stour to the north'. The authors suggest that the translation of the words were at fault but it would seem that the water meadows of Lytchett Matravers and possibly of Lytchett Minster were as suggested those by the Stour. [52]

This right continued into the nineteenth century when it was regarded as being of some value to the possessors, as the meadow land in Lytchett Minster was valued in 1798 as being worth 40s. an acre.[53] In 1832 the rights to these 'foreshares' were sold to an inhabitant of Sturminster Marshall who may have then purchased the other rights from elsewhere.[54] This land paid no tithe according to the tithe assessment

48 Mills, *Place Names of Dorset*, vol.II, *p.33.*
49 Thorn, *Domesday Book*, p.3.
50 Taylor *The Making of the English Landscape Dorset*, p.75.
51 DHC, D-LEE/A1/3.
52 Thorn, *Domesday Book, Dorset*, section.34.5.
53 DHC, D.2301/M/1.
54 DHC, D-LEE/A/3/1.

of Sturminster Marshall which suggests a connection with the church, perhaps pre-dating Domesday and the Conquest.[55]

Another neighbouring parish is Morden. In the Domesday Book three mills are mentioned in that parish. Two of these mills can be traced today along the Sherford River complex but the third reference is of interest: 'from part of a mill 11*d.*'.[56] The mill at Organford bestrode the Sherford River being partly in Morden and partly in Lytchett Minster. The earliest reference to the place name Organford is 1194.[57]

A further complication for Wright was that the manor of Bere cum Lytchett bought by Kitson, which consisted originally of two separate manors until at least the end of the fifteenth century, was only part of the parish.[58] There was another large manor in the parish called the manor of Slepe cum Cockamore, which also originally had been two manors, and was under the control of George Trenchard.[59] Other manors with property in the parish as well as Sturminster Marshall, were Canford, Morden, Newton Peverill (also based in Sturminster Marshall) and Lytchett Matravers. Unlike his approach to Okeford Fitzpaine, Wright, because of the interlocking of Kitson's manor with these others, attempted to provide details of all the cultivated lands in the parish some of which were not part of the Kitson manor. Frequently, not having the necessary permission or information, he had to make an estimate of some of the areas in other hands which at times he clearly found difficult [LM.83].

The parish consists of two halves separated in the centre by part of the important tenement of 'Hell', which became Hill Farm in the nineteenth century [LM.44]. This tenement is mentioned in the 1584 survey as being free of the manor of Lytchett Matravers: the inclosure map shows it as being situated half in Lytchett Matravers with the other part in Lytchett Minster, although this is not mentioned in the survey.[60] The division came almost as far south as the modern Dorchester Road with the tenement called 'Birde Oke' in the survey (though Oke or Oake at a later date) beside the Sherford River being the main connection between the two halves [LM.153].

The inclosure map for Lytchett Minster mentioned above has been chosen to show the areas in relation to the survey. It is dated to the 1820s and therefore almost two and a half centuries after the survey of 1584 but, in spite of this time difference, it is still possible to follow most of the boundary lines with some degree of certainty.[61] The inclosure map was based on a survey of c.1798 by Francis Webb, a

---

55 Taylor *The Making of the English Landscape: Dorset*, p.78.

56 Thorn, *Domesday Book, Dorset*, section.36.15.

57 Mills, *Place Names of Dorset*, vol.II, p.24.

58 Bere cum Lytchett had originally been two manors which were amalgamated in the fifteenth or early sixteenth century.

59 This George Trenchard was the son of Henry Trenchard of Lytchett Matravers who held the manor of Slepe cum Cockamore in the sixteenth century. It was finally bought from the Carew family by another Trenchard, Sir George, in 1605.

60 It is possible to become very confused with the map here for some of the numbers for the areas of Lytchett Matravers at this point are the same as those for Lytchett Minster therefore the former numbers have been omitted in the copy of the map.

61 The inclosure map for Lytchett Matravers and Lytchett Minster is based on an Act of

surveyor from Wiltshire. This provides details of all the areas and owners/occupiers for the parish at that time with other useful information.[62] The map which was made to accompany it has not been found but this matters little for a later surveyor, Robert Page from Wimborne, based the inclosure map on it using the same numbering and the same measurements. Page's map has useful additions to Webb's survey for it shows the areas of land which were not inclosed in 1798, i.e. all those many areas affected by the Inclosure Act together with buildings erected between the 1798 survey and the map of the 1820s. Francis Webb's numbering went up to c. 650. All the areas with higher numbers were inclosed after 1798 and have been conveniently shown by Page in fainter lettering that helps to identify easily the later additions.[63]

The details of the inclosures were not finalised until 1829 but the map, though not dated, is earlier: it was made initially, it is thought, before a second map also by Page, around 1824-1825. The latter accompanied the sale of all the Trenchard owned lands in Lytchett Minster still in the hands of that family to Sir Claude Scott, a banker from London. Before this Scott had made substantial purchases in the parish and from November 1824 became the effective owner of the bulk of the lands there.[64] Accompanying the second map is a survey of the parish by Robert Page.[65] This survey describes each of the areas of land with their names and state of cultivation, including lands that were not owned by Scott. It also provides a list of all the separate tenements in alphabetical order of the names of the tenants - with details of the rents and heriots paid with the terms and the lives involved. This extra information is also of value in helping to identify the details of the 1584 survey. The maps and descriptions of 1824 show a very complex landscape with many tenements having scattered lands in different areas. In the majority of cases the older tenements can be shown to have the same form in 1824 as they did in 1584.

Because of this history the houses in Lytchett Minster were much more dispersed than those in Okeford Fitzpaine: the character and structure of the two parishes were very different. The road system for Okeford Fitzpaine was centred on the village. The road system for Lytchett Minster was a more complex series of through routes, but it was this road system which Thomas Wright used in his division of the parish, describing his division between the roads as 'precincts'.

2. A walk through Lytchett Minster in 1584

The most prominent feature in Lytchett Minster was the Beacon. The survey was written only four years before the Spanish Armada, a time when many the beacons of

---

Parliament of 1818 and the inclosure award of 1829. The map was produced around 1824. DHC, I.5.

62 DHC, D.2301/17/1.

63 These later numbers which have been omitted from the copies of the map in this book with the exception of a few in the village.

64 J. Palmer 'Sir Claude Scott and the Development of Lytchett Minster' *Proc. DNHAS*, (2014) vol.135, pp.33-45.

65 DHC, D-CRL/B11/3/1.

England, especially in the vulnerable coastal areas, were lit to warn of an imminent invasion. The Beacon stood in an area of heath land, part of Lytchett Common which covered about half of the parish. No detailed description is given of this common land for the survey begins with the cultivated land to the north of what is today called Dorchester Road in Precinct One.

Precinct One, is described as being between the common to the east and 'Criche' (later Creech) Lane.[66] To the south was the 'Queen's highway' going through the village; the line of the road changed in the twentieth century due to the extension of the grounds of South Lytchett House and the building of the bypass through the village in the 1960s.[67] The principal tenements here in 1584, held by Thomas Barnes, William Mudge and Emma Henning, more or less converge on what is called in the survey George Cross, but whether a cross was still there at the time of the 1584 survey is not known. On either side of the junction was a tenement with unenclosed areas called from the fifteenth to the nineteenth century 'the George' but no reference to any inn on the site has been found [LM.8, LM.12]. The position of Bakers Lane is shown by a line of trees on the inclosure map.

Precinct Two is similarly bounded by roads: Creech lane to the east and the way leading from the church to Blandford on the west, now part of a drive within the bounds of Lytchett Minster school. Much of the latter does not exist now as a public road but is the driveway leading from Dorchester road to Lytchett Minster School and was once called Church Lane. It is noticeable that there were several sites in this Precinct that were free lands associated with other manors. William Knappe held land which was part of the manor of Newton Peverley to the south and separately, to the north of Pitt Bridge, over forty-six acres of land.[68] For a long period this was called Pitt Farm but is now the site of Lytchett Heath House. We do not know the complete size of William Knappe's stock as no inventory is available but he had at least fifty-four sheep and eight 'rother' beasts mentioned in his will which was proved in 1607 in which he is described as a yeoman [LM.16, LM.17].[69]

The large manor of Canford owned the most important tenement in Lytchett Minster, now part the site of Lytchett Minster school. In 1584 this area of around sixteen acres was owned by Sir Francis Wyllyby. The Willoughby family (the more usual spelling) were prominent landowners from the Midlands [LM.35]. The descendants of the Willoughbys sold it to Thomas Barnes in the seventeenth century.[70] It was bought by John Jeffery MP of Poole from the Barnes family at the end of the eighteenth century and sold to Claude Scott in 1812. It was never owned by any member of the Trenchard

---

66 This name continued into the nineteenth century. It is called Randalls Hill today after a later occupant of the farm house.

67 The position of what is now known as the Courtyard Centre and previously Cottage Farm illustrates this: Cottage Farm is shown on the inclosure map as being south of the main through road.

68 DHC, D/DAS/4558, a plan of this plot dated 1781.

69 TNA, PROB 11/109 William Knapp, yeoman, 6 March 1609.

70 DHC, D-DAS 4276-8.

family who bought the manor of Lytchett Minster cum Bere in 1604 from the Kitson family and therefore it could not be the manor house of that manor in the sixteenth century. It could only be called a manor house in the nineteenth century when, because of the activities of Sir Claude Scott, it became part of the manor of Lytchett Minster.[71]

Precinct Three covered the village to the north and west of the main through road and also a large area of mainly freely held land to the west as far as King Lane (now Fox's Lane). Julian Gould had one of the most important sites in the village with twenty acres of land around the church; the house itself could have been of some size for he had at least five servants. [LM.37]. In the surviving records his name is mentioned more frequently than any other villager for he acted as a bailiff for Thomas Kitson and was also described as an 'accomptant' in documents on the sale of trees.[72] The wills of Gould and his wife survive.[73] He gives every appearance of being a 'yeoman', but he was described as a 'husbandman' in an earlier document of 1562, when he leased Holton in Wareham parish at the other side of the Sherford River.[74] He also held the site of the house in Lytchett Minster now known as North Holton Farmhouse with some land in that area.

The largest area in Precinct Three [LM. 44] was the freely held site known as 'Hell' throughout most of its long history and was held at this time by Christopher Antill [elsewhere Anketill] as part of the manor of Lytchett Matravers. Nearby was the site of the manor called Cockamore [LM.41].

Precinct Four is to the west of King Lane beginning with three coppices [LM. 52, 53, 54] and then to the west of these was the large site of Bere Manor [LM.56]. The present house possibly stands on the site of the old manor house but whether any old walls remain from an earlier building is not known nor has any document been found which might indicate when the lord of the manor last lived there. It was the only tenement held by lease according to the valuation of 1565, but the name of the lessee was not given. It was the most important manor in the parish as can be seen by the detailed description in the survey and its land remained more or less intact until the nineteenth century. The description of the boundaries is of interest: to the west was the Queen's highway leading from Wareham to Lytchett Matravers, but to the south was the Common of Newton, when one would have expected a reference to a road or track which followed approximately the line of the A35 today. Here and elsewhere in the parish were several areas of common, frequently marshy, on each side of the roads and particularly at the road junctions.

Precinct Five covered the area west of the Lytchett Matravers to Wareham road as far as the common land on the boundary of Lytchett Minster and Morden.[75] One of its principal sites was Newton which was not 'new' in 1584. 'Niweton' goes back

71 J. Palmer 'Sir Claude Scott and the development of Lytchett Minster' in *Proc. DNHAS*, (2014) vol.135 pp.33-45.
72 SRO, 449/1/E3/15.51.
73 TNA, PROB 11/76 Gilian Goold or Goolde, 6 Nov. 1590; Anne Gould widow 11 Oct.1597.
74 DHC, D-RGB/1650 John Leweston to Julian Gould lease of Holton Farmhouse in Wareham.
75 This boundary was subject to disputes at times e.g. DHC, D-WPC/M/3 dated 1769.

to at least 1332 and originally covered an area now both south and north of the present main road and east of the Organford to Wareham road.[76] Part of the site in Precinct Five was held by John Browning [LM.57], part by Nicholas [LM.58, LM.59] and Eleanor Lucas [LM.60]. The Lucas family held several sites in this part of the parish. Within the bounds of Newton is a lake and the deeds for this area in the early eighteenth century contain reference to a 'swanyard'. In the early seventeenth century Sir George Trenchard was granted by King James I various rights including that to the swans landing on his territory.[77] To the north of this Precinct there was a considerable area of common land.

To the west was the large old site of Bulbury, or *Bulrebury* in 1306.[78] Half of it, about sixty acres [LM.68], was held by Augustine Lawrence who was the holder of a large area in Precinct Six. The other half was mostly woodland and was retained by the lord of the manor and let out by him by indenture. South of Bulbury was, according to the 1584 survey, 'the common of Littchett', but called on the inclosure map 'the common of Slepe'.

An asset not mentioned in the survey, but which was included in the valuation of 1565, was the 'sundry quarries of stone' 'very apt for building' which the valuer thought might provide Thomas Kitson with an annual revenue. Quarr Hill in Precinct Five and Quarr Farm in Lytchett Matravers might be clues to their whereabouts in this area. There is no information for Lytchett Minster on the building materials for the houses in the sixteenth century for no houses survive from this period: they would probably have been timber with wattle and daub infilling or of cob rather than stone except possibly for the most prestigious houses.

Precinct Six on the south side of the road was the largest Precinct but divided into two halves by a stream and described separately. It continued eastward as far as the road to Wareham from Lytchett Matravers. The western apart included land in Morden parish. It would seem that most of the land of the manor of Slepe itself was west of the stream. Organford, one of the oldest settlements in the parish, was by 1584 a complex area of small sites some of them freely held. This complexity was possibly due to the presence of a mill which was a part of the manor of Bere. The mill was held in 1584 by Nicholas Lucas while his brother, Richard, held adjacent land which was also part of Bere manor. Some of the land in this Precinct was south of the river Sherford and in Morden parish.

Precinct Seven consisted of a further considerable amount of land south of the river Sherford which was within Morden parish. Most of this was heathland described in the survey as 'Goore Hethe' and a description of the boundaries is given in the survey. In 1584 it was held by Bere Farm.

Precincts Eight and Nine contain the land between Precinct Six and the road from Lytchett Matravers to Wareham over the King's Bridge with a lane called Broad

---

76 Mills, *Place Names of Dorset*, vol.II, p.34.
77 DHC, D-LEE/D9/1. The document is a 1827 copy.
78 Mills, *Place Names of Dorset*, vol.II, p.33.

Lane dividing the two Precincts. These two areas also contained areas of common land - Organford common remained mostly intact until the time of the inclosure Act. In Precinct Eight there was a large area of free land, estimated in 1584 as being forty acres which formed the basis for the land owned later by the Pike and Pitt families who lived at what was later called Organford house [LM.144]. In 1584 the house and land were held freely by John Sherman but were sold at the end of the sixteenth century to the Chisman family. The principal site in Precinct Nine was called 'Birde Oke' in 1584 and later Oke or Oake. It is first mentioned in sixteenth century documents referring to Gold Court in Precinct Eleven. The land by King Bridge, also known as Clay Bridge, on the road to Wareham was very marshy.

Precinct Ten stretched from King Bridge eastward as far as one of the pathways in the area called Balso Lane. Because of the risk of flooding most houses in the areas were some distance from the river. The nearest and the first site to the west, containing two cottages, was part of the manor of Slepe and is mentioned under the heading of George Trenchard [LM.159]. This is the site now of *The Bakers Arms*. There is no smithy mentioned in 1584 in Lytchett Minster as there is in Okeford Fitzpaine but, in the eighteenth century, the Barnes family were the blacksmiths in Lytchett Minster having the smithy on part of this site. According to the sixteenth century court papers of the manor of Slepe cum Cockamore a Thomas Barnes took this site towards the end of the sixteenth century and a John Barnes was there according to the survey of 1625.[79] It may be that the Barnes family were already blacksmiths at the end of the sixteenth century and maintained their trade in the same position for the next two centuries. Webb's survey of 1798 refers to the building here as 'copthall', presumably the term refers to an unusual shaped roof. Adjacent to this site was the one held by Julian Gould. The house, rebuilt in the eighteenth century, is today called North Holton Farmhouse. The houses south of Wullverstone Lane are some of the most attractive in the village but only one has a date possibly earlier than the eighteenth century.[80]

Precinct Eleven lay immediately to the north of Wullverstone Lane, which formed the principal route to the farmhouses in the east of the parish, but is now blocked by the dual carriage way. Several small sites around the lane were described in the survey as being freehold within the manor of Sturminster Marshall and some of this land was owned by Richard Wolfrey .[LM.186-188] Richard owned the site of the oldest inn in the parish, *St Peters Finger*. It may be the successor of the 'church house' mentioned in the rental for Lytchett Minster of 1590 and described as 'town house' in the survey of c.1587. In other parts of the country some of the buildings or sites of the 'church houses' in which ales had been brewed for church celebrations, developed into inns. Mattingly considers that 'a significant number of [church houses] became inns'.[81]

79 DHC, D-LEE-C/1/1.

80 NHLE, ID 108991.

81 J. Mattingly, 'Built to last? The rise and fall of the church house.' *The Local Historian* 2012, vol.42, p.115.

The most significant site in Precinct Eleven was the land held by George Trenchard. This is perhaps where the manor house for Lytchett Minster was earlier located. The manor house was not on the major triangular site [LM.35] which is commonly considered the site of the manor today. The only other property to which the title of 'manor' was attached in the sixteenth century was 'the old manor house called Gold Courte', sometimes called Gould's.[82] It is not mentioned in the 1584 survey by this name but is described in Precinct Eleven as a large area of land which Wright estimated as sixty-two acres and the house on it is described as being a 'new house', though no indication is given in the survey as to how long this 'new' house had been in existence. [LM.183] The position of this 'new house' can be traced in succeeding documents. Today the site of this 'new' house lies directly under the modern bypass where it crosses the old Watery Lane.[83] But this new house might have been built in a different position from the original. Trenchard's site extended northwards as far as 'the Queen's highway near George Crosse' that is to the old line of the Dorchester Road (before the construction of the bypass and the bridge over it altered the road alignment at this point). To the north of this land is a site later called 'Pond Close, or Pound Close, alias Court Close' in a document of 1715.[84] The word 'Court' is the name given to the central sites of the old manor of Durweston and of Okeford Fitzpaine and is a word used for the site of a manor house. This site also included an old 'roofless tenement' and 'old walls which have fallen down'. Could these have been the remains of the old manor house of Lytchett Minster?[85] No name is given in the survey for the tenant of this new house and its land but by the survey of 1625 James Gerrard held 'the ancient Manor House called Gold Courte' at a rent of 17s. a year.

Precinct Twelve lay to the east of Precinct Eleven. South of the present Dorchester Road were East Marsh and Eastern Brook, the area of George Trenchard's new development [LM.195]. Whether the six cottages there today were completed by this George Trenchard is uncertain. There were some houses around here by the time of the survey of the manor of Slepe cum Cockamore in 1625. Two of the oldest houses in the parish exist in Marsh Lane and are thought to be part of Trenchard's development. One is dated 1681 but part of its fabric may be earlier.[86]

South of this area was a complex set of sites forming part of what is now known as French's Farm. Simon Chesmond [LM.196], John Mudge [LM.197], John Barnes [L.M.202] and Simone Henning, widow, [LM.198] not only held land here but they also shared with three others the right to about sixty-four acres in the Rushe Grounde, a valuable area from where rushes were obtained. Some of Simone's land was adjacent to the creek, she held an area later called the boat ground and another called the Salterns. Salt making was conducted around Poole harbour especially in Purbeck

82 DHC, D-LEE/C5/32, D-DAS/4405, D-DAS/4685.
83 Number 314 on the inclosure map.
84 DHC, D-DAS/4333 dated 1715.
85 The inclosure map reference numbers for this site are 325, 330-333.
86 NHLE, ID: 431010 and 431011.

where it flourished from the fourteenth century.[87] To the east was heathland with one or two isolated sites of development. Also included in Precinct Twelve are three islands in Lytchett Bay called Furgoore, Utter Hethe and Brakney. These islands were held in common by the principal tenants in Precinct Twelve.

The will of Joan Barnes, dated 1617, illustrates some aspects of daily life within the manor. She was probably the widow of the John Barnes who held land in Precincts Eight and Twelve. In this many of her friends are mentioned and we can reconstruct one of the social circles which existed in the village at that time. Her possessions are also of interest especially as described by her. Daughter Julian inherited her 'best' red petticoat whereas daughter Edith had the 'worser', but Edith was compensated by inheriting her 'best' gown and 'best' hat. Joane had a 'better' feather bed, a 'lesser' feather bed was inherited by her son, William but he obtained her 'best' great chest, the 'best' cupboard, all the corn growing on the living and he shared the residue of the estate with his brother-in-law, George Mudge. A great deal of thought had been given by Joane in her attempt to please all her children. It is a will which brings to us some glimpse of what life was like in Lytchett Minster at the time.[88]

Durweston cum Knighton

1. The origins and administration of the manors

Durweston.cum Knighton is a combination of two parishes that were amalgamated in 1381. Knighton church was to be used by the united parish while the body of Durweston church was ordered to be destroyed except for the chancel which the rector was to maintain and to say mass yearly within it.[89] Two separate surveys were made by Wright but with one preamble and included in one manuscript.

The arrangement for these surveys and the vocabulary used are the same for both as Durweston and Knighton were similar in structure. Thomas Wright decided to organise the surveys in the same way as for Lytchett Minster, rather than for Okeford Fitzpaine, by describing separate areas of land. Because he was dealing with a parish that had kept its common strip field system, he used not only the road system where applicable, but also the boundaries of the adjacent strips, to divide the areas. For the headings to the areas that contained the strips, or had contained strips, he used the word '*stadium*'. In the areas where no strip fields were present, for example in the village which contained houses but no strip fields, he used the word 'Precinct' as in Lytchett Minster. The word *stadium* has been left in its Latin form. The origin of the

---

87 L. Keen 'Medieval Salt Workings' *Proc. DNHAS*, (1988), vol.109, pp.25-28.
88 Other wills of interest include: TNA, PROB 11/88 John Barne 20 Oct. 1596; PROB 11/113 Henny Hemminge 7 Feb.1609; PROB 11/109 William Knapp, yeoman, 6 March 1609; PROB 11/80 Thomas Francklinge or Frankling 22 Nov. 1593; PROB 11/ 241 John Geale 17 Oct 1654; PROB 11/268 Stephem Emberlie or Emberley, yeoman 31 Oct. 1657 and PROB 11/286 Joane Emberley, widow 31 Jan. 1659.
89 Hutchins, vol I, p.266.

word goes back to classical Greece- a *stadion* was a Greek measure of length about 607 feet long.[90] This measurement is fairly close to the amount of 220 yards of an English furlong which was regarded as being a comfortable length for a plough team to plough in one stretch before turning and was the word used in the terminology of open fields: many of the strips illustrated in Durweston and Knighton seem to be of the approximate measurement of 220 yards.

The strips themselves can be seen be seen on an extant map which covers part of the parish. Such a map is very rare for this period; it is rather crudely drawn and now faded.[91] It is drawn to a scale of about 24-25 inches to one mile. At first it gives the impression of a sketch map rather than a fully detailed survey, but when looked at more closely, it can be seen that measurements of those lengths of roads which exist today are approximately the same and that a fairly careful survey was originally attempted, although some of the boundary lines between the tenements do not fit with the measurements given.

The map covers approximately 600 acres, or about one third of the parish, as against the 1824 acres in a survey of circa 1593. The main area missing is that to the east and south with a smaller area to the west. The village itself is shown as is the river Stour, the island with its withy beds is shown as is the mill in the position it occupies today. Much of the arable land is missing as also are the large areas of common downland as well as woodland. In particular most of the land, amounting to some 291 acres according to the survey of c.1593, which was the demesne for Knighton, held by the Powlden family, is not shown on the map although the central site of the old manor house of Knighton is there.

The map provides the layout of the houses in the village although it is doubtful whether the drawings of the houses give their true appearance for they are all almost identical. The only apparent differences are the manor house of Knighton and the rectory for which two chimneys are provided with the majority have only one: barns and other buildings which were not houses are shown without a chimney. None of the houses from 1585 survive in the village although it could be possible that a few of the older ones may have some remnants of walls or other features from that period.

Two other surveys exist for Durweston cum Knighton: one was produced about the same time or slighty later than the 1585 survey printed here[92]; the other was presumably produced around 1593 from evidence in changes in the tenancies in Durweston and Knighton and the dates of births in the Frampton family.[93] This latter survey gives very useful details of the individual tenements including the numbers of sheep and cattle and some information on how the land is divided into pasture, arable

---

90 *Collins English Dictionary of the English Language,* ed. Patrick Hanks, 1979.

91 SRO, 449/8/4.

92 Herts RO, Gorhambury Collection XI/4. Surveys for Okeford Fitzpaine and Lytchett Minster also exist in the same collection. The majority of the personal names coincide with those in the 1585 survey.

93 SRO, 449/1/E3/15.102/2.1.

and meadow which is not clear in the surveys for Okeford Fitzpaine and Lytchett Minster for, if the surveyor did not know what use the holder was going to make of the land, he classified it under 'pasture or inclosed land', therefore the amount of arable land is underestimated.

The next extant map, together with an enlargement of the village part, for Durweston cum Knighton is dated 1801. Accompanying it is a list of land areas with the names of the two principal farmers who held the majority of the land. This map and accompanying document were accepted by the Tithe Commissioners as the Tithe map for the parish. This is surprising because the map is of poor quality, in particular crude colouring has obscured some of the boundary lines. There is also a problem in dating the accompanying list where several of the fields are described as glebe lands: these glebe lands fit very well with those described in the 1584 survey and the 1580s map, but not with the position in 1801. For example the 1801 map has been coloured to show the glebe in one complete area after an agreement was made with the rector in 1784 to exchange lands and to consolidate his holding, but the wording of the accompanying document still has the glebe land elsewhere.[94]

The village itself, like Okeford Fitzpaine, was compact but the administrative affairs of the two manors were kept partially separate even after they came under Kitson's control. The boundary line is clearly shown on part of the 1580s map. In the village it went through the middle of what is now Water Lane (a road which went as far as 'Church Lane' in that period) with Knighton on the south side and Durweston on the north. But its continuation westward from the rectory westward (Milton Lane, as it was called in 1801) was not the boundary. The sites to the south of Milton Lane including the rectory, were in Durweston. The two manors each had their own sheep downs so the vital decisions on the management of the sheep were made separately. There are several references at the end of the surveys for both Knighton and Durweston giving details of the various downland areas which could be used for the animals of the tenants. This separation of the two former manors could have caused complications but unlike Okeford Fitzpaine and Lytchett Minster, no other outside manors had land in the parish.

2. A walk through Durweston cum Knighton in 1585

Pevsner writes lyrically of Durweston: 'Durweston is the first village above Blandford in the valley of the Stour and, as one comes from the south, appears handsomely, crowned by the church above the flat meadows, surrounded by the generous curves of the downs'.[95] In this sentence he includes several features that defined the history of the parish. The proximity of Blandford, the broad river Stour with its mill and meadows, the sheep dotted downs and the central church were the key components. What was not there in 1585 was the predecessor of today's A351 which bisects the village road and makes it more difficult to decide where the original sites were then.

94 TNA, CRES 39/86.
95 J. Newman and N. Pevsner *The Buildings of England. Dorset* (London, 1999) p.191.

Thomas Wright, in 1585, began his description of the Knighton part of the parish with the manor house at the corner of Church Lane [K1.1]. From there he continued eastward along what is now Water Lane and part of Milton Lane: at the time one continuous street described in the text as the highway from the Stour to Ockford.

The manor house for Knighton and the land which formed the demesne was held throughout a large part of the sixteenth century by members of the Powlden family: It was rebuilt in the eighteenth century so its appearance in the sixteenth century is not known. Most of the houses in Knighton were immediately to the east of the manor house. Several of the areas with the houses are around one rood in extent suggesting that this was part of a planned settlement at some time in the past. All include gardens but those which are almost twice the size include 'crofts', smalled hedged plots, in a parish consisting of strip fields and common pasture.

A few of the occupiers are mentioned here to illustrate the information available in the documents and to give idea of the variety in the tenements. Next to the manor was the house of William Stone with garden containing one rood, thirty-two perches. [K 1.2]. According to a copy of court roll dated 6 June 1572 his cottage and land consisted of one close called Southclose of one acre, a close of either pasture or arable called Long Close of two acres and seven acres of arable land in South field with one acre in North Field for which he paid a fine of £13 7s.[96] In the rental of 1590, he paid 7s. a year but his name was later crossed out and that of his widow, Joan, inserted. The survey of 1593 mentions that the tenement consisted of around fourteen and a half acres of which ten were arable and he had the right to have thirty-two sheep on the common, and it would seem, four beasts in the 'field' and two in the meadow.[97]

In Durweston cum Knighton several widows held land after the deaths of their husbands. One was Christiana Loder [K1.6] whose son John took on the tenement containing twenty acres of arable and three of pasture with the right to keep sixty sheep and four draught animals. Nearby was Emma Pelle [K 1.8] with John Pelle next door [K1.7] their relationship is not known. John held only ten acres of arable and pasture with the right to keep thirty-four sheep: whereas Emma held forty-four acres one of the largest amounts for copyholders in the parish.

William Domine, who is described in the section on 'Trees' as a specialist in forestry, held a property [K1.9] which was twice as large as the majority, containing a 'croft'. In the rental of 1590 William's name is crossed out and the name of Ellen his widow substituted. By the survey of c 1593 she was aged eighty: the holding was too much for her to manage so she obtained a licence to let it out paying 12d. for the privilege. In this survey it is described as having eleven acres of arable, fifteen acres of pasture, one acre of meadow and the right to have ninety sheep on the downs, the rent being 12s. After Robert Skott [K1.10] there were no more houses closer to

96 SRO, 449/1/E3/15.53/1.1.
97 The numbers given in Knighton are for the number of beasts allowed on the meadow after reaping and on the common grazing.

the Stour. There are other houses south of the church and the cemetery and east of
the road to Bryanston belonging to Knighton. Of these, James Privet held twenty-
two acres comprising one acre of meadow and ten acres of pasture and eleven of
arable according to the survey of c. 1587. Near to the southern boundary was in an
inclosure called Bugkes Close where the Powldens had built some cottages [K1.9]. As
the cottages are not included in the rental of 1590 they presumably were under John
Powlden's lease and probably built for his workmen. New cottages were being built
at this time in all the manors. To the east of the road was the land by the Stour which
contained excellent meadow land: Powlden holding sixteen acres with the remaining
tenants having about an acre each. A few areas were held by Durweston men but it is
noticeable that they, unlike the Knighton tenants, were not allowed to pasture their
cattle upon it after the hay had been cut. 'Ilandes' [K4.5] may have been an area that
remained dry when the remainder was flooded by the Stour.

The land to the west of the Bryanston road was mostly in strips where the land
was suitable. There was some higher sloping land not suitable for strips and these
were left unfenced for general use. There was also an area of trees.

The description of Durweston in the 1585 survey begins with the rectory in
Precinct One and on the south side of the Stour to Okeford road. The main village area
is described under Precinct D7 and D8 the mill being the first building mentioned.
The mill house was rebuilt in the late eighteenth century. The necessary maintenance
of the mill was costly and possibly frequent. There were substantial repairs to the mill
in 1482-1483[98] when much of it had to be rebuilt and further maintenance in 1490-
1491.[99]

In 1582 the grant to Robert Oliver was for 'two grist mills under one roof'
for which he had to pay an entry fine of £110.[100] Later he gained permission for
building a new house, which, in the rental of 1590 was described as having been built
at the west end of his mill: on the contemporary map there is a drawing of a building
which has been crossed out close to the mill. The rent in 1593 for the whole was
£7 13s. 6d.. Oliver did not occupy the mill all the time for there are two references
to his paying fines to allow him to sub-let.[101] He also held a meadow nearby called
the Millhams adjacent and a small island called Gasthams. Meadow land near the
river in Durweston was scarce and the majority went with the mill. Edward Bennett
had one acre on land beside the river. The only meadow in the vicinity was three
acres in 'Twitchings' (i.e the land near the 'cross roads', which is the meaning of the
name) which belonged to John Standley. A larger area of 'meadow' land in Norden is
described in the memoranda at the end of the survey.

The site of the old church of Durweston of which the chancel was kept when
the rest of the church was demolished in 1381 is possibly described in the reference
to the cottage held by the Rector called Chappell Hay [D7.8]. The remains of the

98 SRO, 449/1/E3/15.53/2.3.
99 SRO, 449/1/E3/15.102/1.1.
100 SRO, 449/1/E3/15.53/3.2.
101 SRO, 449/1/E3/15.53/3.2.

church would probably have been somewhere in this vicinity because here also was
the site of the manor house of Durweston which may, at one time, have stretched
as far as the corner along the north side of the road. Three sites, those of John Iles,
Roger Ranewe and Richard Prower [D7.5, 6, 7] all included areas called Court Close.
'Court' is the word given to the area around a manor house and can be found in the
surveys for Okeford Fitzpaine and Lytchett Minster. Whether any of the three houses
shown were originally part of the manor house itself is not known, but none are shown
with two chimneys as are the two larger houses in the parish.

John Vallevin [D7.12] had the house by the cross at the cross roads.[102] To the
north of him, on the east side of this road from 'Shillingstone to Bryanston', were
John Shepherd and Edith Rogers, each with the usual rood, then a small piece of
land of Richard Prower and finally Alice Dennis with over two roods. Two of the three
attractive cottages nearby are possibly of seventeenth century origin, but it could be
that some contain earlier features, and these cottages may be on the sites of those
of the inhabitants mentioned above.[103] The last person on this side of the road was
John Rogers whose tenement was larger being of one acre [D7.17]. Between the road
and the river to the east were various inclosures shown on the map together with a
withy bed on an island in the river which again was shared between the tenants of the
manor.

On the west side of the Shillingstone to Bryanstone road are several other
tenements. Most of these are rather larger than the one rood tenements found on
the Knighton side of the village road. The first of these is somewhat puzzling for
it would appear to be that of John Stevens which is the corner house on the map
with no tenement to the east but a cottage belonging to the rector, Walter Coshe, is
mentioned in the 1585 survey. Further down the road is a cottage of William Howsley
[D21.1] so small that no area is given. It would seem from the map to be in the middle
of the road.

The map shows more of the Durweston part of the parish than that shown for
Knighton. Missing are the wooded and common areas near the northern boundary of
the parish and some of the *stadia* and the common land to the west. In this area also
are several areas of trees. In the 1593 survey for Durweston cum Knighton seventy-
eight acres of wood are mentioned. The largest of these was Filgrove.

Some of the most important land in both Knighton and Durweston was the
downland on which the animals were pastured and on which the holders of land had
certain definite rights. The Durweston tenants had rights to 435 acres of common
grazing for sheep. In Knighton the tenants had access to 207 acres and the leased
Knighton demesne had a further eighty-eight acres of 'sheep ground'. For all the
other tenements apart from the demesne, the number of sheep allowed to be kept was
specified in the 1593 survey. In total the number of sheep in the parish amounted to
more than 2,260 suggesting about three to four sheep per acre. There are also some

102 This is the junction of the two principal roads before the main road built in the 1790s.
103 NHLE, ID 103119.

references to residual feudal services and obligations. In Durweston cum Knighton, as in Lytchett Minster, tenants owed working days to the lord of the manor and were also invited to a communal Christmas dinner.

Fortunately one of the few wills which exist for this period is that of the rector, Walter Coshe, who died in 1597.[104] He was the rector at the time of the 1585 survey He also held the living of Shillingstone and altogether would have had a considerable income. The glebe of Durweston cum Knighton consisted of about sixty acres in 1584. It is possible that his curate, Mr Thomas Whitelocke, looked after Shillingstone for him because he was given all the 'stuffe and timber' he had in that parish. The impression given is that of of a kind thoughtful man who spent considerable time deciding how his goods would be disposed, so that his friends and those who had served him would benefit most, but he did not forget the poor of his parishes. Richard Meade, described as a servant, was left a black colt, all his books, a cloth gown, hose and doublet, his best cassock and the lesser bedstead, together with the feather bed, in the parlour. The reference to the rooms gives us some idea of the size and function of the house. Tamazin Bodman, had the great brass pan (which was white) together with the cupboard in the hall next the chamber door plus one cow, whereas Margaret Polden, another servant, had the best brass pan, one cow and the great cupboard in the hall with a press in it. The two latter also shared the linen and all the silver spoons not given elsewhere. At some point he had borrowed money from both of them, £10 in the case of the latter, and to this he added a further £10.

He was particularly concerned with the future of the youngsters, William and Walter Coshe, (the former whom he spoke of as his servant) and who were presumably relatives. He asked his executors (including the then Archdeacon of Dorset) 'to have care and regard' that their portions 'be used to their best profit till they come to one and twentie years of age and that their mother have nothinge to doe with it'. The executors were to be rewarded for their pains: the Archdeacon was given a bedstead with feather bed which Walter Coshe himself used in the parlour together with a black bound chest and a silver cup and 40s.; Mr Peter Barker, the vicar of Stourpaine, had the bedstead above in the little chamber and the cupboard and counting board and 40s.; and Robert Frampton a corn mill, a bullock and all the chairs, forms and stools in the house with the boards that lie on both the cocklofts and forty shillings.

From these bequests we discover that the rectory possessed downstairs, a parlour in which were two beds, a chamber and a hall which had a great cupboard in it and possibly the pans mentioned and other kitchen equipment. Upstairs was one little chamber and two cocklofts and there may have been also other rooms not mentioned and other furniture, It would seem that we have a house with possibly one dormer window, if not more although no dormers are shown on any of the stylised houses on the map. The will also contains many references to his animals and to corn, some of which was growing in the parsonage ground in Knighton field. Barley, oats, dredge, peas and vetches were other crops grown. He had to make an

104 TNA, PROB 11/90 Walter Coshe 14 June 1597.

alteration to his will before he died, because by the time of his death he had used the corn he had left to the poor of the parish and, in compensation, he left all the barley and other grain then in the ground. He would appear to have been a man of some consequence beyond his own parish and may have had some influence on church affairs in Dorset.

The Purpose of the Surveys

The 1584 surveys, printed in this volume, are excellent documents, providing a full picture of the land arrangements and they were produced for a specific purpose: to provide the final audit of inclosed land within the manors. 'Enclosing and engrossing (holding more than one tenement) were two of the most controversial topics in sixteenth century England' writes Joan Thirsk. She adds that 'they provoked animated discussion in the alehouses, inspired outspoken sermons from the pulpit, and stirred passions and community loyalties in the fields as men ploughed their strips side by side in the common fields and muttered imprecations against the selfish and rich'.[105] There is evidence from elsewhere in Dorset that some of the common fields and the common heath or downland were being inclosed at this time and during the previous century.[106] At Long Bredy the lord and tenants agreed to enclose "a good part of the commons and waste ground of the manor" in 1597.[107] Excuses were made for abandoning the perambulation of the boundaries of parishes like Netherbury and Long Burton because of the difficulty caused by 'the new inclosures and multitude of hedges'.[108] Kitson, the Goldings and Wright were acting, like many other landlords and estate mangers, to improve the profitability of their lands.

Landlords in the later sixteenth century looked to maximise their profits: inflation had reduced the value of their fixed customary rents. The majority of their income came from the entry fines when new tenants were added to existing copyhold agreements. Customary tenants held their land for a term of lives rather than a term of years. A man might hold his land for the term of his life and those of two of his sons, when he died the eldest son might add his own child to the copyhold on payment of a fine that dwarfed the annual rent.[109] It was costly and inefficient to hold regular manor courts to administer a complex range of land disputes arising from scattered land holdings and easier for tenants and landlords to work and administer consolidated holdings. Poorer tenants did not benefit from the inclosures, as less common land and waste was available to them, but they did not control the process. As long as the wealthier tenants saw advantages the landlord was likely to succeed.

---

105 J. Thirsk (ed.) *Agricultural History of England and Wales*, vol. IV p. 200.
106 Taylor, *The Making of the English Landscape: Dorset*, pp.119-130.
107 Taylor, *The Making of the English Landscape: Dorset*, p.128.
108 J. H. Bettey 'Parish Life in Dorset in the Early Seventeenth Century' *Proc. DNHAS*, (1992) vol.114, pp.9-12.
109 Examples of the copyhold agreements for Okeford Fitzpaine may be found in Appendix A.

Thomas Kitson came of age and inherited his estates in 1561 and it seems likely that they had been poorly managed for some time previously. He was able to accrue vast sums from entry fines which enabled tenants to add further lives to their copyholds. These are detailed in an account roll of 1564, concerning the manors which Kitson held across the country, starting in Devon, Dorset and Somerset, followed by other manors elsewhere.[110] The entries for these West Country manors are longer and more complex than those for the remainder. Reference is made to instructions given to Edward Golding by Thomas Kitson dated 25 April 1564 to hold a meeting at Ipplepen. The report of the meeting begins with an account of the usual affairs of a normal court but is followed by a paragraph entitled 'Fines for land'. This contains the names of fifty-three tenants of the manor who had agreed to pay varying sums amounting to the enormous sum of £3,375. A further paragraph in the report of this court gives details of when all or a part of this money was to be paid. In most cases the amount was to be paid in three instalments during the next two to three years. Torbryan follows with similar details, the sum involved here being £1,352.

Okeford Fitzpaine is next: instructions had been given to Golding on the 26, April 1564 and a court was held in the parish on the 8th June 1564. Eighteen of the tenants agreed to pay fines varying from £6.13s. 4d. to £60 making a total of £474. This sum is much less than that of Ipplepen but again an extraordinarily large amount.[111] The manors of Durweston cum Knighton and Lytchett Minster cum Bere follow. Large sums could be made from fines, but only occasionally when the tenants wanted to add new lives; in the intervening years the tenants might be left to manage their own affairs and pay the small customary rents.

A survey dated 1582 provides more details of the above agreements made at Okeford Fitzpaine with many other agreements which were made during the preceding half century.[112] The author is given as Thomas Golding, the brother of Edward; it would seem that Edward had either died or retired by this time.[113] There is one reference to Thomas having acted as a surveyor in Okeford Fitzpaine earlier and it seems likely that he was the man who did most of the surveying in the three manors prior to the meetings of 1582.[114] By that time he had possibly taken over the overall management of the Dorset and Somerset manors. The Okeford Fitzpaine section is headed with the words: 'An abstracte of the Coppyes of the said manor taken the 26th May 1582' by Thomas Golding' and is printed in Appendix A. At this court it was necessary for Thomas Golding to have the original text of the transactions so these could be verified.

This document contains several references to open fields in Okeford Fitzpaine that are not present in the 1584 survey: William Whyte had seven acres of arable lying

---

110 SRO, HA 528/24.

111 A further document exists consists of torn and partly illegible pieces of paper which confirms the above and provides more details of the agreements reached SRO, 449/1/E/15.103/1.1.

112 SRO, HA/528/27.

113 TNA, C2/Eliz/M15 dated 1558-1603.

114 SRO, HA/528/27. A Thomas Golding was involved in a Chancery Case as a defendant with Thomas Kitson HD/1778.

in two fields, while Alice Lyndsey held arable land that was "inclosed". The terms are precise: fields were open fields and inclosures were recently enclosed. After half of the entries the abstract changes from English to Latin and the same distinction is maintained with the use of "inclausum" and "campus". The fields had gone two years later when Wright surveyed. They had been replaced by inclosures and from these it is possible to map the process. The working papers contained sufficient detail for the Goldings to manage the manors: they detailed the entry fines, rents and the outstanding lives, but they only estimated the size of the tenements. The 1584 surveys produced by Wright are precise and reliable: they are a definitive description of the manors immediately post inclosure. At the Hertfordshire Record Office there are three short surveys which are not dated but appear, from an examination of the changes in the names of the people involved, to be slightly later at around 1587.[115] These seem to have been compiled as working documents for the use of the steward when dealing with those aspects of the manor that are not included in the 1584 surveys.

There is no precise evidence of when the inclosure process began. It is likely that Kitson and Golding took an overview of the estate in the 1560s and decided to sweep away some of the archaic structures which made it difficult to administer. For the process to have been completed by 1584 this was an achievable timescale: agreements would have been sought with the tenants, a scheme devised for each manor, and thousands of hurdles produced to divide those fields, commons and waste. Presumably each manor was inclosed in sections, one field or Precinct at a time, to minimise the disruption to the farming calendar. The result was a consolidated land holding which could be worked without reference to neighbouring tenements, and could be easily sold or leased by the tenant. Kitson gained a structure that required minimal administration and which included additional arable and pasture that had formerly been commons.

The importance of the inclosures in the history of each parish varied: for Okeford Fitzpaine the effect was the most drastic. The houses and the village itself changed little, apart from the building of some new cottages possibly on the old demesne land and one new house in West Street but the inclosures of the land around had a major effect not only on the lives of the people concerned but also on the landscape. Almost every aspect of their lives was touched. Close to the village the inclosure of the 'Westwood' and the loss of many trees in that area would be obvious every time they wandered beyond the built up areas. The inclosure and fencing of much of the common land would restrict their movement and would be noticed especially by those with little land. Whenever they climbed the largest remaining common land, 'The Hill', the changes below them would be very apparent. The effect it had on the reorganisation of the land areas and the less need for cooperation between the tenants also had a direct affect on the social make-up of the parish. The

115 Herts RO, Gorhambury Collection XI.4. The names useful for dating are John Henning the elder in Lytchett Minster who died in December 1584, and 1590 when Julian Gould died.

enclosures could well have been was the most radical event in the history of Okeford Fitzpaine.

In Durweston cum Knighton the changes were major but of less significance to the villagers themselves although of considerable significance to John Powlden. In the parish the majority of the strip fields remained and the comparatively small area of land taken from the commons was not of much consequence though the lack of common land beside the roads could have been a nuisance when animals were moved around. The major change here came in the eighteenth century when the strips disappeared, not through any official inclosure but because of the policy of the landowners. In the eighteenth century the owners of the manor pursued a policy of amalgamating the tenements to produce larger units. This was done gradually: when a tenancy fell in it was kept in hand until it could be joined to another to make a larger unit and remove the need for the strips. As the century progressed there were less copyholders and leaseholders named in each successive survey and more cottages paying a rack rent. By 1784 enough land was in hand for an exchange to be made with the rector so that the glebe could be brought together into one unit instead of in the many parts as described in the survey of 1585. This was not only more practical for the landlord but also for the rector as his land was next to his rectory to the south of Milton Lane.[116]. The result of this policy and the two major farms created can be seen clearly on the map of 1801. This process of amalgamation was of great benefit to the landlord but unfortunate for those who had been copyhold or leasehold tenants with their own land. Some of the rights held by the parishioners on the common land did survive until the pioneering agriculturalist, Lord Portman, in the nineteenth century arranged for a whole area of common land, to be called Shepherd's farm, to be transformed, as he said, into good agricultural land by dint of excessive hard labour.[117] There exists in the National Archives a board of wood divided into squares which is a plan of the area before the work started and gives the names of all the tenants and the areas of land over which they had rights which they lost under Lord Portman's scheme and for which they were compensated'

The major change in Lytchett Minster occurred later than in the other two parishes following the inclosure Act of 1818 and the activities of Sir Claude Scott. These events have been discussed elsewhere.[118] Between 1584 and the 1820s surprisingly little seems to have changed in the boundaries of the tenements. There was some inclosure of the heathland and some building along the side of the roads, but only after 1820 did the main phase of inclosure take place. Over the next two centuries almost all the heathland to the east of the village was gradually developed with new houses and an area, now called the town of Upton, has arisen containing the majority of the population: in the twenty first century the population has risen to over

116 TNA, CRES 38/86.
117 T. Ward, 'Archdeacon Anthony Huxtable (1808-1883) Radical Parson, Scientist and Scientific Farmer. in *Proc. DNHAS*, (1980) vol.101, pp.7-23.
118 J. Palmer, 'Sir Claude Scott and the development of Lytchett Minster in the nineteenth century' in *Proc. DNHAS*, (2014) vol.135, pp.33-45.

ten thousand. New amenities have and are being developed producing a popular and pleasant community noted for its attractive floral displays, close to the countryside and the inlet of the sea yet convenient for the ever growing area of Poole.

The Changes in Okeford Fitzpaine

In Okeford Fitzpaine the survey makes a clear distinction between a *clausam*, an ancient inclosure, and *inclausam*, a recently inclosed area. In 1584 no common fields remained in Okeford Fitzpaine as a direct result of the process of inclosure over the preceding years when the new inclosures were created.

It is impossible, through lack of space, to give more than a few examples of how tenants were affected by these land transactions but Appendix A details the copyhold agreements which present the position in 1582 prior to the inclosure of some tenements. The copyholds may be compared with the entries in the 1584 survey. To do this various factors must be considered: measurements in the copyholds are all described as 'estimated' and therefore, are seldom exactly the same as those in Thomas Wright's survey when, possibly for the first time, a proper measurement of the land was conducted. The inclosures were of mainly arable and pasture land, little definite information is given on how the meadow land was affected. Much of the arable had been in the common strip fields. Discovering where this land was in Okeford Fitzpaine can be difficult from the records available from this period. There are only a few entries which provide some clues as to the whereabouts of the strip common fields. The Historic Monuments Commission refer to the remains of strips in Hebed, in land near to Garlands and in Fiddleford, but concludes that nothing is known of the open field structure and arrangement.[119]

The evidence of Domesday Book is for extensive arable in the eleventh century. The 1584 survey does not mention land use, between then and the late eighteenth century; no document which provides details of the full picture has been found, although court roll entries give individual amounts. The most useful document, is a survey compiled in the nineteenth century but which refers back to the late eighteenth century and is especially useful as it has the same numbering as the map of 1782.[120] The majority of the areas of arable land in the 1800s survey can be found between the numbers, 330-420 on the map of 1782, and most of these areas were described as 'inclosures' in the 1584 survey.[121] It can be seen that most the arable land was close to the village, mainly to the south west and south east with a few pockets elsewhere.

With most of the arable being in the strip fields before 1584 much of the remaining land, with the exception of the woodland, was used for pasture. Several of the wealthier tenants had their own inclosed land before the 1560s. Most of these copyhold tenants are mentioned in the survey as having *terra nata*, that is land to

---

119 RCHM, *An Inventory of Historical Monuments in the county of Dorset, Volume 3, Central Dorset,* (1970) part 2, p.206.

120 DHC, D-PIT Acc 9202 Box 3 item 4.

121 The numbering was the same in the 1800s survey as on the 1782 map although it was changed for the Tithe map of 1838.

which they had a right by birth. They are sometimes called customary tenants, in other words tenants who held their land by the customs of the manor and who were admitted in the manor court. This land could be used as the holder wished for either arable or pasture and therefore its classification was not known. It is estimated that in 1584 about 250 acres of land had been held in this way.

The task of dividing up the common land in Okeford Fitzpaine to form the inclosures was complicated by the terrain itself, the road system and by the presence of the existing 'closes' which were fixed areas and could not be part of the process. Additionally other areas of land in Okeford Fitzpaine proved an obstacle to any attempt to re-draw the boundaries. The freehold lands, including over 100 acres owned by the Yeovil almshouse, were not under Kitson's jurisdiction and were not therefore part of the process of inclosure. Much of this freehold land and the old closes were in the south west of the parish. The families who held these properties were generally the more prosperous and the impression given is that these areas had long been in existence as distinct entities. Southley was a compact area of about fifty-three acres in several closes at the far south west of the parish which was held by Edward Howe, the successor of the John Howe mentioned in Golding's notes. He was one of the largest holders of land having about ninety-two acres in 1584, part of which was in this area [Go 571-578], and was described as a customary tenant in the survey. Another customary tenant was Edward Phillips who held land nearby which consisted at that time of one large close, part of the area called Stroud, which was about thirty-nine acres and contained many trees. By the time of the 1782 map this land was divided into nine areas [Cl 479-487].

Another such tenant, with one of his two tenements in this area, was John Iles, whose name is the first in the survey and coincidentally held the first land on the south west side of the parish. From his own tenement as far as the road to Dorchester he held a series of inclosures. These appear on the first inspection to be scattered without any forming any specific pattern. But, on further examination of the map, it can be seen that the inclosures were deliberately planned in this area. Those belonging to John Iles, and the other tenants, were adjacent to one another and arranged to facilitate movement of stock between them, without having to enter the land of a neighbour, to enable easy access to a road or common land. John Iles, starting from his tenement [Fu 469, 472, 478] could lead his animals through his inclosures for about half a mile without trespassing on his neighbours as far as the road along which it was an easy distance to his house in the village or on to the Downs.

His neighbour, Edward Phillips, had the same advantage along a similar, but more contorted route from his tenement of Stroud again as far as the road [Cl 470, 467, 463 to close 425]. Joan Osmond's land comes next and again along a similar line of inclosures more irregular in shape, takes her not in this case as far as the road to Dorchester but up to Redlake Lane near to the village. Those with less land had their tenements nearer to the road to which access was arranged. Considerable thought was given therefore to the boundary lines and what appears haphazard on the map was carefully planned. This arrangement provides an explanation why the tenement of John Iles and others remained more or less intact for the next two hundred years: it would have been very difficult to have detached some of the land without blocking access to the remainder.

Other areas show considerable thought in the planning process. Three sites to the north west of Yeovil almshouse site were all part of the land called Gobson. The arrangement for these three tenants, William White senior, Henry Ford and John Shotto near the boundary of the parish on the north east side, was cleverly designed to allow all three access to the area of Gobson which is described as The Common on the 1782 map: the land was tapered so that access was made possible for each.

The land in the east of the parish had a somewhat different composition. There were less pre-existing closes here and therefore more inclosures distributed among many tenants. There had been some land already in closes including land belonging to the rector. The glebe was extensive in Okeford Fitzpaine and the rector had a right to some of the inclosed land that was to be found close to his original land. His agreement presumably was obtained to the whole process although there are no references to this in the documents mentioned although the list of his land is given in the survey.

When all these factors are considered it is not surprising that the whole process took twenty years to complete. By 1564 agreement had been reached with twenty-eight tenants of Okeford Fitzpaine; a sufficient number to allow the process of division to begin. Other tenants joined in later and the whole system seems to have been ratified at the meeting in May of 1582 when the tenants produced their copies of the original documents. The following year Thomas Wright was sent to Dorset to make a complete record of the results, including the full measurements necessary to prevent any disputes in the future.

There were a few minor alterations in the next few years as some of the tenants exchanged small areas of land with their neighbours. The rental of Okeford Fitzpaine of 1590 is unusual in that it contains references to these exchanges and gives the details of how the various rents were slightly altered by them.[122]

One somewhat surprising omission from the survey is that of the rights of the tenants over the common land, in particular the number of animals they were allowed to keep there. With the enclosure of the land one would have expected that a new arrangement would have been necessary but no mention of one is given. Durweston cum Knighton is the only manor that provides this information. Subsequent documents for Okeford Fitzpaine, especially the court documents of the eighteenth century sometimes mention common rights but it is difficult to extract definite amounts that might have been allowed in 1584. The 1800s survey does provide more information, although again the allocations of sheep and 'beasts' to each tenement would appear to have changed over the previous two hundred years but a total of over 800 sheep can be deduced from this document. The land on which they grazed was 'The Hill' thus giving an approximate estimate of four sheep allowed per acre. Gobson was used

122 SRO, HA/528/86.

for the 'beasts' - draft horses and oxen. Here there was a more democratic approach for it would seem that originally every tenement (possibly excluding the new cottages) had the right to keep one 'beast' on Gobson, allowing very approximately one acre per animal.

It is clear that the process of inclosure was complete in Okeford Fitzpaine by 1584. No common fields remained and each tenant had a discrete tenement in a structure that was sufficiently productive for many to remain intact until the survey of 1792 and beyond. The process of inclosure had not been haphazard for it is evident that each tenant's field inter-linked to form continuous areas linking them with the drove roads and commons.

The Changes in Durweston cum Knighton

Durweston cum Knighton in the 1585 survey was a parish containing open strip fields many of which are shown on the map dated to the 1580s, so it might be assumed that there had been little change in the structure of the lands here but, when the wording in the survey is examined, it is found that the word '*inclausa*' occurs very frequently these inclosures amount to about 400 acres in the whole parish.

The use of specific words is again of interest. An area containing, or which had contained, a series of strips is called a *stadium* and this description is used for most of the areas of land in both Durweston and Knighton, the word 'Precinct' being reserved for the principal areas containing the houses and where there were no, or very few, strips. In the 1585 survey *stadium* continues to be used even if the area no longer contained any strips or else very few. This is useful because it helps to reveal areas which had previously been part of strip fields.

Knighton

The area K1 is a good example of a Precinct, beginning with the manor house and continuing along the road leading to the Stour with the Knighton houses on the south side with the addition of a few areas of land. Conversely K2, on the east side of Brenson way (the road leading to Bryanston) is described as a *stadium*, but no strips are mentioned. Out of the six entries, there are three 'tenements', held by Robert Frampton [K2.1], Robert Seagar [K2.4] and Thomas Phillips [K2.6] beside the road. *Stadium* K3, which is a continuation of K2 on the same side of the road, likewise contains little reference to strips. Out of the ten entries here three are the tenements of John Frye [K3.1], Robert Hector [K3.2], and Nicholas Evered [K3.4]. The valuable meadow land was to the east of K2, in *stadia* K4-6 and most of this land was in strips with the exception of a large inclosure belonging to John Powlden. At the top of the road James Privett also has a tenement on the west side of the road [K19.1] and beside it is an area where John Powlden, the holder of the demesne, was built four houses [K19.2]. Six of these seven Bryanston Way tenants occur in the court roll entries abstracted by Thomas Golding. They also occur the most frequently in the references to the 'inclosures' mentioned in the Knighton survey of 1584.

The majority of the areas from K4 to K32 are headed with the word *stadium,* although they include some inclosed land. Some of these 'inclosures' are near to the downland and it would seem they were taken from that uncultivated area: for example K32 is described as in the area lying between Knighton Cowpasture and the Sheep Down, with two of its twelve areas described as closes, the remainder as 'inclosures'. The whole covered forty-four acres over half of which was held by the Bryanston Way tenants.

The fine which Thomas Phillips, one of the Bryanston Way tenants, paid for his copyhold, dated 1577 was £46 13s. 4d. which is comparable with those of Okeford Fitzpaine for a similar sized property - Phillips was paying for thirty-eight acres of arable land. In the 1585 survey his land is described as containing two inclosures each of around seventeen acres. The remainder of his arable land was in strips.

John Powlden held a lease for the demesne lands of Knighton: the original lands farmed by the lord of the manor and frequently described as the 'farm'. These lands were very extensive. In the survey of 1585 he had his own sheep down containing eighty-eight acres and a few separate areas of land including several acres of meadow but most of the remaining land stretched almost all the way across the southern border of the parish adjacent to Bryanston. [K33.6 to K.33.9]. In the description of these areas in the 1585 survey there is once more a deliberate differentiation between the use of the word 'close' and 'inclosure' and again this is significant. K33.9, beside the Bryanston road, is described in the survey as being in four 'closes' which already existed before the changes were made to the manor. The later map of 1801 is very helpful in differentiating between the arable fields and the 'closes'. For example the word 'close' is used in 1801 for K33.6 to K.33.8; these areas are described in 1585 as inclosures and were some of the better quality land. They were most likely to have been arable in 1585, divided into strips; a large number of these would have belonged to Powlden, but other tenants would have had a share. To consolidate his land John Powlden had to give up the strips he held in the other fields and these strips would have become available in the remaining areas to compensate those who had lost strips and to provide additional strips for the Bryanston Way tenants.

An arrangement was probably reached between Thomas Kitson and John Powlden for his demesne land to be consolidated and free from any association with others. For both Kitson and Powlden this consolidation of the land would have been beneficial for ease of management.

Durweston

What happened in Knighton contrasts with the position in Durweston. Here, according to the 1585 survey, the demesne was divided into five parts each with separate tenants holding by copyhold rather than by lease, as in Knighton, and with the land belonging to the tenants spread across the manor. When this division took place is not known though it is possible not until the 1570s. The first definite reference found to it is in the copies of the court rolls for 1577 when both Edward Bennett and Henry Reynolds took out a copyhold on a fifth part of the farm.[123] Bennett paid a fine of £30 and Reynolds £27.

In the 1585 survey the five tenants of the farm were named as John Henning, Edward Bennet, John Iles, Richard Prower and Roger Ranew.[124] It cannot be a coincidence that the last four all have the same surnames of copyhold tenants in Okeford Fitzpaine and John Henning was associated with that parish as a free tenant of Nash Court in Marnhull. These men in Durweston must therefore be the same men or relations of those in Okeford Fitzpaine. It is possible that Kitson chose to divide the farm to gain a higher rent, or that it was divided and leased to existing tenants to encourage them to accept inclosures elsewhere. There is no reference to a 'house' on the land of either Edward Bennet or John Henning and the other three might have lived in Okeford Fitzpaine or elsewhere. Almost half of the acreage of the inclosures in Durweston, which amounted in total to around 180 acres, belonged to these men.

Many of the inclosures are to be found beside the road leading from the Stour to 'Ockford'. The first section is described as a 'Precinct', followed by the rectory and four 'inclosures' which may previously have been unenclosed common grazing land beside the road as no *stadium* is mentioned.

As in Knighton, the word *stadium* is used for an area which did not contain only strips: the *stadium* D.6 consisted of fifteen acres of land in three 'inclosures', suggesting that here there had previously been strips but this had been inclosed.

The principal Precincts D.7 and D.8 contain almost all the houses in Durweston plus the mill and the site of the manor house. At the northern end of Precinct Seven are several inclosures. D.9 – D.14 are *stadia* forming the field later called Winshead, consisting of strips covering forty-five acres which is shown on the on the 1801 map and still more or less intact today. The land beside the Ockford Way consisted of inclosures matching the inclosures as on the other side of the road with some areas of high ground called the South Cliffe described as vacant.

The remaining areas contain many 'inclosures' some of which were near to the remaining downland and may have been taken from there rather than from the arable. The description ends with D.28 which covers the very large area of the Durweston downlands divided into several areas.

From the analysis of the parish of Durweston cum Knighton it is clear that there were a considerable number of boundary changes with many new areas created. This was caused by the alteration to the demesnes in both Knighton and Durweston, the need to produce more discrete tenements in the parish and the general desire to improve the efficiency of the whole. The extra land needed was obtained from various sources: the inclosures included land beside the roads, former open grazing, former arable, the reorganisation of the demesne and occasionally taking some of the downland into cultivation. The process appeared to start a little later than in Okeford

---

123 SRO, 449/1/E.15.53/1.1.

124 The spelling of this surname was an alternative to that of 'Reynolds' and used in the 1585 survey.

Fitzpaine but possibly was not concluded by 1584 as for the other two manors, for this survey is dated 1585.

This parish is the only one with a map extant. From clues given in the description of this parish it may be possible to deduce the origin of the map. One of these is the reference to Robert Seagar of Knighton who, in 1577, added the name of his son, William, to his copyhold cottage, ten acres of arable land and one close of pasture.[125] The latter was described as 'newly inclosed' but then was added 'newly being inclosed lying near unto the free Downe.' In other words the inclosure of this area was being undertaken when the agreement was written down. This shows that the arrangement for the inclosure of land coincided more or less with the time when the agreements were reached. In Okeford Fitzpaine thirty-eight agreements had been reached by 1564 which suggests that a start was made to dividing this land, possibly as the payments for the fines were collected and much was arranged fairly early in the process. With Durweston cum Knighton the main process would not have been started until the 1570s, for only a few minor agreements had occurred in 1564. In the 1570s Thomas Golding was in the area and it is possible that he was himself responsible for the map, which would be amended as decisions were reached. This explains the many alterations which were made to it and some its inaccuracies for, as the copyholds state, they were based on estimated and not measured figures. The map could then have been used as a guide by Thomas Wright when he was asked to measure the area accurately. Its use, therefore, might have extended over several years, representing a new structure that was yet to take shape on the ground, and perhaps explaining its battered condition. Whether the map ever covered the whole parish is not known for many of the 'inclosures' (excluding those affecting Powlden and those around the Downs) are shown in the extant part.

The Changes in Lytchett Minster cum Bere

The manor of Lytchett Minster was situated in an area of Dorset containing heathland where there were few common strip fields. The survey of 1584, however, is evidence of their presence in the parish of Lytchett Minster because the word *stadium* is used twice in Precinct Six and, as explained earlier; this was the word used by Thomas Wright to describe areas containing strip fields. This word is used for the land south of what is now the road to Dorchester and east of the stream which divides Precinct Six north of the river Sherford; it was divided horizontally by one continuous boundary into what seems to have been a 'North Field' and a 'South Field'.

A large part of Precinct Six was not owned by Thomas Kitson. Much of the other areas of land were freely owned, Richard Russell being the principal owner in this area but Christopher Antill, Benjamin Titchmarsh and others also had land and Augustine Lawrence, gentleman and the principal copyholder in the western part of Precinct Six, was a 'customary' tenant.[126]

---

125 SRO, 449/1/E3/15.103/1.1.

126 It was not unusual in this period for merchants and gentlemen to acquire copyhold land as part of their estates.

It is not known whether the suggestion of inclosure came from Kitson or possibly from Trenchard but, for it to succeed, it needed the agreement of all landowners. This was achieved without apparent difficulty. It occurred after 1565 for the valuation of the manor of Lytchett Minster in that year, which also included the manors of Puddletown and Pulham, made reference to inclosures having occurred in the latter two manors but there was no reference to any in Lytchett Minster. There is also a reference in the Court Book of the manor of Slepe cum Cockamore for 1565 to arable land in the common fields of Slepe.[127] The necessary meeting appears to have taken place about 1567 or 1568, for in the accounts of that year, 5s. was spent on the expenses of the steward coming to court and 'with good conscience conferring with the tenants about the customs'. The steward at this time was Edward Golding. He returned the following year 'concerning a first extract of the court which was signed by men of the homage'.[128]

There are several references to inclosures in the western half of Precinct Six where Augustine Lawrence was the tenant of most of the land owned by Kitson. Some references in the 1584 survey suggest that there had been a substantial area of common here which was shared out between Lawrence, Trenchard and the other freeholders.

No references have been found elsewhere to other strip fields but several Precincts contain references to 'inclosures'. The number of 'inclosures' in the survey of 1584 for the whole of the parish was about forty-four, about half of which were in Precinct Six. The remainder all appear to have been connected with the inclosure of previously uncultivated land. Some of this was the marshy land around the Sherford River, with the aim of turning it into meadow and the rest from the heath. Thomas Barnes and William Furmage had land inclosed from the latter.

The rush land in Precinct Twelve, which is described in the survey of 1584 as belonging to six tenants who had the right to cut these rushes [LM 207] was subject to an agreement soon afterwards whereby the land should be divided so that the tenants had their own particular areas instead of acting in common.[129] The benefits of inclosure were becoming apparent not only to Kitson but also to the tenants.

The inclosure map of the 1820s reveals that little seems to have been done in this respect between 1584 and the 1820s. Some extra land was added on the periphery of the cultivated land and along the side of the roads where new houses were built, but comparatively little until the 1818 Inclosure Act after which the remaining common, covering a large area was finally inclosed. The boundaries changed little over the two and a half centuries, which is very helpful when tracing the position of the areas described in 1584.

127 Slepe Court Book DHC, D-LEE/1.
128 SRO, 449/1/E3/15.51/1.3 and 449/1/E3/15.51/1.4.
129 SRO, 449/E3/15.53/3.2.

Trees

Woodland was a valuable asset which was frequently retained in hand by the lord of the manor. Often tenants acquired the rights to pasture and underwood, while the timber trees remained the property of the lord. At all the meetings of May 1582 woodland was discussed. The woodland areas of all three parishes had the potential of being very profitable, especially those of Lytchett Minster as the valuation of 1565 had stressed. Thomas Golding would seem to have been concerned that the management could be improved. In the notes on the court rolls for 1582 there is a retrospective list of tree sales for all three manors (plus Ipplepen and Downhead), made by Golding himself, back to 1571. He concluded that this list was not complete therefore he asked the homage of each manor to draw up a list of all the sales of trees they themselves could remember over the last decade. They duly did so and this list is dated 29 May. None of the transactions in the tenants' list match those from the court rolls and many have no sale price attached. He must therefore have worried over why he had not been adequately informed and have had some doubts over the trustworthiness of the local men described as 'accomptants' who were responsible for handling the sales: they were Edward Howe for Okeford Fitzpaine, Julian Gould for Lytchett Minster, and Walter Appowell for Durweston cum Knighton .

The most interesting entry for Okeford Fitzpaine in the list from the homage is that which mentions Westwood where as many as 160 trees were felled. These may have been mature trees, as trees not full grown were normally described as 'small'. Westwood was the area surrounding the village to the north and west and, as open land, would have been for many centuries greatly enjoyed and used by the villagers. By 1584 it was divided into many, mostly small, inclosures of about one acre with a few of the more wealthy tenants such as Edward Howe and John Iles having larger areas. The mass felling in itself was a very significant and visible change for the villagers and the landscape would have been greatly altered with the loss of so many trees. There is no record of any payments having been received for these trees.

Possibly the most worrying information concerned Lytchett Minster. The homage reported that someone called Spere had felled and sold an unknown number of trees from the principal woods of the manor, including Berewood, Bulbury and Geynes. It is noticeable that after this meeting the policy changed. The larger transactions were organised by leasing out some of the woodlands and a yearly rent charged. This enabled a sum of money to be initially available together with a regular income for a number of years. In 1582 the tenants of Knighton under William Domine agreed to lease the coppice wood of Filgrove for twenty-one years paying a fine of £20 and a rent of 40s. In the same year in Okeford Fitzpaine William Forde and others agreed to lease the principal wood called Coniger (though the timber trees were excluded from the deal) with a fine of £20 and a rent of £6. This suggests a co-operative effort on the part of the villagers to raise the funds and manage the coppicing. The most important of these leases was that dated 1584 when Thomas Dewey, who leased the farm of the former manor of Bere, agreed to take over Bulbury and Geynes woods for a term of ninty-nine years paying a fine of £160 and a rent of 40s.

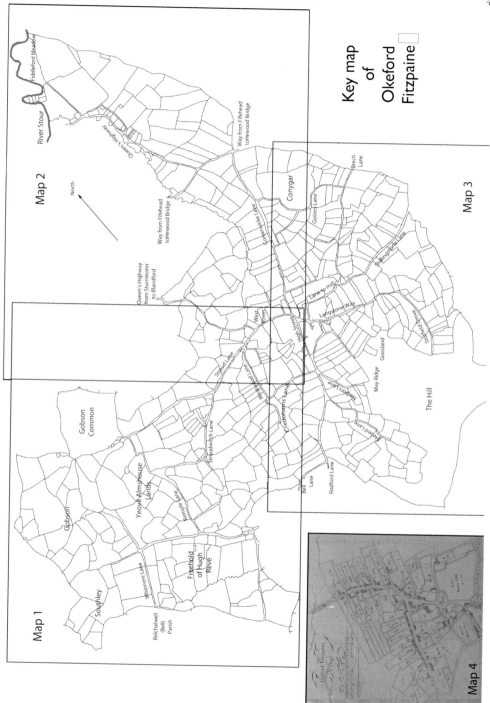

Key map
of
Okeford
Fitzpaine

Map 1

Map 2

Map 3

Map 4

North

River Stour

Fiddleford Meadow

Queen's Highway

Way from Fifehead to Hewood Bridge

Way from Fifehead to Hewood Bridge

Queen's Highway from Sturminster to Blandford

Conygar

Brech Lane

Gollier's Lane

Shillingstone Lane

Corpenlicke Lane

Lane to mill

West Street

High Street

Langstone Way

Stafford Drove

Goosland

May Ridge

Stroud Lane

Highwood Lane

Crebbman's Lane

Naylors Lane

Lidford Lane

The Hill

Streadwich Lane

Bell Lane

Rodford Lane

Gobson Common

Gobson

Yeouh Almshouse Lands

Temple Lane

Whitmere Lane

Freehold of Hugh Reve

Southley

Belchalwell (Bell) Parish

Okeford Fitzpaine Village

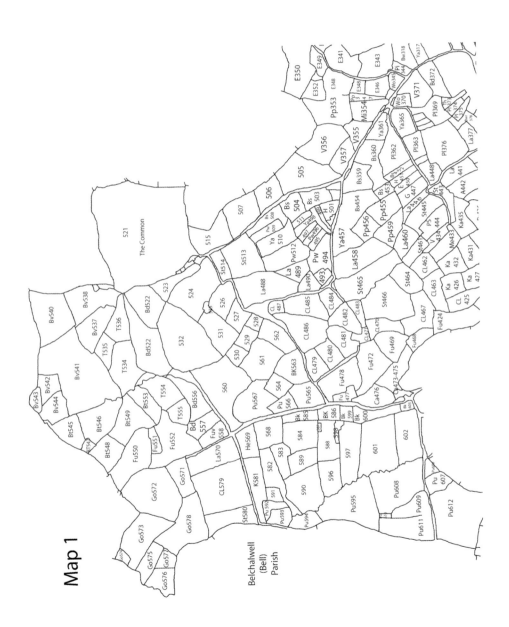

Map 1

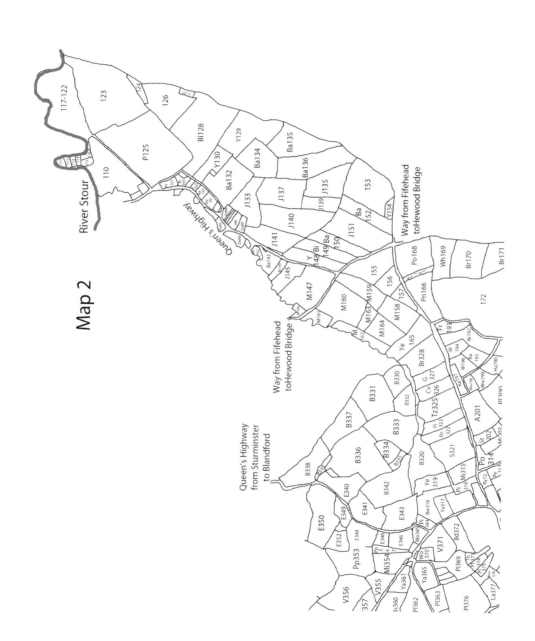

Map 2

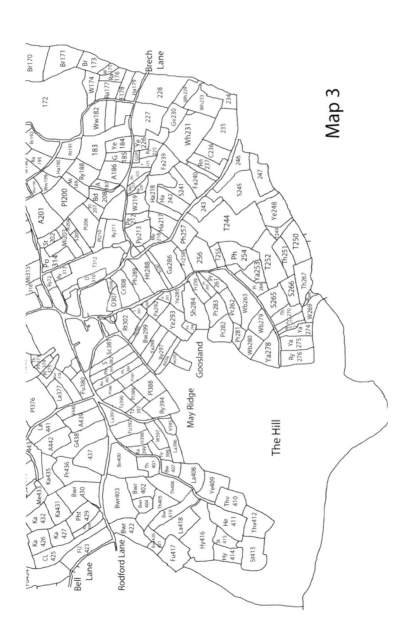

Map 3

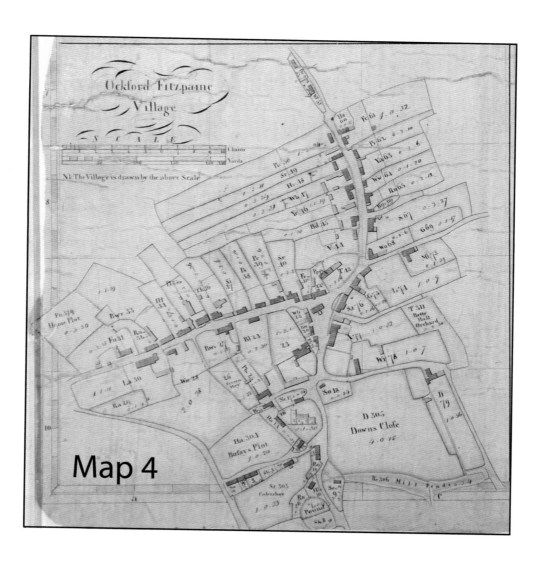

Map 4

The Lytchett Minster maps

The Lytchett Minster maps are based upon the Inclosure map for Lytchett Minster and Lytchett Matravers produced in 1820s (Dorset History Centre reference I.5).

Each entry in the printed survey of 1584 is followed by those numbers on the inclosure map that are thought to correspond with the sixteenth century tenements. These identifications are conjectural and based upon the author's interpretation of the survey and other contemporary documents at the Dorset History Centre and the Suffolk Record Office.

The survey begins with a heading for many of the precincts. This usually starts with a fixed point in the landscape such as a river or highway and then states the direction in which the lands will be described.

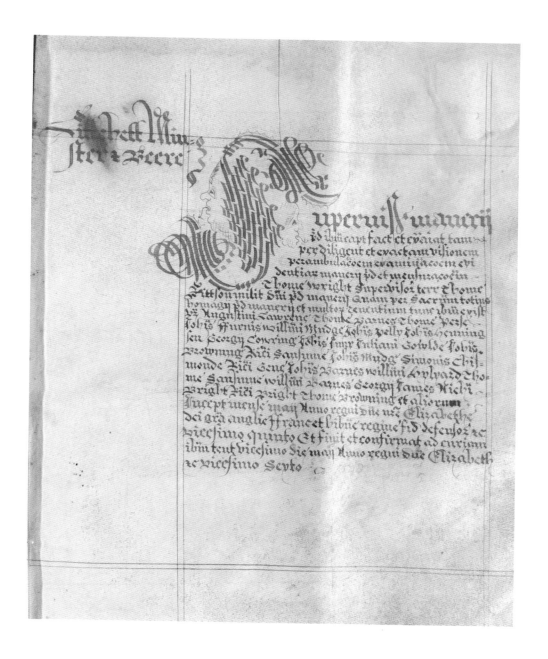

MAPS AND PLATES

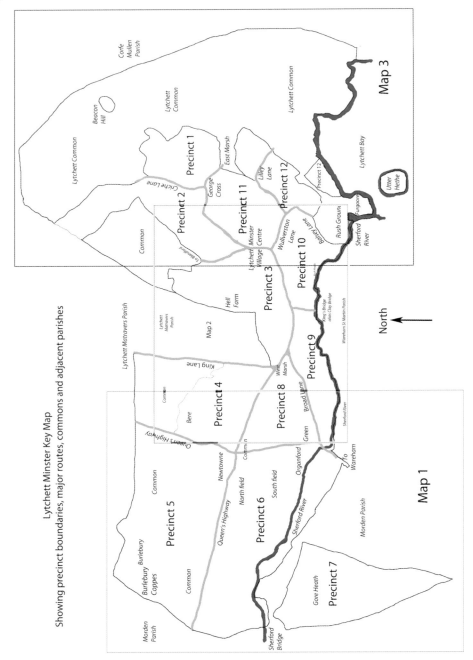

Lytchett Minster Key Map

Showing precinct boundaries, major routes, commons and adjacent parishes

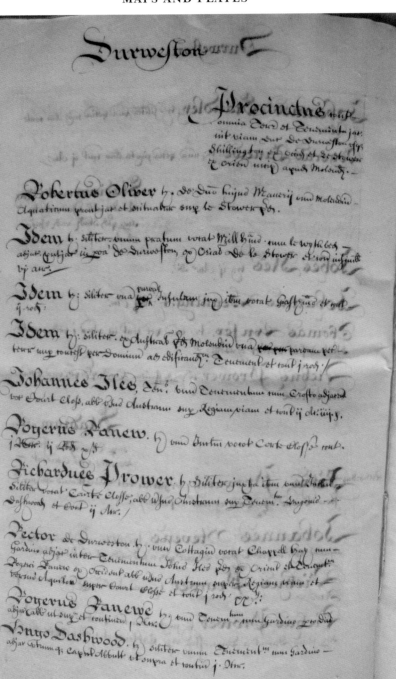

The Durweston cum Knighton map, 1580s

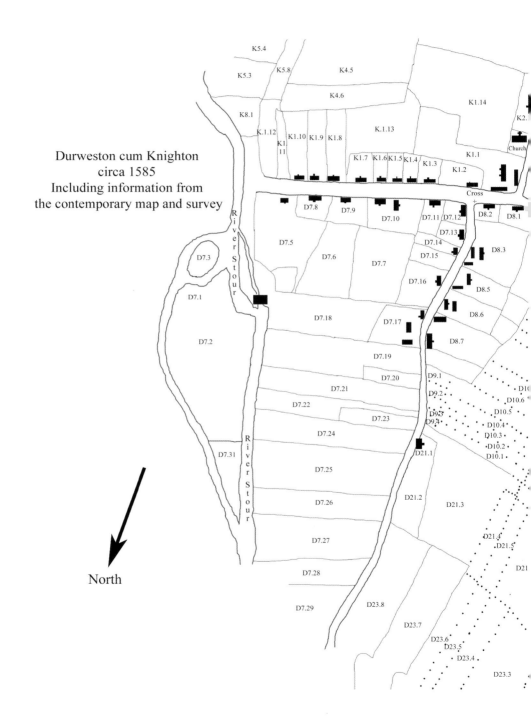

Durweston cum Knighton
circa 1585
Including information from
the contemporary map and survey

North

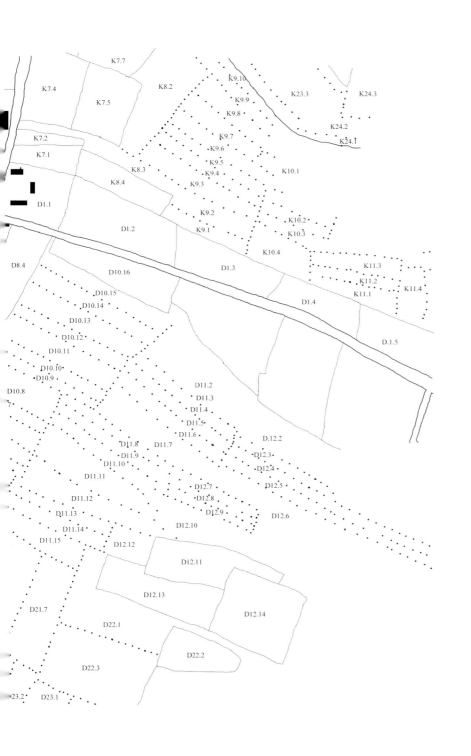

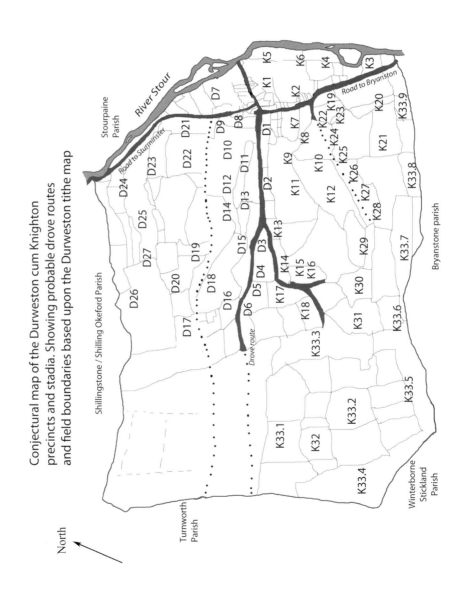

Conjectural map of the Durweston cum Knighton precincts and stadia. Showing probable drove routes and field boundaries based upon the Durweston tithe map

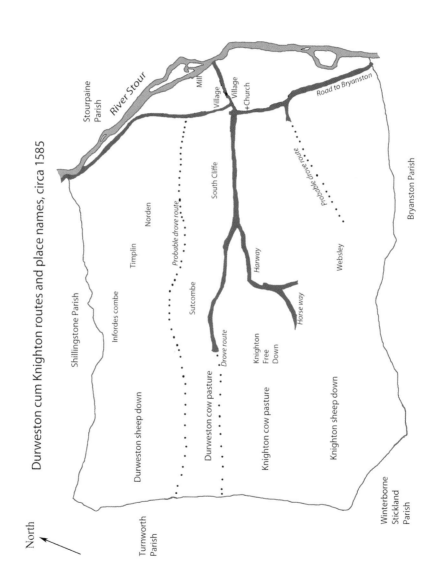

Durweston cum Knighton routes and place names, circa 1585

North

Stourpaine Parish

River Stour

Mill

Village

Village +Church

Road to Bryanston

Bryanston Parish

Shillingstone Parish

Norden

Timplin

Infordes combe

Probable drove route

South Cliffe

Sutcombe

Harway

Probable drove route

Websley

Horse way

Drove route

Knighton Free Down

Durweston sheep down

Durweston cow pasture

Knighton cow pasture

Knighton sheep down

Turnworth Parish

Winterborne Stickland Parish

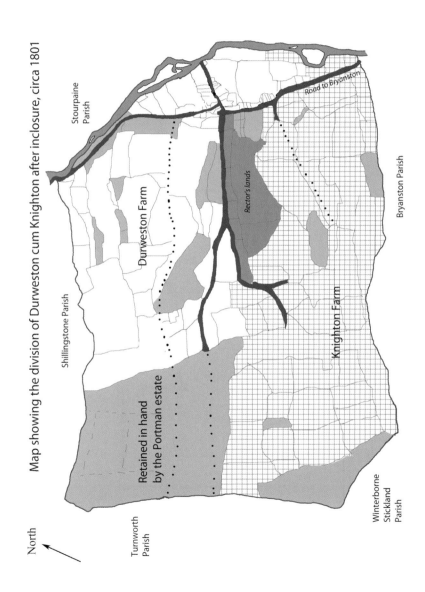

Map showing the division of Durweston cum Knighton after inclosure, circa 1801

Detail from the Durweston cum Knighton map, 1580s

OKEFORD FITZPAINE

Survey of the manor held, made and examined by diligent and exact inspection, perambulation and examination of the aforesaid manor by Thomas Wrighte, surveyor for Sir Thomas Kittson, lord of this manor and with the oaths of the whole homage of the manor and numerous tenants including: Hugh Kene, Henry Forde, Henry Reynolde, Henry Wakeford, John White senior, John Isles, William Chepman, William White, Robert Pope, Richard Prower, William White, Robert Pope, Richard Prower, William White senior, Richard Bute, John Newton, Richard Gobye, Joseph Harrys, Edward Williams, Walter Rose, Robert Hyne, William Phillips, Richard Foote, John Bythewoode, Laurence Frampton, John Pelly, Edward Bennett, Noel Harvye, Thomas Snoke, John Mahew, Richard Powlden, Edward Skott, Henry Bugge, William Forde, George White and others. Begun in the month of April in the 25ᵗʰ year of the reign of her majesty Queen Elizabeth, finished and confirmed at a court held on 27 day of March in the 26ᵗʰ year of her reign [1584]

[OF1.1] John Iles holds by copy one tenement with garden adjacent lying in the Hye Streate beside the land of William Pellye to the north, John's other land to the south and abutting to the east over the Queen's highway leading from Sturmester to Blandford, containing 2 roods, 10 perches. [Fu 31]

[OF1.2] He also holds similarly nearby one inclosure with a small orchard to the north called Lowbrooke lying between the said way to the east, the customary land of Henry Wakeford to the west, abutting to the north over the said tenement and the land of Henry Wakeford and to the south over a certain lane called Credohams Lane, containing 3 acres, 1 rood. [Fu 379, Fu 380]

[OF1.3] He also holds two inclosures lying together called Reyland lying between Bell Lane to the south and the customary tenement of Edward Phillipes to the north abutting to the west over Rodford Lane, containing 5 acres, 2 roods, 4 perches. [Fu 423]

[OF1.4] He also holds similarly three inclosures lying together nearby called Overshott between the land of John Norman lying in the parish of Bell [Belchalwell] to the south, the land of Agnes Mauery in the tenure of Edward Phillipes to the north and abutting to the east over Reyland, containing altogether 6 acres, 1 rood, 35 perches. [Fu 424]

[OF1.5] He also holds near there one inclosure lying between the land of Walter Debyn lying in the said parish of Bell to the south, the customary land of the said Edward Phillipes to the north and abutting to the west over the land lately held by the monastery of Abbotes Burye, containing 2 acres, 3 roods, 8 perches. [Fu 468]

[OF1.6] He also holds near the Strowde one tenement with diverse closes of arable, pasture and meadow land lying together between land lately of the said monastery of Abbotes Burye and Bell Lane to the south and a certain lane leading from Strowde to Fesbury Knappe to the north, containing altogether 23 acres, 1 rood, 22 perches. [Fu 469, Fu 472, Fu 477, Fu 478]

[OF1.7] He also holds similarly one inclosure called Sugestone lying between the customary land of Elizabeth Say to the east, the land of George Trencher, esquire, lying in the parish of Bell to the west, abutting to the south over Southleyes in the tenure of Edward Howe and to the north over the customary land of Robert Poope, containing 11 acres, 1½ roods. [Fu 550, Fu 551]

[OF1.8] He also holds similarly one inclosure called Sandhill lying between the land of George Trencher, esquire, lying in the parish of Bell to the west and land of diverse men of this manor to the east, abutting to the south over Ockford Downes in part and land lying in the parish of Bell in part and to the north over the customary land of Henry Wakeford and Alice Harrys, widow, containing 6 acres. [Fu 417]

[OF1.9] He also holds similarly one inclosure called Whitpitt with appurtenances lying between the customary land of Alice Harrys, widow, to the north and the customary land of William Pelle to the south abutting to the west over Rodford Lane and to the east over the customary land of Edward Williams and Narbures Lane, containing 3 acres. [Fu 392]

[Marginal annotation: total acreage:] 62 acres

*

[OF2.1] William Pellye holds one tenement in the Hye Street lying between the tenement of John Iles to the south, the tenement of Henry Wakeforde to the north and abutting to the east over the Queen's highway leading from Sturmestur to Blandford, containing 1 rood. [Ra 32]

[OF2.2] He also holds similarly one close called Old Coniger lying between the customary land of Richard Birte to the west, the customary land of Richard Gobye to the east, abutting to the north over the land of Richard Birte and to the south over a certain lane called [blank] Lane, containing 2 acres, 1 rood, 30 perches. [Ra 177]

[OF2.3] He also holds similarly one inclosure called Rodford lying between the customary land of John Iles to the north, the customary land of Richard Prower and Hugh Kene to the south, abutting to the west over Rodford Lane and to the east over the customary land of Edward Williams, containing 2 acres, 3 roods. [H 398]

[OF2.4] He also holds similarly one inclosure called Westwood lying near Weste Woode Lane, containing 3 acres, 1 rood, 10 perches. [Pl 365 or Pl 363?]

[OF2.5] He also holds half of one inclosure in the said Westwood, containing 2 roods, 20 perches. [part of H 449, the remainder belonged to Lawrence Frampton]

[OF2.6] He also holds one orchard lying between the croft of Alice Harrys to the west, the land of Henry Reynold to the east, abutting to the north over the orchard of the said Alice and to the south over the way leading from Narburs Elmes to the site of the manor, containing 1 rood. [Ra 29]

[OF2.7] He also holds one inclosure called Rushe Knappe lying between the land of William White senior to the west and the land of Robert Poope, abutting to the south over the land of William White senior and John Newton and to the north over a certain lane called Shillinstone Lane, containing 1½ acres [part of Ph 257?]

[Marginal annotation:] total acreage: 11 acres

*

[OF3.1] Henry Wakeforde holds one tenement in the Hye Streete with garden, orchard and croft adjacent, lying together between the lands of diverse men to the south, the tenement of Henry Reynold and the customary tenement of Edward Howe called Westwood abutting to the west over the customary land of Joseph Harrys, containing altogether 2 acres, 2 roods. [Bwr 33]

[OF3.2] He also holds similarly at the west end of the aforesaid croft one parcel of land called Westwoode lying between the customary land of Joseph Harrys on the west, the customary land of Edward Howe on the east, and abbutting to the south over the croft, containing 2 roods, 10 perches. [part of Pl 376?]

[OF3.3] He also holds similarly one inclosure called Lowbrooke lying between the customary land of John Iles to the east, the tenement of Alice Harrys to the west, abutting to the north over the croft of the aforesaid Henry and to the south over Credohams Lane, containing 2 acres, 10 perches. [Bwr 378]

[OF3.4] He also holds two inclosures lying together by the river called Pinbrooke lying between the customary land of Richard Prower to the north, the customary land of

Agnes White, widow, on the south, abutting to the west over the land of the aforesaid
Richard Prower and to Rodford Lane to the southeast, containing altogether 7 acres,
24 perches. [Bwr 430]

[OF3.5] He also holds similarly diverse closes of arable, pasture and meadow land
lying together called Rodford lying between Rodford Lane and the land lying in the
parish of Bell to the west, the land of diverse tenements of this manor on the east,
abutting over the river bank to the northeast and over the close of John Iles called
Sandhill to the south, containing altogether 19 acres, 2 roods. [Bwr 402, Bwr 403,
Bwr 404, Bwr 420, 421, 422]

[Marginal annotation: total acreage:] 31 acres 3 roods

*

[OF4.1] Henry Reynold holds one tenement with garden and croft adjacent lying
between the tenement of Henry Wakeford on the south, the customary tenement of
Edward How to the north, abutting to the west over the land of the said Henry and
Edward and to the east over the common way leading from Sturmestur to Blandford,
containing 1 rood, 24 perches. [H+ 34]

[OF4.2] He also holds opposite the above tenement one orchard with a pightle
adjacent between the tenement of Robert Poope and Grenhay on the north, the
tenement of Alice Harrys and the way leading from Narbors Elmes to the site of the
manor on the south, abutting to the east over the site of the manor and to the west
towards the tenement of Alice Harrys and William Chipman and the orchard of
William Pelle, containing altogether 2 acres, 18 perches.[Wa 28]

[OF4.3] He also holds similarly one inclosure called Redlake lying between the land
of John Phillipes to the north, the land of Richard Prower to the south, abutting
over Hey Crofte to the west and over the land of the aforesaid Richard to the east,
containing 3 acres, 2 roods, 10 perches. [Me 433]

[OF4.4] He also holds similarly near Rodford Elmes two inclosures with meadow
adjacent between Rodford Lane to the northeast, the land of Agnes Mahoe, widow,
to the south, abutting over the common river bank to the southeast and over Hebed
Lane to the northeast, containing altogether 6 acres 2 roods. [Bn? 400]

[OF4.5] He also holds similarly under the Downes two inclosures lying together
called Hebed between the Downes to the east, the land of William Chipman and his
own lands to the west, abutting to the north over the customary land of Hugh Kene
called Shortland and over the Downes to the south, containing altogether 6 acres, 1
rood. [Thv 410, Thv 412 both cover OF.4.5 & OF.4.6]

[OF4.6] He also holds similarly one inclosure called Hebed between the customary land of Johanna Osmond, widow, to the west, his own aforesaid land to the east abutting to the north over the land of William Chipman and to the south over the Downes, containing 2 acres, 1 rood. [see OF.4.5]

[OF4.7] He also holds one inclosure called Furzey Crofte lying between the customary land of Hugh Kene to the north, the customary land of Walter Rose to the south, abutting to the west over the common river bank and to the east over the way called Comerweck Lane, containing 7 acres, 1 rood. [Br 328]

[OF4.8] He also holds similarly three inclosures lying together called Old Conyger lying between the lord's coppice called Coniger and the customary land of Richard Birte to the south, the land lying in the parish of Shillingston to the north, abutting over the land of William Chipman to the west and over the land of the said Richard Birte to the east, containing altogether 9 acres, 2 roods, 10 perches. [Br 171, Br 173]

[OF4.9] He also holds one cottage in the Hye Street with garden and yard adjacent between the tenement of Agnes Mahoe to the south, the tenement of William White junior to the north, abutting to the west over Hugh Kene's croft and to the east over the aforesaid Queen's highway leading from Sturmestur to Blandford, containing ½ acre. [Si 37]

[OF4.10] He also holds similarly one inclosure called Mill Closse lying between Shillingston Lane on the south, the common river bank on the north, abutting to the west over the land of Margery Skotte, widow, and to the east over the land of Emma Russell, containing 1 acre 3 roods 12 perches. [Me 216]

[Marginal annotation: total acreage:] 40 acres ½ rood

*

[OF5.1] Edward Howe holds by copy one tenement with garden and croft adjacent between the tenement of Henry Reynolde on the south, the tenement of Agnes Mahoe on the north and abutting to the east over the Queen's highway leading from Sturmestur to Blandford, containing 2 roods 5 perches. [Pl 35]

[OF5.2] He also holds similarly by the west boundary of the aforesaid croft one inclosure called Westwood lying in two sections between the customary land of Henry Wakeford, Joseph Harrys and William Chipman to the south, the land of diverse tenements to the north, abutting to the east over the aforesaid croft and the croft of Henry Reynold and to the west over the lands of diverse men, containing 6 acres, 1 rood, 30 perches. [Pl 369, Pl 374, Pl 375]

[OF5.3] He also holds similarly one inclosure called the Castle lying between the land of William White senior to the west, the land of Elizabeth Saye to the east, abutting to the north over the land of the aforesaid Elizabeth and to the south over the land of William White senior and Edward How, containing 7 acres, 3 roods, 20 perches. [Pl 200]

[OF5.4] He also holds similarly two inclosures lying together called Emede between the land of William White senior, Agnes Mahoe and Agnes Whyte to the west, the land of John Shotto to the east, abutting over the aforesaid close called Castle to the north and over the land of Edward How and Agnes White, widow, to the south, containing altogether 6 acres, 3 roods. [Pl 200]

[OF5.5] He also holds similarly one inclosure called Longclosse lying between the aforesaid Emede to the north, the meadow of William Ford to the south, abutting to the east over the meadow of Agnes White called Millclosse and to the southwest over a certain lane leading to the mill called Emede Lane, containing 1 acre, 2 roods, 13 perches. [Pl 210]

[OF5.6] He also holds one inclosure called Narbor lying in two squares between the land of Richard Gobye and William Forde to the south, the tenement of William Chipman and Agnes White to the north, abutting to the west over Narbor Lane and to the east over a certain lane leading to the Downes called Knill Lane, containing 10 acres, 1 rood [Pl 386, Pl 387, Pl 388, Pl 389]

[OF5.7] He also holds several closes lying together called Southleys lying in diverse sections between the land of George Trencher esquire in the parish of Bell to the west, the land of Thomas White esquire lying in the parish of Eberton [Ibberton] and the land of diverse tenements called Whitmere to the east, abutting to the north over the land of John Iles and Elizabeth Saye and over the common river bank to the south west, containing altogether 56 acres, 2 roods, 32 perches. [Go 571 - 578]

[OF5.8] He also holds one inclosure near Horsfoole Plecke lying between the land of Agnes White to the north, the land of Edward Williams to the south, abutting to the east over the common river bank and to the west over Mill Lane, containing 2 acres 2 roods. [Ne 220]

[Marginal annotation: total acreage:] 92 acres, 2 roods, 6 perches

*

[OF6.1] Agnes Mahewe holds by copy one tenement with garden and yard adjacent between the tenement of Edward Howe to the south, the cottage of Henry Reynold to the north and abutting the Queen's highway aforesaid to the east, containing 2 roods, 22 perches. [Th 36]

[OF6.2] She also holds at the west end of the aforesaid yard one inclosure called Westwood lying between the land of Edward Howe to the south, the land of diverse tenants to the north and abutting to the east over the aforesaid yard, containing 1 acre, 1 rood, 10 perches. [Th 373]

[OF6.3] She also holds one inclosure called Comerwicke lying between the land of Robert Hynde to the north, the land of Hugh Bythewood to the south, abutting to the west over the common river bank and to the east over Comerwicke Lane, containing 6 acres, 3 roods and 20 perches. [Th 325]

[OF6.4] She also holds two inclosures lying together called the Coniger between the land of William Chipman to the east, the land of William Ford, Richard Prower and her own land to the west, abutting to the south over the lord's coppice called the Coniger and to the north over land lying in the parish of Shillingstone, containing 7 acres, 3 roods, 30 perches. [Wb 169]

[OF6.5] She also holds one pightle with appurtenances lying between the land of William Ford to the north, the land of Richard Prower to the south, abutting to the east over the land of Richard Prower and to the west over Comerwick Lane, containing 1 acre, 1 rood and 22 perches. [Wb 167]

[OF6.6] She also holds two pightles lying together called Pynwell between the land of Alice Biles to the south, the land of Agnes White to the north, abutting to the west over Stotfold Drove and to the east over the land of Richard Birte and her own land, containing altogether 2 acres, 2 roods. [Th 270]

[OF6.7] She also holds near there one inclosure called Pinwell lying between the land of Agnes White on the west, land lying in the parish of Shillingston to the east, abutting to the north over the land of Henry Ford and Agnes White and to the south over the land of Richard Birte, containing 4 acres, 3 roods. [Th 267]

[OF6.8] She also holds another inclosure called Pinwell lying between the land of Henry Ford on each side abutting to the north over the land of the aforesaid Henry and to the south over the land of Agnes White and her own land, containing 3 acres, 1 rood, 30 perches. [Th 251]

[OF6.9] She also holds one inclosure called Rushe Knappe lying between Stotfeld Drove on the east, the land of Richard Prower on the west and abutting to the north over Rushe Knappe way, containing 4 acres. [see next entry]

[OF6.10] She also holds similarly four closes lying together called Stotfold between Stotfold Drove to the east, the land of Richard Prower and the Downes on the west, abutting to the south over the land of Elizabeth Saye and to the north over the aforesaid close called Rushe Knappe, containing altogether 10 acres. [Wh 279, Wh 280 this includes OF.6.9]

[OF6.11] She also holds three inclosures lying together called Worthe between the land of Henry Wakeforde to the north, the land of William White junior to the south, abutting to the west over the land of the aforesaid Henry and to the east over Hebed Lane, containing altogether 8 acres. [Th 405, Th 406]

[OF6.12] She also holds similarly one inclosure called Shortland between the land of Henry Reynold and her own land to the west, Hebed Lane to the east, abutting to the north over the land of the aforesaid Henry and to the south over Hebed Lane, containing 2 acres, 3 roods and 20 perches.[Th 401]

[OF6.13] She also holds similarly one copyhold tenement in West Streat with garden and croft adjacent between the tenement of Richard Gobye to the west, the lands of Hugh Kene to the east and abutting to the north over the Queen's highway leading from Sturmestur to Blandford, and containing 3 roods. [Wh 47]

[OF6.14] She also holds similarly half of one close called Emede abutting to the south over a certain lane leading to the Mill, containing 3 roods. [S.Wb 205 -this is shared with Agnes White]

[Marginal annotation: total acreage:] 54 acres 2 roods

*

[OF7.1] William Whight junior holds by copy one tenement with garden and yard adjacent between the tenement of Henry Reynold on the south, the tenement of Richard Prower on the north, abutting to the west over the croft of Hugh Kene and to the east over the Queen's highway leading from Sturmestur to Blandford, containing 2 roods, 5 perches. [Ps 38]

[OF7.2] He also holds similarly one inclosure near Horsfoole pleck lying between the land of Christiana Howe to the north, the land of Agnes White to the south, abutting to the east over the common river bank and to the west over Horsfoole pleck, containing 2 acres, 4 perches. [Ph 222]

[OF7.3] He also holds similarly one inclosure called Langstone lying between the land of Emma Russell on the east, the land of Margery Skott on the west, abutting to the north over Le Millway and to the south over Langstone Way, containing 4 acres, 10 perches. [Cr 308]

[OF7.4] He also holds similarly one inclosure called Knill lying between the land of Alice Dallydowne to the north, the land of Alice Lynsye to the south, abutting to the east over the lands of William White senior and Hugh Kene and to the west over the common way leading to the Downes, containing 4 acres, 23 perches. [Bwr 299]

[OF7.5] He also holds similarly one inclosure called Hebed lying between the land of Agnes Mayew to the north, the land of Alice Harrys to the south, abutting to the west over the land of Henry Wakefeild and Alice Harrys and to the east over a certain lane called Hebed Lane, containing 3 acres 2 rood. [Bw 419]

[OF7.6] He also holds similarly once inclosure called Redlake lying between the land of Joan Phillipps to the south, the land of John Osmond to the north and west and to the east over Redlake Lane, containing 3 acres, 2 roods, 28 perches. [Ps 444]

[Marginal annotation: total acreage:] 18 acres 3 roods

*

[OF8.1] Richard Prower holds by copy one tenement lying between the tenement of William White junior to the south, the tenement of John White to the north, abutting to the west over the croft of Hugh Kene and to the east over the Queen's highway leading from Sturmestur to Blandford, containing 2 roods, 10 perches. [Pr 39]

[OF8.2] He also holds similarly one inclosure called Cornepp lying between the land of Agnes Mahoe on the north, a certain lane leading to Coniger on the south, abutting to the west over Comerwick Lane and to the east over the lord's coppice called the Coniger and the land of Agnes Mahoe, containing 8 acres, 20 perches. [Pr 166]

[OF8.3] He also holds similarly one inclosure called Maynow Land lying between the land of Alice Lynsey to the east, Stotfould Drove to the west, abutting to the north over the land of the aforesaid Alice and to the south over his own land, containing 1 acre, 2 roods. [part of Pr 264]

[OF8.4] He also holds at the south head of the aforesaid close one pightle called Broadpitt lying between the above close and the land of Alice Lynsey to the north, the land of Johanna Osmond to the south, abutting to the east over land of Henry Ford and to the west over Stotfold Drove, containing 1 acre 16 perches. [part of Pr 264]

[OF8.5] He also holds four closes lying together called Sandhill between the land of Agnes Mahoe to the east, the land of Hugh Bythewood, Margery Skotte and a parcel of the Downes called May Rige to the west, abutting to the north over Rushe Knappe Way and to the south over the land of the said Agnes Mahoe and the Downes, containing altogether 12 acres, 1 rood. [Pr 261-2, Pr 281-3]

[OF8.6] He also holds similarly one inclosure called Nellstede lying between the land of Hugh Kene on the east, Hebed Lane on the west, abutting to the north over the lands of William Pelle and to the south over Hebed Lane, containing 2 acres, 20 perches. [Ka 399]

[OF8.7] He also holds similarly one inclosure call Rodford lying between the land of the rector of Ockford to the north, the land of Henry Wakeford to the south, abutting to the east over Rodford Lane and to the west over his own lands called Redlake, containing 3 acres, 16 perches. [part of Pr 436]

[OF8.8] He also holds two inclosures lying together to the western end of the previous close between the land of Henry Reynold and Emma Russell and the aforesaid close to the west, the land of William White senior to the east and abutting to the south over the land of Henry Wakeford and his own land, containing 5 acres, 1 rood. [Ka 435?]

[OF8.9] He also holds similarly three inclosures lying together called Redlake between the land of Henry Wakeford to the east, the land of Joan Philleps to the west, abutting to the north over the land of Henry Reynold and his own land and to the south over the land of Edward Bennett and Agnes White, containing altogether 7 acres, 2 roods, 37 perches. [Ka 431, Ka 432]

[Marginal annotation: total acreage:] 41 acres 3 roods

*

[OF9.1] John Whight holds by copy one tenement with garden adjacent lying between the tenement of Richard Prower to the south, the tenement of John Newton and Joan Phillips, widow, to the north, abutting to the west over John Shotto's yard and to the east over the Queen's highway leading from Sturmestur to Blandford, containing 1 rood, 20 perches. [Se 40]

[OF9.2] He also holds similarly one inclosure called Oldwood lying between the land of Edward Williams to the west, the land of the rectory and Brechlane to the east, abutting to the south over the rectorial land and to the north over Cotyers Drove, containing 2 acres, 2 roods, 6 perches. [R+ 180]

[OF9.3] He also holds one pightle near the mill lying between the meadow of Margery Skotte to the east, Millway to the west and abutting to the south over Shillingstone Lane, containing 2 roods, 8 perches. [R+ 214]

[OF9.4] He also holds similarly one inclosure called Pounde Close lying between the land of William Chipman to the east, Culverhaye and a certain lane leading to the

Downe on the west, abutting to the south over the land of Alice Dallydowne and to the north over the Pownde and Langstone Way, containing 3 acres, 1 rood, 20 perches. [R+ 302]

[OF9.5] He also holds similarly one inclosure called Jordaine lying between the land of Margery Skott to the west, Coniger Lane to the east, abutting to the north over the aforesaid lane and to the south over the land of the rectory and William Ford, containing 3 acres. [R+ 191]

[OF9.6] He also holds one pightle which is enclosed by a close called Westwood lying in the close of Agnes White, containing 2 roods. [part of 370 which includes R+, S, Wo and land called High Bench]

[Marginal annotation: total acreage:] 10 acres, 1 rood, 19 perches

*

[OF10.1] John Newton holds by copy one cottage [newly] built with garden adjacent between the tenement of John Whyte to the south, the common bakery of the town to the north, abutting over the yard of Joan Phillips, widow, to the west and over the Queen's highway leading from Sturmestur to Blandford on the east, containing 30 perches. [Fr 41]

[OF10.2] He also holds similarly an inclosure called Jordaine lying between a certain lane leading to the lord's coppice and the lands of diverse tenants to the north, the land of Christiana How to the south, abutting over the aforesaid coppice to the east and over Comerwick Lane to the west, containing 3 acres. [Fr 193]

[OF10.3] He also holds similarly one inclosure called Oldwood between the land of Richard Gobye to the west, the land of Margery Skotte to the east, abutting to the north over the land lying in the parish of Shillingstone and to the south over Cotiers Drove, containing 2 acres, 20 perches. [Fr 178]

[OF10.4] He also holds an inclosure called Rushe Knappe lying between the land of William White senior to the west, the land of the rectory called Broadmead to the east, abutting over the land of diverse tenants to the north and over Langstone Way to the south, containing 2 acres, 4 perches. [Fr 258]

[OF10.5] He also holds similarly one pightle: a parcel of the diverse inclosures called Westwood, containing ½ acre, 33 perches. [?]

[OF10.6] He also holds one inclosure called Rushe Knappe lying between the land of Hugh Bythewoode to the east, the land of Margery Skotte on the west, abutting to the south over the land of Richard Prower and to the north over Langstone Way, containing 2 acres, 1 rood, 8 perches. [Fr 259]

[Marginal annotation: total acreage:] 10 acres, 1 rood 17 perches

*

[OF11.1] Henry Forde holds by copy one tenement with garden adjacent lying by the common bakehouse of the town abutting to the west over the tenement of Joan Phillips and to the east over the Queen's highway leading from Sturmestur to Blandford, containing 1 rood. [T 43]

[OF11.2] He also holds similarly one inclosure called Bawte Hawe lying together in three parts with a newly built house and garden between the land of William Ford and a lane leading to the mill on the north, the land of diverse tenements and of another lane leading to the mill on the south, abutting to the west over the tenement of William Ford and Robert Hynde and to the east over Mill plecke, containing altogether 9 acres, 21 perches. [T 312 + T311?]

[OF11.3] He also holds likewise two inclosures lying together called Longhill between the land of the rector and Robert Poope on the west, the lands of the rector, Robert Poope's land and his own land to the east, abutting to the north over Shillingstone Lane and to the south over Rushe Knap Way, containing altogether 5 acres, 2 roods, 10 perches.[see OF.11.6]

[OF11.4] He also holds similarly three inclosures lying together with a pightle adjacent called Longhill between the land of the rectory and Agnes White, widow, on the north, the land of Robert Pope, Agnes Mahoe and his own land on the south and abutting to the east over the lands lying in the parish of Shillingstone, containing altogether 19 acres, 1 roods, 26 perches. [see OF.11.6]

[OF11.5] He also holds similarly nearby one meadow also called Longhill between the land of Agnes Mahew and his own and to the east, the land of diverse tenements to the west and abutting to the south over the land of Joan Osmond and Agnes White, widow, containing 6 acres, 2 roods, 16 perches. [see OF.11.6]

[OF11.6] He also holds similarly nearby one inclosure called Fishers Close between the land of Agnes Mayew to the west, land in the parish of Shillingstone to the east,abutting over his own pightle to the north and over the land of the aforesaid Agnes to the south, containing 5 acres. [The last 4 entries cover T 244,T 249-T 252, T 255 +? T 267]

[OF11.7] He also holds similarly two inclosures lying together called Sugestone lying lengthways between the land of William White senior, Robert Poope and Elizabeth Say to the west, the land of John Shotto to the east, abutting to the south over the land of Elizabeth Say and to the north over the land of the William White and the lord's common pasture called Gobson, containing altogether 28 acres, 1 rood, 10 perches. [T 534 T 535 T 536 T 554 T 555]

[Marginal annotation: Total acreage:] 74 acres 1 rood, 4 perches

*

[OF12.1] Alice Harris, widow, holds by copy one tenement with garden and yard adjacent between a certain small lane leading to the church to the north, abutting to the east over the land of Henry Reynold and William Pelle and to the west over the Queen's highway leading from Sturmestur to Blandford, containing 1 acre, 1 rood, 24 perches. [La 30]

[OF12.2] She also holds similarly one inclosure called New Closse between the lands of Henry Wakeford to the east, the land of Richard Shotto and Joseph Harrys to the west, abutting to the north over the land of Henry Wakeford and to the south over Credohams Lane, containing 3 acres. [La 377]

[OF12.3] She also holds similarly one inclosure called Credohams on each side of the river bank lying between Credohams Lane on the south, the lands of diverse tenants on the north, abutting to the west over Westwood Lane and to the east over the land of John Shotto and the common river bank, containing 2 acres, 2 roods, 8 perches. [La 448]

[OF12.4] She also holds one meadow called Bradmeade between the land of William White senior on the south, Credohams Lane on the north, abutting to the east over the land of William White senior and Joan Phillips, widow, and to the west over the common river bank, containing 4 acres, 1 rood, 8 perches. [La 441]

[OF12.5] She also holds one inclosure called The Goore lying near the land of John Iles, abutting to the west over Rodford Lane and to the east over Narbors Lane, containing 2 acres, 16 perches. [La 391]

[OF12.6] She also holds one inclosure called Shortland between the land of Christiana Howe on the northwest, the land of Hugh Kene to the southeast and abutting over Hebed Lane to the southwest, containing 3 acres, 3 roods. [La 408]

[OF12.7] She also holds one inclosure called Harcliffe between the land of Edward Williams and Hugh Kene on the west, the land of Joan Phillips and the lord's common pasture called the Downes on the east, abutting over her own land and that of Christiana Howe to the south and over Narbors Lane to the north, containing 3 acres, 3 roods, 17 perches. [La 396]

[OF12.8] She also holds similarly one inclosure with an adjacent pightle called Sandhill lying between the land of William White junior on the north, the land of Robert Hynde and John Iles to the south, abutting over the land of Robert Hynde to the east and over the land of Henry Wakeford to the west, containing altogether 6 acres, 16 perches. [La 418]

[OF12.9] She also holds similarly one inclosure lying between the land of Walter Rose on the north, the land of Joan Osmond on the south, abutting to the west over the land of Alice Dallidowne and to the east over Redlake Lane, containing 2 acres. [La 446]

[OF12.10] She also holds one inclosure lying between the land of Alice Dallidowne to the north, the land of Joan Osmond to the south and abutting with a headland over the land of Joan Osmond, containing 4 acres, 25 perches. [La 460]

[OF12.11] She also holds similarly one inclosure lying between the land of Joan Osmond on the south, the land of Alice Lynsey and Alice Dallidowne on the north, abutting over the land of Alice Dallydowne to the east and over Stroudwitch Lane to the west, containing 9 acres, 19 perches. [La 458]

[OF12.12] She also holds similarly one inclosure called Weststrowde lying between the land of Joan Osmonde and Laurence Frampton to the north, a lane leading from Strowde Elme to Remple on the south, abutting to the east over the land of Yeovil Almshouse and Laurence Frampton and to the west over Remple Lane, containing 16 acres, 3 roods, 6 perches. [La 488, La 489, La 490]

[OF12.13] She also holds similarly one inclosure called Whitmere lying between the land of Edward Phillips to the south, Whitmere Lane to the north, abutting to the west over the land of Edward How called South Leys and to the east over Whitmere Lane, containing 6 acres, 10 perches. [La 570]

[Marginal annotation: Total acreage:] 65 acres, 9 perches

*

[OF13.1] William Chipman holds by copy one tenement with garden adjoining between the orchard of Henry Keynes to the north, a small lane leading to the church to the south and abutting to the west over the Queen's highway leading from Sturmestur to Blandford, containing 36 perches.[part of Wa 28]

[OF13.2] He also holds similarly four inclosures lying together called Old Coniger between the tenement of Henry Reynold to the east, the land of Agnes Mahew to the west, abutting over the Coniger to the south and over the land lying in the parish of Shillingstone to the north, containing 8 acres, 1 rood. [Br 170]

[OF13.3] He also holds similarly one pightle lying between Pownd Closse on the west, the land of Hugh Bythewood to the east, abutting to the south over the land of Alice Dallidowne and to the north over Langstone way, containing 3 roods, 20 perches. [Sh.t ? 301]

[OF13.4] He also holds similarly two inclosures lying together called Hebed between the land of Robert Hynde to the west, the land of Henry Reynold and Joan Osmond to the east, abutting to the north over the land of Henry Reynold and Hugh Kene and to the south over Hebed wood, containing 7 acres, 30 perches. [He 411 +?]

[OF13.5] He also holds nearby by indenture one inclosure called Hebed wood between the aforesaid close to the north, the land of Robert Hynde to the south, abutting over the land of Robert Hynde to the west and the land of Joan Osmond to the east, containing 2 acres, 2 roods, 20 perches. [S.t 415]

[OF13.6] He also holds similarly one inclosure called Westwood containing 2 roods, 20 perches. [?]

[OF13.7] He also holds similarly one pightle called Narbor lying between the land of Richard Poope to the north, the land of Edward How to the south, abutting to the east over the land of Agnes White and to the west over Narbors Lane, containing 1 acre, 1 rood, 20 perches. [Bw 384]

[Marginal annotation: Total acreage:] 21acres, ½ rood, 6 perches.

*

[OF14.1] Robert Poope holds by copy one tenement with cottage adjacent between the orchard of Henry Reynold to the south, the tenement of Emma Russell to the north, abutting to the east over Grenhay and a garden belonging to John Say and to the west over the Queen's highway leading from Sturmestur to Blandford, containing 2 roods, 34 perches. [Bwv 27]

[OF14.2] He also holds similarly one inclosure called Narbur lying between the land of William Chipman and Agnes White to the south, the land of Agnes White to the north, abutting to the east over the lane leading to the Downe and to the west over Narbor Lane, containing 2 acres, 3 roods, 24 perches. [S 382 or Ph 383 ?]

[OF14.3] He also holds similarly two inclosures lying together called Stonyford between the land of William Pelle to the west, the land of Henry Ford to the east, abutting to the south over the land of diverse men and to the north over Shillingston Lane, containing 3 acres, 33 perches. [Ph 257]

[OF14.4] He also holds similarly two inclosures lying together between the lands of Henry Ford to the west, the land of Alice Lynsey to the southeast, abutting over the land of Henry Ford to the northeast and over the land of Alice Lynsey to the south, containing altogether 5 acres, 2 roods and 30 perches. [Ph 254]

[OF14.5] He also holds similarly one inclosure called Sugestone formerly in diverse pieces with appurtenances lying between the land of Henry Ford to the east, the land of George Tremenher esquire in the parish of Bell to the west, abutting to the south over the land of John Iles and Elizabeth Saye and to the north over the land of William White senior, containing 33 acres, 5 perches. [Bt 545-549, Bt 553]

[OF14.6] He also holds similarly one inclosure called Westwood lying nearby abutting to the east over the land of Edward Howe called Westwood, containing 2 roods, 10 perches.

[OF14.7] He also holds similarly one inclosure called Nethway with a house recently built lying in two squares between the land of Hugh Bythewoode and the common river bank to the west, the land of Alice Lynsey and Agnes White to the east, abutting to the north over the customary land of Hugh Kene and to the south over the Queen's highway leading from Sturmestur to Blandford, containing 4 acres, 2 roods, 9 perches. [Bwv 318]

[Marginal annotation: Total acreage:] 51 acres 2½ roods 14 perches

*

[OF15.1] Emma Russell, widow, holds one tenement with a garden and yard adjacent between the tenements of Robert Poope and John Saye to the south, the rectory of Ockford to the north and abutting to the west over the Queen's highway leading from Sturmester to Blandford, containing 2 roods 19 perches. [Bl 24]

[OF15.2] She also holds similarly one inclosure lying between the land of Margery Skott on the east, the land of Henry Reynold to the west, abutting to the north over the common riverbank and to the south over Shillingston Way, containing 2 acres 2 roods, 27 perches. [Ha 217]

[OF15.3] She also holds one inclosure called Langstone lying between the land of William White junior to the west, the land of Alice Biles to the east, abutting to the north over Mill pleck and to the south over Shillingstone Way, containing 4 acres, 1 rood, 25 perches. [Ph 289]

[OF15.4] She also holds similarly one inclosure called Redland lying between Redlake Lane on the west, the lands of diverse tenants on the east and abutting to the north over Credohams Lane, containing 2 acres, 3 roods, 12 perches.[S.t. 443]

[OF15.5] She also holds one inclosure called Filgrove lying between the land of Margery Skotte to the west, the land of Agnes White to the east, abutting to the north over the land of Margery Skotte and to the south over Shillingstone Lane, containing 2 acres, 3 roods, 30 perches. [Ha 242]

[Marginal annotation: Total acreage:] 13 acres 1 rood and 13 perches

*

[OF16.1] Richard Birte holds by copy one cottage with garden adjacent between the Queen's highway on the west, the smith's forge on the east, abutting to the south over the rectory and to the north over the Queen's highway, containing 30 perches. [Wb 22]

[OF16.2] He also holds similarly one inclosure called Oldwood between the lord's coppice called the Coniger to the west, the land of William Pelle to the east, abutting to the north over the land of Henry Reynold and to the south over Cotiers Drove, containing 2 acres, 3 roods. [W 174]

[OF16.3] He also holds similarly near there one pightle of meadow lying in a triangular form between the land in the parish of Shillingstone to the north, the land of William Pelle and Richard Gobye to the south and abutting to the west over the land of Henry Reynold, containing 3 roods, 20 perches. [W 175]

[OF16.4] He also holds similarly one inclosure called Jordaine lying between the land of Richard Gobye on the east, the land of Edward Bennett and Comerwick Lane on the west, abutting to the north over the land of Edward Williams and to the south over a lane leading from Coniger, containing 3 acres. [W 196]

[OF16.5] He also holds similarly one pightle with appurtenances lying between the land of Alice Lynsey to the south, the land of Alice Biles to the north and abutting to the west over Stotfeld Drove, containing 3 roods, 10 perches. [see next]

[OF16.6] He also holds similarly at the eastern end of the aforesaid pightle two further pightles lying together between the Downes to the southeast, the land of diverse tenants to the northwest and abutting to the east over land lying in the parish

of Shillingstone, and containing altogether 2 acres, 2 roods.
[OF16.5 and 16.6 include W 272, 273, 268, 269]
[Marginal annotation: Total acreage:] 10 acres ½ rood

*

[OF17.1] George Whight holds similarly by copy one cottage lying to the east of the smith's forge, abutting to the south over the rectory and to the north over the Queen's highway, containing ½ rood. [Pb 19]

*

[OF18.1] John Saye holds one cottage newly built lying between the croft of Emma Russell to the north, Grene Hay to the south, abutting to the west over the land of Robert Poope and to the east over the church path, containing 30 perches. [Phv 25]

*

[OF19.1] Alice Hyne holds one cottage lately held by John Saye near the church pathe. [Pe 15?]

*

[OF20.1] Joan Cole holds by copy one cottage near the church pathe. [Ne 17?]

*

[OF21.1] Joseph Harrys holds by copy one small cottage lying near the cemetery of the church of Ockford. [Sr 13]

[OF21.2] He also holds similarly one pightle called the Combe lying near the Downe, between May Ridge and Goosland, and abutting to the north over the land of John Shotto, containing 1 acre, 1 rood, 20 perches. [H+ 295]

[OF21.3] He also holds similarly one pightle called Westwood lying between the land of Alice Harrys and Henry Wakeford to the east, the land of diverse tenements to the west, abutting to the south over the land of John Shotto and to the north over the land of Edward Howe, containing 1 acre, 1 rood. [part Westwood Pl 376]

*

[OF22.1] John Abrabin holds by copy near the Church Litten and the cottage of the aforesaid Joseph Harris.

*

[OF23.1] Robert Bythewoode holds the third part of a small cottage in the lane leading from Narbors Elmes to Cookwell.

*

[OF24.1] John Hussey holds the second part of the above cottage.

*

[OF25.1] Elwe Curson holds the third part.

*

[OF26.1] Agnes Bythewood holds similarly by copy one small cottage near there.

*

[OF27.1] Margery Skotte, widow, holds by copy one tenement with garden and yard adjacent, with one inclosure on the opposite side of the tenement with a cottage built in the west part of the tenement lying together between the common way leading to the mill to the west, the land of William White junior to the east, abutting to the north over the aforesaid way leading to the mill and to the south over Longstone Waye and Cookwell, containing altogether 8 acres, 2 roods, 10 perches. [D 305, 307, 309, 79 ? Ry 306]

[OF27.2] She also holds similarly opposite the above tenement one inclosure called Bawtye Hawe with appurtenances lying between the land of Henry Ford to the north and the lane leading to the mill on the south each side abutting over the land of the said Henry Ford, containing 2 acres, 1 rood, 3 perches. [D 310]

[OF27.3] She also holds similarly the site of the manor called Corte Closse with a certain barn lately built lying between the land of Henry Reynold and Grene Hay to the west, the lane leading from Narbors Elmes and upto Cookwell to the east, abutting to the north over the cemetery of Ockford and to the south over the aforesaid lane, containing 1 acre, 1 rood, 30 perches. [Ha 304 + Ha 14?]

[OF27.4] She also holds one inclosure called Langestone lying between the land of William White senior to the east, the land of Alice Biles to the west, abutting to the south over Langstone Way and to the north over Shillingstone, containing 1 acre 2 roods. [Sc 287]

[OF27.5] She also holds similarly one corn mill. [Rv 82]

[OF27.6] She also holds one meadow called Mill Mead lying between the common river bank to the south, the land of William White senior to the north and abutting to the west over the mill pleck, containing 3 acres, 8 perches. [Pp 213]

[OF27.7] She also holds similarly on the other part of the river bank one pightle of meadow lying between the meadow of John White to the west, the land of Henry Reynold to the east, abutting to the north over the common river bank and to the south over Shillingstone Waye, containing 1 rood. [?]

[OF27.8] She also holds one inclosure called Fillgrove lying between the land of Emma Russell on every part, abutting to the north over the common river bank and to the south over Shillingstone Waye, containing 2 acres, 20 perches. [part 218]

[OF27.9] She also holds similarly one close similarly called Fillgrove between the common river bank to the northwest, the land of Emma Russell and Agnes White to the southeast and abutting to the south over the aforesaid inclosure called Fillgrove, containing 3 acres, 2 roods, 20 perches. [part 218?]

[OF27.10] She also holds similarly three inclosures with meadow adjacent lying together called Church Ways between the common river bank, the land of Robert Hynde and the land of the rectory called the Great Breage to the northeast, the land of the rectory called Churchwayse and the land of Richard Gobye, William Phillips and her other land to the southeast, abutting over the land of William Phillips to southwest and over land lying in the parish of Shillingstone to the northeast, containing in total 17 acres, 1 rood, 35 perches. [Wh 229, Wh 231, Wh 232, Wh 233]

[OF27.11] She also holds similarly one pightle lying between the land of William Phillips on each side abutting to the south over Shillingstone Lane, containing 1 acre. [Wh 238]

[OF27.12] She also holds holds similarly one inclosure called Oldwood lying between the land of John Newton to the west, Brech Lane to the east and abutting to the south over Cotyars Drove, containing 2 acres 1 rood. [Ha 179]

[OF27.13] She also holds similarly one inclosure called Jordaine lying between the land of Elizabeth White to the west, the land of John White to the east, abutting to the north over the lane leading to Coniger and to the south over the land of Elizabeth Saye and William Ford, containing 3 acres. [Ha 190]

[OF27.14] She also holds similarly one inclosure near the site of the manor lying between the land of Agnes White to the south, the lane leading from Narbors Elme and to Cookwell on the north and abutting to the east over the lane leading to the Downes, containing 3 acres, 1 rood, 10 perches. [Si 381]

[OF27.15] She also holds similarly one cottage called the Smithyes Forge lying between the tenement of Richard Birte on the west, the cottage of George White on the east, abutting to the south over the rectory and to the north over the Queen's highway, containing ½ rood. [Bu 20]

[OF27.16] She also holds similarly one inclosure with coppice adjacent between the land of John Newton and Richard Prower to the east, the land of Hugh Kene to the west, abutting to the south over Mayridge and to the north over Langstone Way, containing 5 acres, 3 roods and 28 perches. [Sb 284]

[Marginal annotation: Total acreage:] 55 acres, 3½ roods.

*

[OF28.1] Noel Harvey holds by copy one cottage newly built near the mill lying near the land of Henry Ford called Bawtry Hawe.

*

[OF29.1] Edward Williams holds by copy one tenement with garden and yard adjacent lying between a certain lane leading from the cemetery to the mill to the east, the yard of William White senior and the land of Henry Ford to the west, abutting to the north over the land of the aforesaid Henry and to the south over the tenement of William White senior, containing 1 acre, 2 roods. [Wr 78]

[OF29.2] He also holds one inclosure called Oldwood lying between the land of John White to the east, the land of Elizabeth White to the west, abutting to the south over the land of the Rectory and to the north over Cotyars Drove, containing 2 acres, 20 perches. [W 181]

[OF29.3] He also holds similarly one inclosure near the mill lying between the land of Edward Howe to the north, the land of William White senior to the south, abutting to the east over the common river bank and to the west over Brech Lane, containing 1 acre, 1 rood, 16 perches. [W 219]

[OF29.4] He also holds similarly one inclosure called Hartliffe lying between the land of Alice Harrys to the east, the land of diverse tenants to the west, abutting to the south over the land of Hugh Kene and to the north over Narbors Lane, containing 2 acres, 2 roods, 35 perches. [W 397]

[OF29.5] He also holds similarly one inclosure called Westwood lying between the land of William Chipman to the north, the land of John Shotto to the south, abutting to the east over the land of Joseph Harrys and to the west over the common river bank, containing 1 acre, 20 perches. [part of 376]

[OF29.6] He also holds similarly one close called Jordaine lying between the land of Christiana Howe to the north, the land of diverse tenants to the south and abutting to the east over Comerwick Lane, containing 2 acres, 2 roods. [W 194]

[Marginal annotation: Total acreage:] 11 acres, 1 rood, 11 perches.

*

[OF30.1] William White senior holds one tenement with cottage, garden and yard adjacent next to the tenement of Edward Williams and abutting to the south over the Queen's highway, containing 3 roods. [A 77]

[OF30.2] He also holds similarly one inclosure called Castle lying between the land of Edward Howe to the east, Comerwicke Lane to the west, abutting to the south over the land of Joan Osmond and Elizabeth Saye and to the north over the land of Elizabeth White and the lane leading to Conyger, containing 8 acres, 1 rood, 14 perches. [A 201]

[OF30.3] He also holds similarly near the same one pightle called Emede between the land of Edward How to the east, the land of Elizabeth Saye to the west, abutting to the south over the tenement of Agnes Mayew and to the north over the close called Castle and the land of Edward Howe, containing 2 roods, 20 perches. [A 204]

[OF30.4] He also holds similarly one inclosure called Horsfole lying between the land of Williams Phillips to the southwest, the land of Walter Rose to the northeast and abutting to the east over Horsfole Pleck, containing 3 acres, 5 perches. [A 186]

[OF30.5] He also holds similarly one inclosure near the mill lying between the meadow of Margery Skott called Mill Mead to the south, the land of Edward Willliams to the north, abutting to the west over Breche Lane and to the east over the common river bank, containing 1 acre, 3 roods, 32 perches. [Pe 212]

[OF30.6] He also holds similarly two inclosures lying together called Langstone lying between the land of Margery Skotte to the west, the land of William Pelle and John Newton to the east, abutting to the south over Langstone Way and to the north over Shillingstone Lane, containing 5 acres, 2 roods, 20 perches. [Ga 286]

[OF34.5] She also holds similarly one inclosure called Stotfold lying between the land of William Ford to the south, the land of Alice Lynsey to the north, abutting to the east over the Downe and to the west over Stotfold Drove, containing 3 acres, 10 perches. [Ya 275 + part of ?]

[OF34.6] She also holds similarly opposite the aforesaid lane one inclosure also called Stotfeld between the land of Agnes Mahew to the north, Stotfeld Drove to the east and abutting to the south over the Downe, containing 4 acres, 3 roods, 20 perches. [Ya 278]

[OF34.7] She also holds similarly one inclosure called Westwood Closse lying between the free land of Hugh Kene to the east, the common riverbank to the west and abutting to the south over the land of John Bythewood, containing 4 acres. [part of Pl 362]

[OF34.8] She also holds similarly one pightle nearby between the freehold land of Hugh Kene to the west, Westwood Lane to the east, abutting to the south over the land of John Bythewood and to the north over her own land, containing 2 roods, 7 perches. [part of Pl 362]

[OF34.9] She also holds similarly at the northern end of the aforesaid pightle another close called Westwood Closse between the common riverbank to the northwest, Westwood Lane to the south and over the freehold land of Hugh Kene and her own land, containing 1 acre, 3 roods. [part of Pl 362 all the last three areas were small parts of the area called 'High Bench' the remainder was freely held by Hugh Kene]

[OF34.10] She also holds similarly one inclosure called Cockes Hay between the tenement of Alice Dallidowne to the northeast, the land of Joan Phillips to the west, abutting to the north over the land of Alice Dallidowne and to the south over Strowde Lane, containing 3 acres, 1 rood. [Mi 354]

[OF34.11] She also holds likewise one inclosure called Horsfoole between the land of Edward Howe called the Castle to the west, the land of William Ford to the east, abutting to the south over the land of John Shotto and to the north over the land of Margery Skotte, containing 2 acres, 1 rood. [Mi 189]

[OF34.12] She also holds similarly two inclosures lying together called Sugestone, of which one contains many trees, lying together between the land of Edward How called Southleys and Whitmere Lane to the south, the land of diverse tenements to the north, abutting to the west over the land of John Iles and to the east over the land of John Shotto, containing altogether 12 acres, 1 rood, 20 perches. [Fuv 552 + Fuv 558]

[Marginal annotation: Total acreage:] 40 acres, 12 perches.

*

[OF35.1] William Forde holds by copy one tenement with garden and yard adjacent between the tenement of Elizabeth Say and the yard of Robert Hynde to the south, a certain lane leading to the mill on the north, abutting to the east over the land of Henry and William Ford and to the west over Comerwick Lane, containing 1 acre, 1 rood. [Ry 72]

[OF35.2] He also holds similarly one pightle lying near his tenement called Bawtye Haw between the land of Henry Ford and the aforesaid lane leading to the mill called Emede Lane to the north, abutting to the east over the land of Henry Ford and to the west over his own tenement, containing 1 acre, 20 perches. [Ry 313]

[OF35.3] He also holds similarly one inclosure called Long Closse lying between the land of Elizabeth Say and Joan Osmond to the north, the lane leading to the mill called Emede Lane to the south, abutting to the east over the land of Elizabeth Say and to the west over Comerwick Lane, containing 4 acres, 4 perches. [Po 314]

[OF35.4] He also holds similarly one inclosure called New Crosse between the land of Agnes Mahew to the east, Comerwick Lane to the west, abutting to the south over the land of Agnes Mahew and to the north over the common way leading to Heward Bridge, containing 9 acres. [Po 168]

[OF35.5] He also same holds similarly one inclosure called Horsfole between land of Elizabeth Say on the west, the land of the rector on the north east, abutting to the south over the land of William Phillips and William White senior and to the north over the land of Margery Skotte and John White, containing 4 acres, 3 roods. [Ry 188]

[OF35.6] He also holds similarly one inclosure called Play Cross between the land of Edward Howe called Narbor to the north, Narbors Lane to the south, abutting to the west over the land of Richard Gobye and to the east over the Downes, containing 4 acres, 2 roods. [Ry 394]

[OF35.7] He also holds similarly one inclosure called Knill between the land of Alice Lynsey on the north, the land of John Shotto to the south, abutting to the east over the land of Hugh Kene and to the west over the lane leading to the Downes, containing 3 acres, 1 rood. [Ry 297]

[OF35.8] He also holds one inclosure called Stotfold between the land of Elizabeth Saye to the north, the Downes to the south, abutting upon the Downes to the east and over Stotfold Drove to the west, containing 4 acres. [Ry 276]

[OF35.9] He also holds similarly one meadow called Mill Closse lying near the mill between the land of Edward How, Agnes White and the lane leading to the mill and Brech Lane to the south, containing 3 acres, 15 perches. [Ry 211]

[OF35.10] He also holds similarly one pightle of meadow between the land of Hugh Kene to the north, the land of Christiana How to the south, abutting to the west over the land of Walter Rose and to the east over the common riverbank, containing 1 acre, 1 rood. [Ry 225]

[Marginal annotation: Total acreage:] 36 acres, ½ rood

*

[OF36.1] Agnes Whight, widow, holds by copy one tenement with garden and yard adjacent between her cottage, the yard of Walter Rose and Comerwicke Lane to the east, her own land to the west and abutting to the south over the Queen's highway leading from Sturmestur to Blandford, containing one acre, 30 perches. [S.67 + ? the lane to the west and the small cottage Buv 66?]

[OF36.2] She also holds likewise one other tenement, near the first, between that tenement to the west, Comerwicke Lane to the east, abutting to the north over the yard of Walter Rose and to the south over the Queen's highway, containing 28 perches. [part of 316]

[OF36.3] She also holds similarly near there one inclosure called Netherway between the land Elizabeth Saye to the north, the land of diverse tenements to the south, abutting to the west over the land of Robert Poope and Hugh Bythewoode and to the east over Comerwick Lane, containing 1 acre, 2 roods, 12 perches. [B 136]

[OF36.4] She also holds similarly near the above two inclosures lying together, with a certain lane leading to them, lying between the land of Elizabeth Saye to the south, the land of William Phillips to the north, abutting over the land of George Trencher esquire lying in the parish of Bell and the freehold land of Hugh Kene to the west and over Comerwick Lane to the east, containing altogether 9 acres, 3 roods, 12 perches. [S 321]

[OF36.5] She also holds similarly one meadow called Mill Closse lying between the land of Edward How and John Shotto to the north, the meadow of William Ford and Edward How to the south and abutting to the east over Breche Lane, containing 3 acres, 3 roods, 20 perches. [Ph+ 209]

[OF36.6] She also holds similarly half of one meadow with Agnes Mahew, widow, containing 3 roods, 6 perches. [S. Wb 205]

[OF36.7] She also holds similarly one inclosure called Fillgrove between the land of Emma Russell to the west, the land of William Phillips to the east, abutting to the north over the land of Margery Skotte and William Phillips and to the south over Shillingstone Lane, containing 3 acres, 4 perches. [S 241]

[OF36.8] She also holds similarly one pightle called Langshere between the land of the rector to the east, west and south and to the north over Shillingstone Lane, containing 3 roods, 10 perches. [part of S 245]

[OF36.9] She also holds similarly two inclosures lying together called Langshere between the lands of Henry Ford, the rector and her own land to the west, the land of the rector to the east and north and to the south over the land of Henry Ford and her own land, containing altogether 7 acres, 2 roods, 30 perches. [S 245]

[OF36.10] She also holds similarly near there one pightle between the land of William Phillips to the south, the land of the rector and her own land to the north, abutting to the east over land in Shillingstone and to the west over the land of Henry Ford and her own land, containing 3 roods, 20 perches. [part of S 245]

[OF36.11] She also holds similarly one inclosure called Pinwell lying between the land of Agnes Mahew to the east, the land of Joan Osmond and her own land to the west, abutting to the north over the land of Henry Ford and to the south over her own land, containing 3 acres, 1 rood, 20 perches. [S 266]

[OF36.12] She also holds similarly one pightle between the land of Agnes Mahew to the south, the land of Joan Osmond to the north and abutting to the west over Stotfold Drove, containing 1 acre 8 perches. [part S 265]

[OF36.13] She also holds similarly one inclosure lying between the land of Margery Skotte to the north, the land of Robert Poope to the south, abutting to the east over the lane leading to the Downe and to the west over Narbors Lane, containing 3 acres, 1 rood, 20 perches. [S 382]

[OF36.14] She also holds near there one inclosure called Narbor between the land of the said Robert Poope to the north, the land of Edward How to the south, abutting to the west over the land of William Chipman and to the east over the lane leading up to the Downes, containing 1 acre, 3 roods. [Ph+ 383]

[OF36.15] She also holds similarly one inclosure called Rayland between the land of Edward Bennett to the south, the land of Henry Wakeford and Richard Prower to the north, abutting to the west over the land of Edward Bennett and to the east over the land of Henry Wakeford and Rodford Lane, containing 4 acres, 2 roods, 21 perches. [Ph+ 429]

[OF36.16] She also holds similarly one inclosure called Cowle Crosse lying between the Queen's highway leading from Sturmestur to Blandford to the east, the land of Alice Dallidowne to the west, abutting to the north over the common river bank and to the south over Strowde Lane, containing 1 acre 2 roods. [?]

[OF36.17] She also holds similarly two parts of one inclosure called Westwood abutting to the west over Hay Bench, containing 1 acre, 2 roods, 10 perches. [part of 370]

[OF36.18] She also holds similarly near Horsfole Pleck one pightle between the land of William White junior to the north, the land of Edward How to the south, abutting to the east over the common river bank and to the west over Horsfole pleck, containing 1 acre. [Wo 221]

[Marginal annotation: Total acreage:] 48 acres, 11 perches

*

[OF37.1] William Phillips holds by copy one tenement with garden and yard adjacent between the land of Agnes White to the east, the land of Elizabeth White to the west, abutting to the north over the land of Agnes White and to the south over the Queen's highway leading from Sturmestur to Blandford, containing 2 roods, 20 perches. [Ru 650?]

[OF37.2] He also holds similarly one inclosure called Comerwick lying between the land of Agnes White to the south, the land of Hugh Bythewood to the north, abutting to the west over the land of George Trencher esquire and to the east over Comerwicke Lane, containing 3 acres, 3 roods, 36 perches.[Ru 322]

[OF37.3] He also holds similarly one inclosure called Horsfoole lying between the land of William White senior to the northeast, a certain lane leading to the land of William Ford and others to the northwest and abutting to the southeast over Horsfole Pleck, containing 2 acres, 20 perches. [A 187 and A 186?]

[OF37.4] He also holds similarly one inclosure called Fillgrove lying between the common riverbank to the northwest, the land of Margery Skott, Agnes White and his own land to the south and abutting over the land of Margery Skotte to the northeast, containing 3 acres, 20 perches. [Fa 239]

[OF37.5] He also holds similarly one inclosure near the previous entry between the land of Agnes White to the west, the land of Margery Skott to the east, abutting to the north over the aforesaid inclosure and to the south over Shillingstone Lane, containing 4 acres, 2 roods. [Fa 240]

[OF37.6] He also holds similarly near the above one inclosure lying between the land of Margery Skott to the west, the land of Richard Gobye to the east and abutting to the south over Shillingstone Lane, containing 3 acres. [Ru 237]

[OF37.7] He also holds similarly one pightle called Westwood lying between the land of Alice Biles to the south, the land of diverse tenements to the north and abutting to the east over the land of Edward How, containing 2 roods. [part of Ru 237?]

[OF37.8] He also holds similarly one meadow called Langshere lying between the land of Henry Ford to the west, land lying in the parish of Shillingstone to the east, abutting to the north over the land of Agnes White and to the south over the land of Henry Ford, containing 5 acres, 3 roods. [Ye 248]

[Marginal annotation: Total acreage:] ~~33 acres 2 roods 16 perches~~ 23 acres, 2½ roods

*

[OF38.1] Elizabeth White, widow, holds by copy one tenement with garden and yard adjacent between the tenement of William Phillips to the east, the tenement of Alice Lynsey to the west, abutting to the north over the land of Agnes White and to the south over the Queen's highway leading from Sturmestur to Blandford, containing 2 roods, 10 perches. [Ww 64]

[OF38.2] She also holds similarly three pightles of land lying together between the land of the rector called Upper Brech to the south, Gotiers Lane to the north, abutting over the land of Edward Williams to the east and over Coniger Lane to the west, containing altogether 5 acres, 10 perches. [Ww 182]

[OF38.3] He also holds similarly one inclosure called Jordaine between the land of Margery Skott to the east, the lane leading to Coniger to the west, abutting to the north over the same lane and to the south over the land of William White senior and Edward How, containing 3 acres, 35 perches. [Ww 198 and Ww 199]

[Marginal annotation: Total acreage:] 8 acres, 3 roods, 15 perches.

*

[OF39.1] Alicia Lynsey holds by copy one tenement with garden and yard adjacent between the tenement of Elizabeth White to the east, the tenement of Hugh Bythewoode to the west, abutting to the north over the land of Agnes White and to the south over the Queen's highway leading from Sturmestur to Blandford, containing 2 roods, 10 perches. [Ya 63]

[OF39.2] She also holds similarly two pightles lying together between the land of Robert Poope to the west and the land of Christiana Howe to the east abutting to the north over the land of the said Robert Pope and to the south over the Queen's highway leading from Sturmestur to Blandford, containing 2 acres, 18 perches. [Ya 317]

[OF39.3] She also holds one inclosure with pightle on the northern boundary of her tenement between the land of Robert Poope to the northeast, the land of Richard Prower and Stotfold Drove to the southwest and abutting to the east over the meadow of Henry Ford, containing 2 acres, 7 perches. [Ya 253]

[OF39.4] She also holds similarly one inclosure called Stotfold between the land of Richard Birte to the north, the land of Elizabeth Say to the south, abutting to the west over Stotfold Drove and to the east over the Downes, containing 2 acres, 6 perches. [Ya 274 + Ya 273]

[OF39.5] She also holds similarly one inclosure called Knill between the land of William White junior to the north, the land of William Ford to the south, abutting over Longwayle to the east and over the way leading to the Downes to the west, containing 2 acres, 3 roods, 33 perches. [Ya 298]

[OF39.6] She also holds similarly one inclosure called Cannys Haye lying in a triangular form between the land of Alice Harrys to the south, the land of Lawrence Frampton to the north and abutting to the west over Strowdwitch Lane, containing 5 acres, 12 perches. [Ya 457]

[OF39.7] She also holds similarly one pightle between the land of Yeovil Almshouses to the east, the land of diverse tenants to the west, abutting over the land of John Bythewood to the north and over Strowdwitch Lane to the south, containing 3 acres. [Ya 498]

[OF39.8] She also holds similarly one pightle between the land Yeovil Almshouses on each side and abutting over her own land, containing 3 roods, 20 perches [part of Ya 498]

[OF39.9] She also holds similarly near the same one inclosure with meadow adjacent abutting to the west over a certain drove of Laurence Frampton, to the east over the land of Yeovil Almshouse and her own land, containing altogether 5 acres, 3 roods, 16 perches. [Ya 510]

[OF39.10] She also holds similarly one inclosure called Dockle lying near the land of John Bythewood, over the common river bank to the east and to the west over Strowde Lane, containing 2 acres, 1 rood. [Ya 361]

[OF39.11] She also holds similarly one inclosure called Whitemere lying between Whitmere Lane to the west, the freehold land of Hugh Kene to the east and on each side abutting over Whitmere Lane, containing 8 acres. [K 581]

[Marginal annotation: Total acreage:] 39 acres, 3 roods, 6 perches

*

[OF40.1] Hugh Bythewode holds by copy one tenement with garden and yard adjacent between the tenement of Alice Lynsey to the east, the tenement of Christiana How to the west and abutting to the south over the Queen's highway leading from Sturmestur to Blandford, containing 2 roods, 20 perches. [Pi 62]

[OF40.2] He also holds similarly one inclosure called Comerwicke between the land of William Phillips to the south, the land of Agnes Mayewe to the north, abutting to the west over the common river bank and to the east over Comerwicke Lane, containing 3 acres, 1 rood, 8 perches. [Pi 323]

[OF40.3] He also holds one inclosure called Rush Knappe between the land of Richard Prower to the east, the land of John Newton to the west, abutting to the south over the land of the above Richard and to the north over Langstone Way, containing 1 acre, 1 rood, 17 perches. [Pi 260]

[OF40.4] He also holds one pightle lying lengthways beside Langestone Way between the land of William White senior to the south, Langestone way to the north and abutting to the west over the land of William Chipman, containing 3 roods. [Pa 290?]

[OF40.5] He also holds similarly one pightle called Cold Crosse between the Queen's highway leading from Sturmestur to Blandford on the west, the land of Robert Poope to the east, abutting to the north over the common river bank and to the south over the highway, containing 1 acre, 10 perches. [Pi 344]

[Marginal annotation: Total acreage:] 7 acres, 15 perches

*

[OF41.1] Christiana Howe, widow, holds by copy one cottage with garden, yard and a pightle adjacent between the lands of Alice Lynseye to the west, the land of Hugh Bythewood to the east, abutting to the north over the land of Robert Poope and to the south over the Queen's highway leading from Sturmestur to Blandford, containing 1 acre, 1 rood, 7 perches. [Fe ?]

[OF41.2] She also holds similarly one inclosure called Jordaine between the land of Edward Williams to the south, the land of John Newton to the north and abutting to the west over Comerwick Lane, containing 3 acres. [part of Br 192]

[OF41.3] She also holds similarly another inclosure called Jordaine between the land of Richard Gobye to the west, Conyger Lane to the east, abutting to the north over the land of Edward Williams and her own land and to the south over a certain lane leading to Conyger, containing 3 acres. [part of Br 192]

[OF41.4] She also holds similarly one inclosure lying between the land of Walter Rose and William Ford to the north, the land of William White junior to the south, abutting to the east over the common river bank and to the west over Horsfole Plecke, containing 1 acre 3 roods. [F 223]

[OF41.5] She also holds similarly one inclosure called Shortland lying between Hebed Lane to the west, the land of Alice Harrys to the east, abutting to the north over the land of Alice Harrys and Hugh Kene and to the south over Hebed Lane, containing 2 acres, 32 perches. [Bw 407]

[Marginal annotation: Total acreage:] 11 acres, ½ rood, 19 perches.

*

[OF42.1] Joan Phillips, widow, holds by copy one tenement and garden and yard adjacent lying between the land of John Schotto to the west and the land of diverse tenants to the east abutting to the south over the yard of John White and to the north over the Queen's highway leading from [Sturminster] to Blandford, containing 2 roods, 24 perches. [V 44]

[OF42.2] She also holds similarly one inclosure called Narbors lying between the land of William White senior to the south, Credohams Lane to the north, abutting to the west over the land of Alice Harrys and to the east over Narbors Elmes, containing 2 acres, 20 perches. [V 440]

[OF42.3] She also holds similarly one inclosure called Hay Crofte between the land of Joan Osmonde, widow, to the north, Edward Phillips and Edward Bennet to the south abutting to the west over her own land and to the east over the land of Richard Prower, Henry Reynolde and her own land, containing 5 acres, 24 perches. [V 462]

[OF42.4] She also holds similarly near above inclosure one pightle also called Hay Crofte between the land of William White junior to the north, Henry Reynolde to the south and abutting to the west over the land of Joan Osmond and her own land, containing 1 acre, 1 rood, 24 perches. [V 434]

[OF42.5] The same holds similarly diverse closes lying altogether called the Stroud with one pightle adjacent called Billet with appurtenances lying between the land of George Trencher esquire in the parish of Bell and the land of Alice Dallidowne to the north abutting to the west over the freehold land of Hugh Kene, containing altogether 27 acres, 34 perches. [V 355, V 356, V 357, V 505]

[OF42.6] She also holds similarly one inclosure called Bowaye lying between the land of John Shotto to the east, abutting to the south over the land of Edward Howe and to the north over the lane leading to the Strowde, containing 4 acres. [V 371]

[OF42.7] She also holds similarly half of one close called Westwood lying near the above inclosure, containing 2 roods, 30 perches. [part of V 371]

[OF42.8] The same holds similarly one inclosure called Play Crosse between the Downes to the east and the land of Alice Harrys to the west abutting to the north over Narbors Lane, containing 1 acre, 2 roods. V 395]

[Marginal annotation: Total acreage:] 42 acres, 2 roods, 9 perches.

*

[OF43.1] John Shotto holds by copy one tenement with garden and yard adjacent between the tenements of Joan Phillips, widow, and John White to the east, the tenement of Hugh Kene to the west, abutting to the south over the yard of Richard Prower and to the north over the Queen's highway leading from Sturmestur to Blandford, containing 2 roods. [Bd 45]

[OF43.2] He also holds similarly two inclosures lying together between the tenement of Alice Biles to the east, the land of Joan Phillips to the west, abutting to the south over the land of Agnes Mahew and Edward How called Westwood and to the north over the said Queen's highway, containing 3 acres, 3 roods, 12 perches. [Bd 372]

[OF43.3] He also holds similarly three inclosures lying together called Westwoode between the land of Edward Williams to the north, Credohams Lane to the south, abutting to the west over the land of Alice Harrys and the common river bank and to the east over the land of Joseph Harrys and Alice Harrys, containing altogether 8 acres, 2 roods. [the largest part of Pl 376, Joseph Harrys also has a part]

[OF43.4] He also holds similarly diverse inclosures lying lengthways called Sugestone between the land of Yeovil Almshouses to the east, the land of Henry Ford and Elizabeth Saye to the west, abutting to the south over the land of Elizabeth Saye and Whitmere Lane and to the north over the lord's common pasture called Gobson, containing altogether 33 acres, 3 roods, 7 perches. [Bd 522, Bd 533, Bd 556, Bd 557 and Bd 559]

[OF43.5] He also holds similarly one inclosure called Knill between the land of Joseph Harris and the Downes to the south, the land of William Ford to the north, abutting to the east over the land of Hugh Kene and to the west over the way leading to the Downe, containing 1 acre, 3 roods. [Bd 296]

[OF43.6] He also holds similarly one inclosure called Bullhedge with a sharp ascendant to Horsfoole Pleck lying between the land of Edward Howe to the west, a certain lane leading to the land of William Forde and others to the north-east and abutting to the northwest over the land of Elizabeth Say, containing 3 acres, 1 rood, 8 perches. [Bd 208]

[Marginal annotation: Total acreage:] 51 acres, 2 roods, 7 perches.

*

[OF44.1] Hugh Kene holds by copy one tenement with garden and croft adjacent between the tenement of Agnew Mahew to the west, the tenement of John Shotto and others to the east, abutting to the south over the land of Agnes Mahew and to the north over the Queen's highway leading from Sturmestur to Blandford, containing 1 acre, 16 perches. [Ye 16]

[OF44.2] He also holds similarly one inclosure with meadow adjacent between the land of Robert Poope called Nethway to the south, his own freehold land to the north, to the west over common river bank and his own land and to the east over another way belonging to Agnes White, containing 4 acres. [Ye 319]

[OF44.3] He also holds similarly one inclosure called Furzey Crofte lying between the lands of Henry Reynold to the south, the freehold land of Thomas White esquire called Arthurs to the north, abutting to the west over the common river bank and to the east over Comerwick Lane, containing 7 acres, 1 rood. [Ye 165]

[OF44.4] He also holds similarly one inclosure called Breche between the land of Walter Rose to the south, the land of the rector to the north, abutting to the west over the land of the rector and to the east over Breche Lane, containing 2 acres, 2 roods, 30 perches. [Ye 184]

[OF44.5] He also holds similarly one inclosure lying between the land of the rector called Great Breche and the meadow of Robert Hynde to the north, the land of Walter Rose and William Forde to the south, abutting to the west over Breche Lane and to the east over the common river bank, containing 4 acres, 2 roods. [Ye 226]

[OF44.6] He also holds similarly one meadow called Longwaile between the land of Margery Skotte to the east, the land of diverse tenants to the west, abutting to the south over May Ridge and to the north over Langstone Wey, containing 7 acres, 3 roods. [Ye 293, Ye 294, Ye 285]

[OF44.7] He also holds similarly one inclosure near Hebed Lane between the land of Richard Prower to the west, the land of Alice Harrys to the east, abutting to the north over the land of Edward Williams and William Pelle and to the south over the land of Christiana Howe and Hebed Lane, containing 2 acres, 1 rood. [Ye 399]

[OF44.8] He also holds similarly one inclosure called Shortland between the land of Alice Harrys to the west, the land of Henry Reynold and the Downes to the east, abutting over Hebed Land and over the Downes to the northeast, containing 4 acres, 1 rood, 30 perches. [Ye 409]

[Marginal annotation: Total acreage:] 33 acres, 3 roods, 16 perches.

*

[OF45.1] Richard Gobye holds by copy one tenement with garden and croft adjacent between the tenement of Agnes Mahew to the east, the tenement of Edward Bennett to the west, abutting to the south over the land of Agnes Mahew and to the north over the Queen's highway from Sturmestur to Blandforde, containing 3 roods. [Hv 48]

[OF45.2] He also holds similarly a common bakehouse built with garden adjacent lying between the tenement of Henry Forde to the north, the tenement of John Newton to the south and abutting to the east over the said Queen's highway, containing 30 perches. [Pp 42]

[OF45.3] He also holds similarly one inclosure called Jordaine between the land of Christiana How to the east, the land of Richard Birte to the west, abutting over the land of Edward Williams to the north and over a certain lane leading to Conyger to the south, containing 3 acres. [Ra 195]

[OF45.4] He also holds similarly one inclosure called Old Woode between the land of William Pelle and Richard Birte to the west, the land of John Newton to the east, abutting to the north over the land lying in the parish of Shillingstone and to the south over Cotyars Drove, containing 2 acres, 7 perches. [Ra 176]

[OF45.5] He also holds similarly three inclosures lying together called Narbor between the land of Edward Howe to the north, Narbors Lane to the south, abutting to the east over the land of Edward Howe and William Forde and to the west over Narbors Lane, containing altogether 7 acres. [Tz 390 and 393]

[OF45.6] He also holds similarly two inclosures lying together called Ovenest between the land of Alice Dallidowne to the south, the land of Laurence Frampton to the north, abutting to the east over the common riverbank and to the west over the land of Alice Dallidowne, containing altogether 4 acres, 2 roods. [Pp 455]

[OF45.7] He also holds similarly two inclosures called Churchwayse lying together between the land of William Phillips to the west, the land of the rector called Churchwayse to the east, abutting to the south over Shillingstone Lane and to the north over the land of Margery Skotte, containing together 3 acres, 1 rood. [C 236]

[Marginal annotation: Total acreage:] 20 acres 2½ roods, 17 perches.

*

[OF46.1] Edward Bennett holds by copy one tenement with garden and croft adjacent between the tenement of Richard Gobye to the east, the tenement of Alice Biles to the west, abutting to the south over the land of Agnes Mahew and to the north over the Queen's highway leading from Sturmester to Blandford, containing 3 roods. [Sr 49]

[OF46.2] He also holds similarly one inclosure called Shapehaye lying between the lane leading to Conyger and the land of Richard Birte to the east, Comerwicke Lane to the west, abutting to the north over the land of Richard Birte and to the south over the lane leading to Coniger, containing 2 acres. [Ka 197]

[OF46.3] He also holds similarly one inclosure called Redlake between the land of Richard Prower and John Phillips to the north, the land of Edward Phillips to the south, abutting to the west over the land of Edward Phillips and to the east over the land of Agnes White and his own land, containing 6 acres, 3 roods. [Ka 426, Ka 427]

[OF46.4] He also holds similarly near the above one inclosure called Raylond between the land of Agnes White to the north, the land of Edward Phillips to the south, abutting to the west over the previous close and to the east over Rodford Lane, containing 1 acre, 2 roods. [Ka 428]

[OF46.5] He also holds similarly one inclosure called Westwood lying between Westwood Lane on the west, the lane leading to the lands of diverse tenants in Westwoode to the east, abutting to the north over Westwood Lane and to the south over the land of diverse tenants, containing 3 acres, 3 roods. [Ka 399?]

[Marginal annotation: Total acreage:] 14 acres 3 roods.

*

[OF47.1] Alice Byles, widow, holds by copy a tenement with garden and croft adjacent between the tenement of Edward Bennett to the east, the land of John Schotto to the west, abutting over the land of Agnes Mahew to the south and over the Queen's highway leading from Sturmestur to Blandford to the north, containing 1 acre, 1 rood. [Piv 50]

[OF47.2] She also holds similarly one inclosure called Langstone between the land of Margery Skotte to the east, the land of Emma Russell to the west and abutting to the north over Langestone Wey, containing 4 acres, 3 roods, 5 perches. [Ht 288]

[OF47.3] She also holds similarly one inclosure lying between the land of Agnes Mahew to the north, the land of Richard Birte to the south, abutting to the east over the land of the said Richard and to the west over Stottfould Drove, containing 1 acre, 2 roods, 16 perches. [Piv 271]

[OF47.4] She also holds similarly one inclosure lying between Stroudwitch Lane to the east, the land of Yeovil Almshouse to the northwest and abutting over the land of Laurence Frampton to the southwest, containing 1 acre, 2 roods, 20 perches. [part of Piv 494?]

[OF47.5] She also holds similarly one pightle called Westwood between the land of Alice Dallidowne to the south, the land of William Phillips to the north and abutting to the east over the land of Edward How, containing 3 roods.

[Marginal annotation: Total acreage:] 10 acres, ½ rood.

*

[OF48.1] Richard Foote holds by copy one tenement with garden, yard and diverse closes of arable, pasture and meadow lying together between the land of Alice Dallidowne and the freehold land of George Trencher, esquire, to the northwest, the Queen's highway leading from Sturmestur to Blandford on the east, abutting to the north over the land of George Trencher, esquire, lying in the parish of Bell and to the south over the common river bank, containing 29 acres, 3 roods, 21 perches. [E 346, E 348[1], E 348 [2], E 349, E 350, E 351, E 352]

[OF48.2] He also holds similarly in another part of the said Queen's highway four closes with an adjacent pightle of arable, pasture and meadow between the freehold land of Hugh Kene, a parcel of the the tenement called Browne to the south, over the Queen's highway to the west, abutting to the north over Brownes tenement and to the south over the common river bank, containing altogether 20 acres, 38 perches. [E 340, E 341, E 342]

[OF48.3] He also holds similarly one inclosure between the land of Laurence Frampton to the north, the land of Walter Roose to the south, abutting to the west over the common riverbank and to the east over Westwood Lane, containing 1 acre, 3 roods. [E 450]

[Marginal annotation: Total acreage:] 51 acres 3½ roods.

*

[OF49.1] Alice Dallidowne, widow, holds by copy one tenement with garden, yard and diverse closes of arable, pasture and meadow, lying together, between the land of John Phillips and Elizabeth Saye to the southwest, the land of Richard Foote to the northeast, abutting over the land of George Trencher, esquire, in the parish of Bell to the northwest and over the common river bank to the southeast, containing altogether 9 acres, 2 roods, 12 perches. [Pp 353]

[OF49.2] She also holds similarly one cottage near the same between the common riverbank to the north, Haybenche to the south and abutting to the east over the land of Agnes White, containing 2 roods, 8 perches. [Pp 59]

[OF49.3] She also holds similarly one inclosure called Knill between the land of William White junior to the south, the land of John White and William Chipman to the north, abutting to the east over the land of William White senior and to the east over the lane leading to the Downes, containing 1 acre. [Pp 300]

[OF49.4] She also holds similarly three pightles lying together called Ovenest between the lands of Robert Gobye and her own land to the north, the land of Alice Harrys to the south and abutting on each side on the lands of Alice Harrys, containing 5 acres. [Pp 459]

[OF49.5] She also holds similarly two pightles lying together near the same between the land of Richard Gobye to the east and the land of Alice Lynsey to the west abutting to the south over the land of Alice Harrys and the above Alice and to the north over the land of Laurence Frampton, containing altogether 2 acres, 2 roods, 30 perches. [Pp 459]

[OF49.6] She also holds similarly one pightle called Westwood lying between the land of Robert Poope to the south, the land of Alice Biles to the north and abutting to the east over the land of Edward Howe, containing 2 roods, 16 perches. [Pl 363?]

[Marginal annotation: Total acreage:] 19 acres, 2 roods, 6 perches.

*

[OF50.1] John Bythewood holds by copy one tenement with garden, yard and diverse closes of arable, pasture and meadow lying together between the lane leading to Gobson called Cheslane to the north, the land of Laurence Frampton, Yeovil Almshouse and Alice Lynsey to the south, abutting to the west over the land of Joan Osmonde and to the east over Strowdewitche Lane, containing together 11 acres, 2 roods, 14 perches. [Bs 502, Bs 503, Bs 504, Bs 508]

[OF50.2] He also holds similarly three closes lying together between Strowde Lane to the northwest, the common riverbank to the east, abutting to the south over the land of Laurence Frampton and to the northeast over the land of Alice Lynsey, containing altogether 11 acres, 2 roods, 32 perches. [Bs 453 Bs 359, Bs 360]

[OF50.3] He also holds similarly one inclosure lying between the land of Elizabeth Say and the freehold land of Hugh Kene to the north, the land of Laurence Frampton to the south, abutting to the west over the common riverbank and to the east over Westwood Lane, containing 1 acre, 2 roods. [Bs 452]

[Marginal annotation: Total acreage:] 29 acres, 3 roods, 6 perches.

*

[OF51.1] Laurence Frampton holds by copy one tenement with garden and croft adjacent between the land Yeovil Almshouse to the west, Strowdewitche Lane to the east and abutting to the north over the land of John Bythewoode, containing 1 acre, 2 roods, 20 perches. [H 500 and H 501]

[OF51.2] He also holds similarly one pightle lying between the land of Yeovil Almshouse on each side, abutting to the east over the land of Alice Lynsey and to the west over his own land, containing 2 roods, 30 perches. [Pw 496]

[OF51.3] He also holds similarly one pightle lying between Strowdewitch Lane to the east, the land of Alice Harrys to the west and abutting over the land of Alice Biles to the northeast, containing 1 acre, 3 roods, 36 perches. [part of Pw 494?]

[OF51.4] He also holds similarly one inclosure with meadow adjacent near the same between the land of Alice Harrys to the south, the land of Alice Lynsey to the north, abutting to the west over the land of Joan Osmond and to the east over the land of Yeovil Almshouse and his own land, containing altogether 6 acres, 20 perches. [Pw 512]

[OF51.5] He also holds similarly near the same one inclosure lying between the land of Alice Lynsey on the south, the land of John Bythewoode on the north abutting to the west over the land of Joan Osmond and to the east over the land of John Bythewood, containing 2 acres, 13 perches. [Pw 509]

[OF51.6] He also holds similarly opposite the tenement two inclosures lying together between the land of Alice Dallidowne, Richard Gobye and Alice Lynsey to the south, the land of John Bythewoode to the north, abutting to the east over the common river bank and to the west over Strowdewitche Lane, containing altogether 8 acres, 21 perches. [Bs 453, 454?]

[OF51.7] He also holds similarly one inclosure lying near the land of John Bythewood to the north and the land of Richard Foote to the south, abutting over the common river bank to the west and over Westwoode Lane to the east, containing 1 acre, 3 roods. [H 451]

[OF51.8] He also holds similarly one piece of land lying in Westwoode in one inclosure of William Pelle, which could not be seen, containing by estimation ½ acre. [H 449]

[Marginal annotation: Total acreage:] 22 acres, 3½ roods.

*

[OF52.1] Edward Ramsebutt holds by copy one cottage with garden adjacent newly built lying over Bell Knappe near the land formerly belonging to the Abbot of Abbotsbury and returns per annum 62*d*. [Wg 474]

*

[OF53.1] John Norman holds by copy one cottage newly built with garden adjacent lying by Strowdwitche Lane near the land of Yeovil Almshouse. [K 492]

*

[OF54.1] Edward Phillipes holds by copy one tenement near Strowde lying between the land leading from Strowdewitche Lane to Bell to the west, the land of Joan Osmond to the east and also abutting over Joan's land to the north, containing 2 acres, 1 rood, 30 perches. [Cl 471]

[OF54.2] He also holds similarly on another part of the said tenement one inclosure lying between the land of John Iles to the south, the land of Joan Osmond called Hay Crofte to the north and abutting over the tenement, containing 3 acres, 3 roods. [Cl 470]

[OF54.3] He also holds similarly one meadow called Strowdemede lying between the said close and Haycrofte to the west, the land of John Iles and his own land to the east, abutting to the south over the land of John Iles and to the north over the land of Joan Osmond, containing 6 acres, 2 roods, 10 perches. [Cl 467]

[OF54.4 The same holds similarly one inclosure near the above called Rayland between the land of Joan Phillips to the north and the land of John Iles to the south abutting over Strowdesmede aforesaid to the west, containing 3 acres, 2 roods, 20 perches. [Cl 463]

[OF54.5] He also holds similarly one close near the above inclosure called Rayland between the land of John Iles to the south, the land of Edward Bennett to the north, abutting over the above close to the west and over Rodford Lane to the east, containing 5 acres. [Cl 425]

[OF54.6] He also holds one large close well supplied with trees called Strowde lying opposite the above tenement between Remple Lane on the west, the lane leading from Strowdewitche to Bell Knappe on the east, abutting to the south over the same lane and to the north over the lane leading from Strowde to Remple, containing 38 acres, 3 roods. [Cl 479-Cl 487]

[OF54.7] He also holds similarly one inclosure called Whitmere lying between the land of Edward How called Southleys to the west, Whitmere Lane to the east, abutting to the north over the land of Alice Harrys and to the south over the land of Joan Osmond, containing 15 acres, 2 roods, 20 perches. [Cl 579]

[OF54.8] He also holds similarly two parts of one inclosure called Westwoode containing 1 acre, 1 rood, 20 perches.

[Marginal annotation: Total acreage:] 77 acres ½ rood.

*

The lands lying in Fittleford within the parish of Ockforde which is a certain hamlet belonging to the manor of Ockford.

[OF55.1] John Mahewe holds by copy one tenement with garden, yard and one great inclosure adjacent between the land of Richard Powlden to the east, the Queen's highway to the west, abutting over the tenement and lands of Richard Powlden to the north and over the land of diverse tenants called the Mershes to the south, containing altogether 18 acres, 2 roods, 15 perches. [J 140, J 141, and perhaps J 133 and Pr 84]

[OF55.2] He also holds similarly one inclosure lying between the land of Thomas Snoke to the east, the land of Richard Powlden to the west and abutting to the south over the way leading from Ockford to Hammone, containing 6 acres, 2 roods. [Part of J 152?]

[OF55.3] He also holds similarly one inclosure lying between the land of Richard Powlden to the north, the land of Thomas White esquire to the south, abutting to the west over the common river bank and to the east over the Queen's highway leading from Fittleford to Ockforde, containing 2 acres. [J 145]

[OF55.4] He also holds similarly one yard lying opposite the tenement between the common riverbank to the west and the Queen's highway to the east, containing 3 roods. [Da 88?]

[OF55.5] He also holds 3½ acres in Fittleford meadow. [J 119?]

[Marginal annotation: Total acreage:] 31 acres, 1 rood, 15 perches.

*

[OF56.1] Richard Powlden holds similarly one tenement with garden and yard adjacent lying between the tenement of John Mahew to the south, the free tenement of Thomas White esquire to the north, abutting to the west over the Queen's highway and to the east over his own land, containing 3 roods, 2 perches. [J 90?]

[OF56.2] He also holds similarly one inclosure to the east end of the aforesaid tenement lying between the land of Edithe Bugge to the north, the land of John Mahew and his own land to the south, abutting to the west over the previous tenement and against the tenements and land of Thomas White esquire, containing 5 acres, 16 perches. [J 133]

[OF56.3] He also holds similarly four inclosures lying between the land of John Mahew to the west, the land of Edith Bugge to the northeast, abutting over the previous close to the northwest and over the land of diverse tenements to the southeast, containing altogether 22 acres, 31 perches. [Ba 134?, Ba 136?, J 137?]

[OF56.4] He also holds similarly one inclosure lying between the land of John Mahew to the east, the land of Edith Bugge to the west, abutting to the north over the land of John Mahew and to the south over the way leading from Fified to Hewood Bridge, containing 8 acres. [part of J 151]

[OF56.5] He also holds similarly one inclosure called Smithes lying between the land of Edward Skotte to the north, the land of John Mahewe to the south, abutting to the west over the common river bank and to the east over the Queen's highway, containing 2 acres. [part of J 145 or Bi 144]

[OF56.6] He also holds similarly one small pightle lying between the land of Giles Cabell, knight, in the parish of Chillockford [Child Okeford] to the north, a certain lane lying on the opposite side of diverse tenements and abutting to the east over the same tenements and to the west over the Queen's highway, containing 20 perches.

[OF56.7] He also holds similarly in Fittleford meadow 3½ acres. [J122 or J119]

[Marginal annotation: Total acreage:] 41 acres, 2½ roods.

*

[OF57.1] Edith Bugge, widow, holds by copy one tenement with garden and croft adjacent lying on every side by the riverbank between the land of the Queen on the west, the Queen's highway on the east and abutting over the land of Edward Skotte to the south, containing 1 acre, 2 roods, 20 perches. [Ba 143]

[OF57.2] She also holds similarly one inclosure lying between the land of Thomas Snooke to the north, the land of Thomas White esquire and Richard Powlden to the south, abutting over the lane lying opposite part of the tenement to the west and over the land of Thomas Snoke to the east, containing 6 acres, 34 perches. part of Ba 132?]

[OF57.3] She also holds similarly four closes lying together lengthways between the land of Thomas Snoke to the north, the land of Richard Powlden and Mr Crookhorne lying in the parish of Bell to the south and abutting to the east over the land of George Trencher esquire lying in the parish of Hammone, containing altogether 15 acres, 3 roods, 25 perches. [Ba 134 + Ba 135?]

[OF57.4] She also holds similarly one inclosure lying between the land of Richard Powlden to the east, the land of Edward Skotte to the west, abutting to the north over the land of John Mahewe and to the south over the way leading from Fyfid to Hewad Bridge, containing 5 acres, 3 roods. [Ba 152 or Ba 159?]

[OF57.5] She also holds similarly four acres of meadow lying in Fittleford meadow. [Ba 114 + Ba 116?]

[Marginal annotation: Total acreage:] 33 acres 1½ roods, 18 perches.

*

[OF58.1] Thomas Snooke holds by copy one tenement with garden adjacent between the land of Thomas White esquire to the south, the tenement of Roger Apowell to the north and abutting to the west over the Queen's highway, containing 3 roods, 10 perches. [Ba 101]

[OF58.2] He also holds similarly one yard opposite the aforesaid tenement lying between the land of Thomas White esquire to the west and the common riverbank to the east, containing by estimation 1 rood. [Ba 100]

[OF58.3] He also holds similarly one garden between the land of Edward Skotte on the west, a certain lane lying opposite the tenement to the north and abutting to the south over the land of Edward Skotte, containing 1 rood, 10 perches. [Ba 106]

[OF58.4] He also holds similarly two inclosures lying together in a different part of the tenement with the land of Edith Bugge to the south, abutting over the land of Roger Apowell and his own land to the east and over the said lane to the west, containing altogether 3 acres, 2 roods, 34 perches. [part Ba 134 + Ba 132?]

[OF58.5] He also holds similarly one inclosure lying near there between the land of Roger Apowell to the north, Edith Bugge to the south and abutting to the west over his own land and the land of Edith Bugge, containing 5 acres, 1 rood, 15 perches. [part of 134]

[OF58.6] He also holds similarly three closes lying together between the land of Edith Bugge to the south, the land of George Trencher esquire to the north and abutting to the east over the land of George Trencher esquire, containing altogether 8 acres, 14 perches. [Ba 135]

[OF58.7] He also holds similarly one inclosure lying between the land of John Mahew to the west, the land Christopher Selbye lying in the parish of Bell and the land of Roger Apowell to the east, abutting to the north over the land of Richard Powldon and to the south over the way leading from Ockford to Hammone, containing 5 acres, 15 perches. [Ba 152]

[OF58.8] He also holds similarly 3½ acres of meadow lying in Fittleford meadow. [Ba 118]

[Marginal annotation: Total acreage:] 26 acres 3½ roods 18 perches.

*

[OF59.1] Roger Apowell holds by copy one tenement lying between the tenement of Thomas Snooke to the south, the tenement of Thomas White esquire to the north and abutting over the Queen's highway to the west, containing 1 rood, 16 perches. [Y 102]

[OF59.2] He also holds similarly three inclosures lying together opposite the aforesaid tenement between the land of Thomas Snooke to the south, the land of Edward Skotte to the north and abutting to the east over the land of George Trencher esquire lying in the parish of Hammone, containing altogether 15 acres, 16 perches. [Y 129 and Y 130]

[OF59.3] He also holds similarly one small meadow lying between the land of Thomas White esquire on each side, abutting to the north over the land of George Trencher and to the south over the land of Edward Skotte, containing 3 roods. [Y 127]

[OF59.4] He also holds similarly one pightle lying between the way leading from Ockford to Hammone to the southeast, the land of Mr Crookhorne and Christopher Selbye to the north, abutting to the west over the land of Thomas Snooke, containing 1 acre, 2 roods. [Y154]

[OF59.5] He also holds similarly one inclosure lying between the Queen's highway to the west, the land of Edward Skotte to the east, abutting to the north over the land of John Mahew and to the south over the way leading from Fifid to Hewood Bridge, containing 4 acres, 4 roods, 4 perches. [Y 148]

[OF59.6] He also holds similarly 3½ acres of meadow lying in Fittleford meadow. [Y 120]

[Marginal annotation: Total acreage:] 25 acres 3 ½ roods 16 perches.

*

[OF60.1] Edward Skott holds by copy one tenement with garden adjacent between the tenement of Thomas White esquire to the south, the land of Thomas Snooke and his own land to the north and abutting to the west over the Queen's highway, containing 1 rood, 25 perches. [Bi 105]

[OF60.2] He also holds similarly opposite the tenement one yard lying between the land of Thomas White esquire to the west and the common river bank to the east, containing 1 rood. [Bi 104]

[OF60.3] He also holds similarly near the tenement one pightle between the land of Thomas Snooke to the east, the tenement of Thomas White esquire lying in the parish of Bell to the west and abutting over his own tenement to the south, containing 1 rood 26 perches. [Bi 115?]

[OF60.4] He also holds similarly in another part of the tenement four inclosures with meadow adjacent between the land of Roger Apowell to the south, the land of Roger Apowell and Thomas White esquire to the north and abutting to the east over the land of George Trencher esquire lying in the parish of Hammone, containing altogether 22 acres, 16 perches. [Bi 128]

[OF60.5] He also holds similarly one inclosure lying between the land of Edith Bugge to the east, the land of Roger Apowell to the west, abutting over the land of John

Mahew to the north and to the south over the way leading from Fifid to Hewood Bridge, containing 4 acres, 3 roods, and 4 perches. [Bi 149]

[OF60.6] He also holds similarly one inclosure lying between the land of Edith Bugge to the north, the land of Richard Powlden to the south, abutting to the east over the Queen's highway and to the west over the common riverbank, containing 2 acres, 22 perches. [Bi 144]

[OF60.7] He also holds similarly 3½ acres of meadow lying in Fittleford meadow. [Bi 144]

[Marginal annotation: Total acreage:] 33 acres 2 roods 13 perches.

*

[OF61.1] Henry Bugge holds by copy one cottage with garden adjacent newly built over the waste of the lord in Fittleford between the land of Queen to the east and abutting to the south over the land of Edith Bugge, containing by estimation 1 rood.

*

[OF62.1] The village of Ockforde holds at the will of the lord one house called the Townehouse situated and lying in the town.

[OF62.2] It also holds similarly one inclosure called Grenehay alias Playing Closse lying near the land of Henry Reynold, containing ½ acre.

*

[OF63.1] The lord holds in hand one coppice called the Coniger lying between the land of diverse tenants, containing 34 acres, 1 rood. [172]

[OF63.2] He also holds similarly another coppice called the Cliff lying over the Downes, containing 7½ acres.

*

Land belonging to the rectory of Ockford

[OF64.1] The rectory of Ockford is situated and lies between the tenement of Emma Russell to the south, the tenements of diverse tenants to the north, abutting to the west over the Queen's highway leading from Sturmestur to Blandford and to the east over the common way, containing 2 roods, 16 perches. [23]

[OF64.2] Likewise one close called Upp Breche lying in two squares between the lands of Hugh Kene and William Forde to the southwest, the land of diverse tenants to the north and abutting to the east over Brechlane, containing 6 acres, 3 roods, 14 perches. [183]

[OF64.3] Likewise one close called Great Breche lying between the land of Hugh Kene on the southwest, the land lying in the parish of Shillingstone on the northeast and abutting to the west over Breche Lane, containing 17 acres, 1 rood .[227, 228]

[OF64.4] Likewise one inclosure with meadow adjacent called Church Wayse lying between the land of Richard Gobye to the west, land lying in the parish of Shillingstone to the northeast and abutting to the south over Shillingstone Lane, containing altogether 11 acres, 20 perches. [234, 235]

[OF64.5] Likewise three inclosures of land, pasture and meadow called Lamsher between the land of Agnes White to the west, the land lying in the parish of Shillingstone to the east and abutting over Shillingstone Lane to the north, containing altogether 8 acres, 1 rood, 22 perches. [246, 247]

[OF64.6] Likewise one inclosure called Longhill lying between the land of Henry Ford to the south, Shillingstone Lane to the north and abutting to the west over the land of Henry Ford, containing 3 acres 1 rood 8 perches. [243]

[OF64.7] Likewise one meadow called Broadmead lying between the land of John Newton to the west, the land of Henry Forde to the east and abutting to the south over Langestone Way, containing 5 acres, 1 rood, 12 perches. [256]

[OF64.8] Likewise one inclosure with meadow adjacent called Rodford lying between the land of Walter Roose to the north, the land of Richard Prower to the south and abutting to the east over Rodford Lane, containing altogether 7 acres, 16 perches. [437]

[OF64.9] Likewise two inclosures lying together called Alfett Hay lying between the land of Thomas White esquire to the west, Comerwicke Lane to the east and abutting to the north over the common way leading from Fifed to Hewood Bridge, containing altogether 13 acres, 2 roods. [155, 156, 157]

[Marginal annotation: Total acreage:] ~~83 acres, ½ rood, 8 perches~~ 72 acres 3½ roods

*

Free land belonging to this manor, which is held as a knight's fee, lying in the parish of Ockford.

[OF65.1] Thomas White holds certain freehold land in Ockford called Arthurs lying together between the customary land of Hugh Kene to the south, the way leading from Fifed to Hewood Bridge to the north, abutting to the west over the common riverbank and to the east over the land of the rector of Ockforde called Allfett Hay, containing altogether 40 acres. [M 147, M 158 - M 164]

THE SURVEY OF LYTCHETT MINSTER
COMPLETED IN 1584

Litchett Minster and Beere

A Survey of the said manor here taken, made and examined with much diligence and exact discernment by walking the site and examination of the evidence of the said manor and measuring by Thomas Wright, surveyor of the lands of Sir Thomas Kitson of the said manor by taking the oath of all the homage of the said manor and of many tenants there at that time viz: Augustine Lawrence, Thomas Barnes, Thomas Perse, John Furnis, William Mudge, John Pelly, John Henning senior, George Cowring, John junior [*i.e. John Henning junior*], Julian Gowlde, Robert Browning, Richard Sansume, John Mudge, Simon Chismonde, Richard Gene [*sic Geale?*], John Barnes, William Hylyard, Thomas Sansume, William Barnes, George James, Nicholas Bright, Richard Bright, Thomas Browning and others.

Begun the month of May in the twenty fifth year of the reign of our lady Queen Elizabeth, by the grace of God Queen of England, France and Ireland, Defender of the Faith [1583]. And finished and confirmed at the court of the same tenants on the twentieth day of May in the twenty sixth year of the reign of our Lady Queen Elizabeth [1584].

*

The first precinct contains all the land and tenements lying between Litchett Common on the east and Criche Lane on the west.

[LM.1] Thomas Barnes holds by copy one tenement with garden, yard and other [arable] land, pasture and wood adjacent lying altogether in diverse closes between Litchett Common on the east and a certain lane called Bakers Lane on the west abutting to the north over the Common and to the south over East Marshe and Bakers Crosse, containing altogether 33 acres, 2 roods. [239? part of 240 and 241,243-250,252-253,255,256,257,258- these also include LM.2.4 & 5]

[LM.2] He also holds to the north, one close of land between the common on the east and the common and land of Emma Henninge on the west, containing 5 acres, 1 rood. [239?]

[LM.3] William Mudge holds near there one pightle with a separate way leading to the common to the east and lying between land of Thomas Barnes on every side, containing 1 acre, 1 rood, 10 perches. [part of 241?]

[LM.4] Thomas Barnes holds near there two inclosures with an adjoining pightle lying close to Bakers Lane, containing 7 acres, 2 roods, 7 perches. [part of 241?]

[LM.5] He also holds similarly near there one coppice lying between the said close on the east, the lands of John Furmadge and Emma Henninge on the west, abutting to the north over land of William Mudge and to the south over the said pightle, containing 2½ acres. [part of 240]

[LM.6] William Mudge holds similarly by copy one pightle lying between the land of Thomas Barnes and Bakers Lane on the east, the land of Emma Henninge on the west and abutting to the north over a pightle belonging to Thomas Barnes, containing 3 roods, 8 perches. [part of 241?]

[LM.7] He also holds similarly one tenement with garden, croft and other lands adjacent between Bakers Lane to the east, the lands of Emma Henninge and George Trenchard, gentleman, on the west and abutting to the south over the Queen's highway leading to East Marshe, containing altogether 5 acres, 1 rood, 24 perches. [242]

[LM.8] George Trencharde, gentleman, holds freely of the manor de Cockemoore one pightle lying between the land of Emma Henninge to the north, George Crosse to the south and abutting to the west over Creeche Lane, containing by estimation 3 roods. [227]

[LM.9] Emma Henninge, widow, holds by copy one tenement with garden, croft and other [arable] land, pasture and adjacent meadow between the land of John Furmage to the north, land of George Trenchard and William Mudge on the south and abutting to the west over Creech Lane, containing altogether 21 acres, 1 rood, 8 perches. [228,229,230,231,232,233, 234]

[LM.10] John Firmage holds near there one inclosure called A Reed Pasture between the aforesaid land to the south, Litchett Common and the land of Emma Henninge to the north and abutting to the west over Creech Lane, containing 5 acres, 3 roods, 10 perches. [235,256]

[LM.11] Emma Henninge, widow, holds near there three pightles and pasture lying together between the lands of Thomas Barnes and William Mudge on the east, Litchett Common on the west and abutting to the north over the common, containing 4 acres, 2 roods, 30 perches. [237,238]

*

The second precinct contains all the lands and tenements lying between Creech Lane on the east and the way leading from Litchett Church to Blandford to the west, going towards the west.

[LM.12] George Trenchard holds freely of Cockmore one pightle lying near George Crosse between the Queen's highway on the south, his own freehold land to the north and abutting to the west over the common riverbank, containing 1 acre, 10 perches. [part of 210]

[LM.13] He also holds freely one tenement with garden and croft adjacent abutting to the west over the riverbank and to the east over Creeche Lane, containing 1 acre, 3 roods, 14 perches. [part of 210]

[LM.14] John Firmage holds by copy near there one tenement with garden, croft, [arable] land, pasture and meadow now lying in diverse pieces between the aforesaid tenement to the south, the land of Emma Henninge to the north, abutting to the west over the river bank and to the east over Creech Lane, containing altogether 12 acres, 27 perches. [211,212,213,214,215,216,217]

[LM.15] Emma Henninge, widow, holds similarly by copy one close lying adjacent to the previous entry, abutting at either end as above, containing 3 acres, 10 perches. [218]

[LM.16] William Knappe holds freely of the manor of Newton Peverley one tenement with garden, croft and other lands adjacent between Pitt Bridge to the north, the aforesaid close to the south and on all sides abutting at the end as above, containing 5 acres, 1 rood, 10 perches. [219-224]

[LM.17] He also holds similarly to the north of le Pittbridge certain land and wood lying near to the common of Littchett, containing altogether 46 acres 1 rood 26 perches. [*This is in the parish of Lytchett Matravers*]

[LM.18] John Henning, senior, holds by copy one tenement with garden, croft, meadow, pasture and wood lying together in diverse pieces between the common to the north, free land of John Shereman to the south, abutting to the east over the common river bank and to the west over a way leading towards the common, containing altogether 15 acres, 32 perches. [194, 198]

[LM.19] John Sherman holds freely of the manor of Newton Peverley an adjacent tenement with other [arable] land, pasture and meadow lying near the common river bank and a pightle lying parallel to the Queen's highway, containing altogether 11 acres, 3 roods. [199,200,201,202,208,209]

[LM.20] John Leake holds, by right of his wife, freely of the manor of Canward [Canford] and Newton Peverley nearby one tenement with adjacent croft, containing altogether 4 acres, 2 roods. [205, 206, 207]

[LM.21] Nicholas Medar holds freely of Canvar [Canford] and Newton Peverley nearby one tenement with adjacent croft abutting to the west over the way leading to the common, containing 2 acres, 1 rood. [203,204?]

[LM.22] John Henney holds by copy opposite the said way one pightle abutting to the south over Bakers Lane and to the north over the free land of Nicholas Medar, containing 3 roods, 30 perches. [168,184?]

[LM.23] Nicholas Medar holds freely nearby one cottage newly built, containing 2 roods, 24 perches. [169]

[LM.24] John Sherman holds freely in the same place three pightles of land of the manor of Newton Peverley lying together near to a way leading up to Mills Moore, containing altogether 3 acres, 3 roods, 24 perches. [171,172]

[LM.25] He also holds similarly off the same manor on another part of the said way one close opposite the tenement of John Sherman, containing 3 acres, 1 rood. [193?]

[LM.26] John Henning junior, holds by copy one pightle nearby between the said close on the south and Litchett Common on the north, containing 2 roods, 35 perches. [192]

[LM.27] He also holds similarly near there one pightle with a small meadow adjacent near to Mills Moore between the free land of John Leake and John Sherman on the south and Litchett Common on the north, containing 1 acre, 14 perches. [184]

[LM.28] John Leake holds freely, by right of his wife, near the above one coppice with a pightle adjacent, containing altogether 2 acres. [179]

[LM.29] Nicholas Medar holds similarly near to the same one cottage lying near to Litchett Common on the north part and the said pightle on the south, containing by estimation 1 rood. [182]

[LM.30] He also holds similarly one pightle lying between the tenement of George Cowrynge on the west, the land of John Leake on the east and abutting over Litchett Common to the northwest, containing by estimation 1½ roods. [181?]

[LM.31] George Cowring holds by copy near to the same one tenement with garden, croft, other [arable] land, meadows, pasture and wood altogether lying between Litchett Common on the west, the land of John Penneye and Nicholas Medar to the east, abutting to the south over Bakers Lane and to the north over the lands of diverse men, containing altogether 15 acres, 3 roods, 33 perches. [170?,173,174,175,176, 177,178,180]

[LM.32] John Hening junior holds by copy two pightles of land lying together near to the above between Bakers Lane on the north, the Queen's highway on the south and abutting to the west over the free land of Francis Williby, knight, called Gibbes, containing altogether 4 acres, 10 perches. [part of 162?]

[LM.33] He also holds similarly one tenement with garden and a pightle adjacent between land of Francis Willibye and Lady Horsey on the south, Litchett Common to the north and to the west over the Queen's highway leading from Littchett Church towards Blandford, containing altogether 1 acre, 1 rood, 26 perches. [part 164?]

[LM.34] Lady Horsey holds freely of Newton Peverley near to the same one pightle abutting towards the east over Bakers Lane, containing 3 roods, 34 perches. [part 164?]

[LM.35] Francis Wyllyby, knight, holds freely of Canvard [Canford] near to the same one tenement and all the lands adjacent called Gibbes lying between the land of John Heninge junior to the east and the way leading from Litchett Church to Blandford to the west, containing altogether 16 acres, 1 rood. [parts of 163, 164, 165,166]

[LM.36] John Henning junior holds by copy between the said land one piece of land containing by estimation three roods between land of Francis Wyllyby to the north and the Queen's highway on the south, at both ends abutting over land of the said Francis. [part 164?]

*

The third precinct contains all the lands and tenements lying between the Queen's highway leading from Littchett Church to Blandford on the east and Kings Lane to the west, going towards the west

[LM.37] Julian Golde holds by copy one tenement with garden, croft and [arable] land, pasture and wood lying together between the Queen's highway on the east, the way leading from Strowde Marshe through Littchett Common on the west abutting towards the north towards the Common of Littchett, containing altogether 22 acres, 27 perches. [150,152,153,154,156,157]

[LM.38] James Browning holds by copy one cottage lying between the cemetery of Littchett to the west and the Queen's highway to the east containing by estimation half a rood. [part of 157? or part of what is now the graveyard?].

[LM.39] He also holds by copy near to the same one tenement with garden and croft adjacent between the Queen's highway on the east and the land of Richard Sansome and Julian Gowld on the west abutting towards the north over the cemetery of Littchett and containing 2 acres, 2 roods. [144,147,148,149]

[LM.40] Richard Sansome holds by copy near to the same a tenement with garden and other lands and meadows adjacent lying altogether, between the Queen's highway on the south and the land of Julian Gowld and John Browninge on the north, containing altogether 8 acres, 1 rood, 38 perches. [137,140,141,142,143,151]

[LM.41] George Trencherd, gentleman, holds the site of the manor called Cockmoore lying near to the way leading from Strowde Marshe up to Littchet Common, containing by estimation 12 acres. [82, 104,105,106,107,109]

[LM.42] William Hillyard holds by copy, by right of his wife, one pightle called Okhayse between the coppice of Christopher Antill esquire on the north, the site of Cockamoore manor to the south and west and to the east over Littchet Common, containing 3 roods, 20 perches. [108]

[LM.43] Christopher Antill esquire holds freely of Littchett Matrevis one tenement newly built called Balland between the common of Littchet on all sides, containing with the land adjacent 5 acres, 1 rood. [130?]

[LM.44] He also holds similarly one tenement called Hell Fearme with diverse [arable] lands, pastures, meadows and wood lying together between the site of Cockamoore manor and the lane leading from Strowde Marshe to Littchet Common to the east and King Lane and the Common to the west, containing by estimation 168 acres. [This includes land in Lytchett Matravers and most of the remaining land in precinct 4 apart from the areas mentioned.]

[LM.45] Alice Sansome holds freely of Canvard one tenement with garden and croft adjacent between Strowde Marshe on the east, a little lane leading to Hell Farm to the west and abutting to the south over the Queen's highway, containing by estimation 5½ acres lying in the parish of Canvar. [83]

[LM.46] She also holds freely of Newton Peverley one tenement called Brookewoode with two closes lying adjacent called Millhay between the lane to Hell Farm to the east, the land of George Trenchet on the west and abutting towards the south over the Queen's highway, containing by estimation 8 acres. [85,86,87,92,93]

[LM.47] George Trencherd holds freely one meadow lying lengthways beside the Queen's highway to the south and land of Alice Sansome to the north, containing by estimation 5 acres. [83,75?,76?]

[LM.48] He also holds freely near the same one inclosure lying between Millhay to the south and land of Christopher Antill to the north, containing by estimation 6 acres. [82,84,85?]

[LM.49] Alice Sansome, widow, holds freely of Newton Peverley one coppice with a meadow adjacent between the above close to the east, the land of George Trencher to the west and abutting to the north over Caris Coppice, containing by estimation 5½ acres. [77,78?]

[LM.50] George Trenched, gentleman, holds freely near to the same one coppice lying between Caris Coppice to the south and land of Christopher Antill to the north, containing by estimation 3 acres. [79, 80]

[LM.51] Christopher Antill esquire holds freely near to the same one meadow lying between Litchett Common called West Marshe to the south, Caris Coppice and his own land to the north and abutting to the west over King Lane, containing by estimation 5 acres 3 roods. [?]

*

The fourth precinct containing all the lands and tenements lying between Kinge Lane on the east and the Queen's way leading from Warham to Littchet Matrevis [Matravers] on the west, going towards the west.

[LM.52] Richard Barnes son of John Barnes holds by copy one coppice lying between the coppice of Richard Russell to the north, West Marshe to the south, abutting to the east over King Lane and to the west over Meedhams, containing 2 acres, 2 roods. [71]

[LM.53] Richard Russell holds freely of this manor nearby one coppice abutting to the east over Kinge Lane, containing 10 acres, 1 rood. [70]

[LM.54] George Trencherd gentleman holds freely of this manor one coppice nearby called Calfswoode between the above coppice to the south, Litchett Common to the north and abutting to the west over King Lane, containing by estimation 4½ acres. [69?]

[LM.55] The lord of this manor holds in hand one coppice called Berewood lying between Bere Fearme to the south and Litchett Common to the north, containing 31 acres, 3 roods, 22 perches. [32,33,51,52,53,54,55,56,57]

[LM.56] The site of this manor with buildings, yards, gardens, orchards and other [arable] lands, pastures, meadows and woods adjacent lying together between the Queen's highway leading from Warham to Littchett Matrevis to the west, the coppices of Richard Barnes and Richard Russell to the east, abutting to the north over Berewood and to the south Litchett Common at Bere Lane and Litchett Common called Newtowne, containing altogether 103 acres. [34,35,36,37,38,39,40,41,43,44, 45,46,47,48,49,50,55,56,57]

*

The fifth precinct contains all the lands and tenements lying between the way leading from Warham to Littchet Matrevis to the east and Littchett Common on the west, going towards the west.

[LM.57] John Browning holds by copy one tenement with two adjacent closes lying altogether between the land of Nicholas Lucas to the west, Litchett Common to the east, abutting to the north over Nicholas Lucas's coppice and to the south over the Queen's highway, containing altogether 8 acres, 20 perches. [541,542,543?]

[LM.58] Nicholas Lucas holds similarly by copy one cottage with two closes adjacent between the above tenement to the east, the coppice of Eleanor Lucas and the little lane leading to the common to the west, abutting to the south over the Queen's highway and to the north over Nicholas Lucas's coppice, containing altogether 6 acres, 28 perches. [545]

[LM.59] He also holds similarly by copy near to the same one coppice, lying between Common of Littchett on the north and the lands of diverse tenements to the south and on each side abutting the Common, containing 4 acres, 2 roods, 11 perches. [544]

[LM.60] Eleanor Lucas holds by copy one coppice lying between the land of Nicholas Lucas to the east, Litchett Common to the west abutting to the north over the said coppice and to the south over the way leading to the Common, containing 2 acres, 1 rood, 20 perches. [546]

[LM.61] George Trencherd gentleman holds freely of Cockmore one tenement with close adjacent between the Queen's highway to the south, Litchett Common and the said way leading to the Common to the north, containing by estimation 4½ acres. [547,548]

[LM.62] John Browning holds near the same one coppice with close adjacent between the land of Michael Hamper and the coppice of Nicholas Lucas to the west, a certain lane leading as far as the common to the east, abutting the Queen's highway on the south and with Litchett Common to the north, containing altogether 12 acres, ~~13~~ 15 perches. [549,550,551,553]

[LM.63] Michael Hamper, widow, holds by copy near to the same three pightles between the coppice of John Browninge to the east, the land of George Trencher gentleman to the west and abutting towards the south over the Queen's highway, containing 7 acres, 3 roods, 32 perches. [554,555]

[LM.64] Nicholas Lucas holds near to the same one coppice lying between the land of Michael Hamper to the south, Litchett Common to the north and abutting to the east over the coppice and land of John Browninge, containing 5 acres, 6 perches. [552]

[LM.65] George Trencherd gentleman holds freely of Cockmoore near to the same one inclosure with coppice adjacent lying between the said land to the east and Litchett Common to the west, containing by estimation 5 acres. [558]

[LM.66] John Browning holds by copy near there one pightle between Litchett Common to the east, the land of George Trencher to the west, and abutting to the south over Bereway, containing by estimation 3 roods. [?]

[LM.67] George Trencherd, gentleman, holds freely near to the same two pightles lying together between the said pightle on the east, Litchett Common to the west and abutting to the south over Bereway, containing by estimation 3 acres. [556,557]

[LM.68] Augustine Lawrence, gentleman, holds more to the north by copy diverse closes lying together between Common of Littchett on each side, abutting towards the west over the lord's coppice called Burlebury Coppes, containing altogether 59 acres, 2 roods, 39 perches. [7-26,28]

[LM.69] The lord of this manor holds in hand one coppice near there between the said land on the east and Litchett Common on the west, on each side abutting over the said common, containing 63 acres, 3 roods. [1-6]

*

The sixth precinct containing all the the lands and tenements lying between Sherford Bridge on the west and way leading from Warham towards Littchett Matrevis to the east, going eastwards.

[LM.70] Augustine Lawrence, gentleman, holds by copy one tenement with barn built there, garden and yard adjacent in Morden parish between the land of Edward Lawrence esquire on the west, the land of Thomas Earle on the east, abutting to the north over the land of Edward Lawrence and to the south over Litchett Common, containing by estimation ½ acre. [*in Morden parish*]

[LM.71] He also holds similarly an inclosure called Skuttsherne lying in the parish of Littchett, lying between Litchett Common on the north, his own land to the south, abutting to the east over the lord's coppice called Geynes Wood and to the west over Litchett Common, containing 7 acres, 2 roods. [614]

[LM.72] He also holds by copy one coppice between his own land on three parts and abutting to the west over Litchett Common, containing 1 acre, 1 rood. [615]

[LM.73] He also holds similarly by copy an inclosure near to the same called Skutsherne between the said coppice to the north, the land of Benjamin Titchborne esquire to the south, abutting to the west over Litchett Common and to the east over the lord's coppice called Geynes Wood, containing 5 acres, 3 roods. [616]

[LM.74] Benjamin Titchborne esquire holds freely of this manor an inclosure between the land of Augustine Lawrence on every side, containing 8 acres, 3 roods, the yearly rent is 4s. [618]

[LM.75] Augustine Lawrence holds by copy nearby two inclosures lying together, containing 11 acres, 32 perches. [620, 621]

[LM.76] He also holds by copy one close of meadow and alders lying between the river bank on the south, the said two closes on the north, abutting to the west over the way leading to Sherford Bridge and to the east over the customary land of Augustine Lawrence, containing by estimation 9½ acres. [622-624?]

[LM.77] He also holds by copy an inclosure between the said land on the west, the land of Christopher Antill called Rodmore on the east, abutting to the south over the common river bank and to the north over Geynes Woode, containing 6 acres. [605,606]

[LM.78] The lord of this manor holds in hand near to the same one coppice called Geynes Wood between the land of Augustine Lawrence and Christopher Antill to the south, Michael Hamper's coppice and Lyttchett common to the north and abutting to the east over the common, containing 20 acres, 34 perches. [606?,607,608,609.610,611,613]

[LM.79] Michael Hamper, widow, holds one coppice between the said coppice to the south, Litchett Common to the north and abutting to the west over the said coppice, containing 1 acre, 1 rood. [612]

[LM.80] Chistopher Antill esquire holds freely of this manor an inclosure called Rodmore between the land of Augustine Lawrence on the west, Michael Hamper's coppice and the land of George Trencher to the east and abutting to the south over the common river bank, containing 10 acres, 2 roods, 24 perches, the annual rent is 8d. [603, 604]

[LM.81] Michael Hamper, widow, holds one coppice lying between the said land called Rodmoore to the west, the land of George Trencher gentleman to the east and abutting to the north over Litchett Common, containing 1 acre, 1 rood, 10 perches. [601?]

[LM.82] Augustine Lawrence, gentleman, holds by copy near to the same and near to Hitchens a meadow lying between the common river bank on every side, containing by estimation 2 acres. [630?, *Morden parish*].

[LM.83] Memorandum that George Trencher, gentleman, holds diverse tenements and his land lying altogether near to the common river bank of which we with so little information but we now wish to say that nothing of any of this belongs to this manor and we have omitted any attempt to provide estimates of the separate areas, except to say that the whole contains about 90 acres. [512,513,587,590, 595,597-600,602 + land in Morden parish]

[LM.84] George Trencherd, gentleman, holds freely to the north one inclosure lying between Litchett Common on every part, containing by estimation 6 acres. [587]

[LM.85] John Browninge holds by copy one pightle called Canvas Acre lying between Bere Way to the north, the land of George Trencher on the south, abutting to the east over the land of George Trencher and to the west over Litchett Common, containing 1 acre. [585]

[LM.86] George Trencher holds freely near the above two tenements lying together between the said pightle and the common ways on all parts, containing by estimation 13½ acres. [577,580,584]

[LM.87] He also holds freely similarly opposite a lane diverse tenements lying together with the said two tenements. [570,578]

[LM.88] John Warner holds freely of this manor one piece of land lying between the land of Richard Russell to the west, the land of Michael Hamper to the east, abutting to the south over the land of George Trencher and to the north over the Queen's highway, containing 1 acre. [567?]

[LM.89] Michael Hamper, widow, holds by copy one piece of land called Fursacre on each side abutting as above, containing 1 acre. [569]

[LM.90] She also holds by copy close to the same one tenement between the said piece of land on the west, Dunne Crofte to the east and abutting to the south over the land of George Trencher, containing 1 acre, 2 roods, 30 perches. [part 573 + 569]

[LM.91] She also holds by copy and John Warner holds freely one close near to the same called Duncrofte between the land of John Warner to the north, the land of George Trencher to the south and abutting to the west over the said tenement, containing 2 acres, 28 perches. [part 573 + 569-570?]

[LM.92] John Warner holds freely of this manor one pightle lying near the said close called Dunne Croft and abutting to the south over the land of George Trenchard, containing 1 rood, 14 perches. [566]

[LM.93] He also holds freely of this manor one tenement with garden and croft adjacent between the said close called Dunn Croft on the south and the land of Michael Hamper on the north and abutting to the west over Litchett Common, containing 1 acre, 1 rood, 34 perches. [567]

[LM.94] Michael Hamper holds by copy near to the same one pightle the western end abutting as above, containing 2 roods, 30 perches. [565]

[LM.95] John Warner holds freely of this manor next to the same one pightle the west end abutting as above, containing 2 roods, 30 perches. [564]

[LM.96] Michael Hamper holds by copy one close near to the same lying parallel close to the Queen's highway abutting to the west over the Common, containing 1 acre. [563]

[LM.97] John Warner holds freely of this manor towards the eastern head of the said close an inclosure, lying parallel, close to the Queen's highway, containing 3 acres, 2 roods. [518]

[LM.98] Michael Hamper, widow, holds by copy near to the same one close abutting to the east over the lands of George Trencher, gentleman, containing 3 acres, 1 rood. [519]

[LM.99] George Trencherd gentleman holds freely near there an inclosure containing by estimation 6½ acres. [520, 521]

[LM.100] He also holds freely near to the same one pightle lying between the said three closes to the west, the land of Michael Hamper on the east, abutting to the south over the land of Michael Hamper and to the north over the Queen's highway, containing by estimation 3 roods. [522]

[LM.101] Michael Hamper, widow, holds by copy an inclosure near here, the north end abutting over the said way, containing 2 acres, 34 perches. [523]

[LM.102] John Warner holds freely of this manor an inclosure near here, containing 1 acre, 2 roods. [527?]

[LM.103] John Geale holds freely an inclosure of the manor of Cockymore, now of George Trencherd, containing 2 acres, 3 roods, 8 perches. [524]

[LM.104] Richard Russell holds freely near there an inclosure of the manor of Cockymoore, containing 3 acres, 3 roods, 30 perches. [525]

[LM.105] Eleanor Lucas, widow, holds, near there, one tenement with garden, croft, other [arable] lands and pasture adjacent in diverse pieces between the said close on the west, Littchet Common called Newtonne and the land of Richard Russell and George Trenchard on the east and abutting to the north over the Queen's highway, containing altogether 20 acres, 1 rood. [526-532]

[LM.106] Richard Russell holds freely of this manor near there one cottage newly built with close adjacent, containing 2 acres, 36 perches. [533, 534 +537?]

[LM.107] George Trencharde, gentleman, holds freely of this manor two small pieces of land lying altogether near to the same place, containing 1 acre, 16 perches. [535, 536]

*

Stadium containing diverse closes abutting over the said *stadium* towards the north, going towards the west.

[LM.108] Nicholas Lucas holds by copy an inclosure lying between the Queen's highway on the east, the land of George Trencher on the west, abutting to the south over his own tenement and to the north over the said small pieces of land, containing 4 acres, 8 perches. [490, 491 + 489?]

[LM.109] George Trencherd, gentleman, holds freely of this manor an adjacent inclosure, containing 4 acres, 2 roods, 12 perches. [492, 493]

[LM.110] Richard Lucas holds by copy near there two inclosures lying together by the Stert descending to the common, containing altogether 6 acres. [495, 496]

[LM.111] Richard Russell holds freely of this manor certain land now lying in diverse pieces, containing altogether 20 acres, 1 rood, 10 perches. [497-501]

[LM.112] He also holds freely of the manor of Cockymoore an inclosure near adjacent abutting to the south over the common river bank, containing by estimation 9½ acres. [504, 505]

[LM.113] John Geale holds freely of the manor of Cockymore an inclosure near adjacent, containing by estimation 4½ acres. [506?]

[LM.114] John Warner holds freely of this manor an inclosure near Sleape abutting to the south over the common river bank and to the north over his own land and land of Michael Hamper, containing 4 acres, 18 perches. [507 + 508?]

[LM.115] Michael Hamper, widow, holds by copy an inclosure nearby, near Sleape, between the said close to the east, the land of George Trenchard to the west and abutting to the south over the common river bank, containing 5 acres, 1 rood, 6 perches. [509]

[LM.116] George Trencherd gentleman holds freely the remaining lands and tenements lying near to the common river bank as far as Rodmoore and Michael Hamper's coppice, containing altogether by estimation [blank]. [*This repeats most of the land mentioned in LM.83*]

*

Stadium lying near to the common river bank abutting towards the north over the above closes, going towards the east.

[LM.117] Nicholas Lucas holds one meadow lying between the common river bank to the south and the land of Richard Russell to the north, containing 2 acres, 2 roods, 30 perches. [502]

[LM.118] Memorandum that there is one common called Common Moore which is common to five houses only, viz: to the tenements of Nicholas Lucas, Richard Lucas, George Trenchard, Richard Russell and Agnes Russell, containing by estimation 3 acres. [503?]

[LM.119] Richard Russell holds freely of this manor, near to the above, one inclosure, containing 1 acre, 3 roods, 24 perches. [495?]

[LM.120] He also holds similarly at the eastern head of the said close one pightle, containing 1 rood. [part 494 ?]

[LM.121] Richard Lucas holds by copy, at the northern head of the said pightle, one pightle between the land of Richard Russell on each side, containing 1 rood, 4 perches. [483]

[LM.122] Richard Russell holds freely of this manor one pightle with the north end abutting as above, containing 1 rood, 2 perches. [part 494?]

[LM.123] Richard Lucas holds by copy one pightle lying at the southerly head of the said pightle abutting to the south over the said common, containing by estimation 1 rood. [483?]

[LM.124] George Trencherd, gentleman, holds freely one pightle lying lengthways near to the lane leading to the common, containing 3 roods. [484?]

[LM.125] Richard Lucas holds by copy one tenement with garden and croft adjacent, containing 3 roods, 30 perches. [485,486]

[LM.126] Richard Russell holds freely of this manor one tenement with garden and croft adjacent abutting to the east over the tenement of George Trenchard, containing 2 roods, 24 perches. [486]

[LM.127] George Trencherde, gentleman, holds freely of this manor, near to here, one tenement formerly Waddhams with garden adjacent abutting to the east over Litchett Common, containing by estimation 1 rood. [part 485]

[LM.128] Nicholas Lucas holds by copy near to the same one tenement with garden and croft adjacent between the said two tenements to the south, his own land and that of George Trenchard to the north and abutting towards the east over Litchett Common, containing 1 acre, 1 rood, 24 perches. [487,488, 488a?485]

[LM.129] Agnes Russell, widow, holds freely of this manor, near to the mill, one tenement with garden and croft adjacent between the way leading to the common to the north, the common river bank on the south and abutting over the way leading to the mill, containing 1 acre, 1 rood, 34 perches. [480]

[LM.130] Nicholas Lucas holds near there by copy of the lord of this manor one water mill situated and lying near to the land of Agnes Russell. [644,645]

[LM.131] Agnes Russell, widow, holds freely of this manor near there one inclosure between the said Millway on the west and Orgin Grene to the east containing 2 acres, 2 roods, 8 perches. [475,476, 477?]

*

The Seventh precinct containing all the lands lying on the south of the common riverbank in the parish of Morden

[LM.132] Richard Lucas holds by copy an inclosure called Snales Brech lying between Gooreheth Field to the south, Roughmore to the north and abutting towards the west over Hittchams, containing 7 acres, 3 roods, 10 perches.

[LM.133] There is there a marsh called Roughmore lying between the said close and Hittchens to the south and the common river bank on the north, containing by estimation 8 acres.

[LM.134] There is near there one cottage with diverse lands of pasture and marsh adjacent parallel to the common river bank lying between Goorhethe Field to the south and the said river bank and Roughmore to the north, containing altogether by estimation 30 acres. It belongs to the site of this manor called Beare Fearme.[637-640+?]

[LM.135] There is near there another cottage belonging to the same site lying near Sherford Bridge between the river bank to the north and Goreheth Feild to the south, containing 4 acres. [627-629?]

[LM.136] Memorandum that the lord of this manor holds near there one separate common called Goore Hethe belonging to the tenement called Bere Fearme whose bounds are as follows: from Sherford Bridge towards a certain place called Great Ovens and it is in length to that said place 480 perches [*the remainder is in English*] from thence to the uttermost corners is the Meting of the Ways leading to Warham near unto Sanford bridge 240 perches. From thence in the Way to Little Ovens 408 perches, from thence to Orgyn Ford 220 perches, containing 827 acres.

*

The eighth precinct containing all the lands and tenements lying between Broad Lane and the north, beginning at Orginford going east.

[LM.137] William Barnes holds by copy near Orgin Grene one cottage with garden adjacent lying between the common on every part, containing 1 rood, 16 perches. [464,467]

[LM.138] George James holds similarly by copy one cottage near there between Orgin Grene to the south, the land of Alice Sansome to the north and abutting towards the west over the Queen's highway, containing 2 acres, 4 perches. [465]

[LM.139] Alice Sansome holds freely of this manor one coppice with two small areas of land together lying abutting towards the west over the said common, containing altogether 5½ acres. [455]

[LM.140] Eleanor Lucas, widow, holds by copy near there, two inclosures lying together called Whiteherne between the land of John Sherman on the east, Litchett Common called Newtonne on the west and abutting towards the south over the Queen's highway, containing altogether 12 acres, 1 rood, 10 perches. [459,460,461]

[LM.141] George James holds by copy near there one pightle lying lengthways beside Bere Lane, containing 1½ acres. [458]

[LM.142] Thomas Sansome holds by copy near there one coppice abutting to the south over Whiteherne and to the north over Bere Lane, containing 7½ acres. [457]

[LM.143] Richard Barnes holds by indenture one coppice lying between the aforesaid coppice to the west, the freehold land of John Sherman to the east and on each side abutting as above, containing 3 acres, 3 roods, 12 perches. [456]

[LM.144] John Sherman holds freely of this manor one tenement with diverse lands and woods adjacent between the aforesaid coppice and Whiteherne to the west, the land of George Trenchard and Thomas Sansome to the east, abutting to the south over Broad Lane and to the north over Bere Lane, containing altogether by estimation 40 acres. [439-446,452 454,462,466,468-474]

[LM.145] George Trenchede, gentleman, holds freely, between John Sherman's land one coppice abutting to the north over Bere Lane, containing by estimation 1 acre, 1 rood. [part 451]

[LM.146] He also holds similarly one inclosure near there abutting to the north over West Marshe, containing 4½ acres. [part 451?]

[LM.147] Thomas Sansome holds, near there, by copy one tenement with adjacent garden and an inclosure to the north end called Long Croft lying between the land of George Trenchard and John Sherman to the west, the land of George Trenchard to the east, abutting to the north over West Mershe and to the south over the Queen's highway, containing altogether 6 acres, 3 roods, 36 perches. [447, 450]

[LM.148] George Trencherd holds freely near to the same an inclosure lying parallel to the Queen's highway to the east and Long Croft to the west, abutting to the north over West Marshe, containing 2 acres. [448,449]

*

The Ninth Precinct contains all lands and tenements between the common river bank towards the south and the Queen's highway towards the north, beginning near Orgin Ford and going eastwards as far as King Bridge alias Clay Bridge.

[LM.149] First of all there is in the same place one meadow called Bere Meade belonging to the said site lying along, by and near to the common river bank, abutting to the west over Orgin Ford and to the east over the land of Thomas Sansome, containing 8 acres, 32 perches. [433]

[LM.150] William Barnes holds by copy near there an inclosure lying between Orgin Grene on the west, the coppice of George James on the east, abutting to the south over Beare mead and to the north over Orgin Grene, containing 4 acres, 1 rood. [434]

[LM.151] George James holds one coppice near to the same lying between the said close on the west, the land of Thomas Sansome on the east, abutting to the north over Broad Lane and to the south over Beare mead, containing 3 acres. [435]

[LM.152] Thomas Sansome holds by copy near there certain arable land, pasture, meadow and marsh lying together in two inclosures called Hasell Goore adjacent lying together between the common river bank to the south, the Queen's highway to the north, abutting to the west over the said coppice and Bere mead and to the east over the land of George Trenchard, containing altogether 33 acres, 1 rood, 34 perches. [426-432,436 437]

[LM.153] George Trencherd holds freely near there one tenement called Birde Ocke with diverse lands and marsh adjacent between the common river bank to the south, the Queen's highway to the north and abutting towards the east over Kinge Bridge, containing by estimation 40 acres. [421-425]

*

The tenth precinct contains all the tenements and lands lying between the Queen's highway and a certain lane called Wullverston on the north and the common river bank and le Rushe Grounde on the south beginning near Kinge Bridge going eastwards to Ballso Lane.

[LM.154] Alice Sansome, widow, holds freely of Newton Peverley near Kinge Bridge one meadow lying lengthways along the Queen's highway, containing 2 acres, 30 perches. [418,419]

[LM.155] Julian Golde holds by copy near there one meadow lying between the said meadow on the west and the meadow of George Trenchard on the east, abutting to the north over the land of George Trenchard and to the south over the common river bank, containing 4 acres, 5 perches. [417]

[LM.156] George Trencherd, gentleman, holds freely near there one meadow, containing 3 acres, 3 roods. [408]

[LM.157] William Hyllyarde holds by copy near there one meadow abutting on the north over his own land and Richard Geale's land and to the south over the common river bank, containing 1 acre, 3 roods, 30 perches. [407]

[LM.158] Richard Geale holds by copy nearby one meadow, containing 2 acres. [406]

[LM.159] George Trencherd, gentleman, holds freely two cottages lying together abutting to the north over the Queen's highway and to the south over the land of Julian Goulde, containing 1 acre, 3 roods, 28 perches. [415,416]

[LM.160] Richard Barnes son of John Barnes holds by copy near there one garden lying near to the Common on three sides, containing by estimation ½ rood. [414]

[LM.161] Julyan Golde holds by copy near there one tenement with croft and an adjacent pightle between a small lane leading to Julyan Golde's meadow on the west, the land of William Hillyarde on the east, abutting to the south over the land of George Trenchard and to the north over the Queen's highway, containing altogether 1 acre, 3 roods, 24 perches. [411-412]

[LM.162] William Hillyard holds similarly by copy an inclosure abutting with its head to the north as above, containing 1 acre, 1 rood. [409]

[LM.163] Richard Geale holds similarly by copy near there an inclosure, containing 1 acre, 1 rood, 28 perches. [405]

[LM.164] Christopher Antill, esquire, holds freely one tenement near there with garden and croft abutting to the south over the land of Richard Sansome and to the north over the Queen's highway, containing 1 acre, 1 rood. [404]

[LM.165] Richard Sansome junior holds freely of Sturminster Marshall one tenement with diverse lands lying together between the aforesaid tenement and the land of

Richard Geale on the west, Hatbye Lane on the east, abutting to the south over the common river bank and to the north over the Queen's highway, containing altogether by estimation 10½ acres. [390?,391,395?,396-398,401,403]

[LM.166] Richard Geale holds by copy near there one inclosure lying between Hatbye Lane on the west, the land of William Hillyard on the east, abutting to the north over the Queen's highway and to the south over Rushe Grounde, containing 1 acre, 3 roods, 26 perches. [part 368?]

[LM.167] William Hillyard holds by copy an inclosure near there at the northern end of the above inclosure abutting as above, containing 2 acres, 1 rood. [part 368?]

[LM.168] Richard Geale holds by copy near there an inclosure called Brome Close between the aforesaid close and Rushmore on the west, Woodmead on the east, abutting to the north over the aforesaid land of William Hyllyard and to the south over Rushgrounde, containing 4 acres, 1 rood, 24 perches. [part 366?]

[LM.169] William Hilyarde holds by copy near there one tenement with adjacent garden and close, containing 3 acres, 1 rood, 20 perches. [parts 366/367?]

[LM.170] Richard Geale holds by copy one inclosure near there called Ockfeild between the aforesaid close on the south, the Queen's way on the north and abutting to the east over Wood mead, containing 2 acres, 20 perches. [part 367?]

[LM.171] Julian Gould holds similarly by copy one inclosure near there called Wood mead between the aforesaid inclosure on the west, the lands of diverse tenements on the east, abutting to the south over Rushground and to the north over the Queen's highway, containing 5 acres, 3 roods, 10 perches. [369,370]

[LM.172] William Hillyard holds by copy one pightle near Wullverston between the Queen's highway to the north, the land of John Leake to the south, abutting to the east over the land of Christopher Antill, esquire, containing 2 roods, 28 perches. [371]

[LM.173] John Leake holds freely of Sturmester Marshall an inclosure near there, containing 3 acres. [372]

[LM.174] Richard Sansome holds freely of Sturmester Marshall an inclosure lying near to Woodmead, containing by estimation 1½ acres. [373]

[LM.175] Simone Henninge, widow, holds by copy one meadow near there called Grene Meade between le Rushgrounde to the south, the land of Richard Sansome and John Leake to the north and abutting to the east over Anvyles Grove, containing 2 acres, 30 perches. [374]

[LM.176] John Leake holds freely near to the same two pightles with adjacent coppice, containing 2 acres, 1 rood. [375?]

[LM.177] Nicholas Medar holds freely of Sturmester Marshall near the above two pightles lying together containing by estimation 2 acres, 1 rood, 30 perches. [376?]

[LM.178] Christopher Antill, esquire, holds freely an inclosure lying parallel to and near to the way called Wullverston, containing 1 acre, 1 rood. [377]

[LM.179] George Trenchard, gentleman, holds freely one cottage with garden adjacent lying near to Wullveston way, containing by estimation 1 rood. [378]

[LM.180] Nicholas Medar holds freely near there one tenement with certain land adjacent abutting over the Wullverston way, containing by estimation 3 acres, 3 roods. [379?]

[LM.181] George Trenchard, gentleman, holds freely an inclosure near there called Anviles Grove, containing by estimation 2 acres. [380]

[LM.182] Simone Henninge, widow, holds by copy one meadow near to the same lying between the land called Anvells Grove as above and the land of Nicholas Meder to the west, a certain lane called Balse Lane on the east and abutting to the south over Rushgrounde, containing 3 acres, 3 roods. [381]

*

The eleventh precinct contains all the lands and tenements lying between the Queen's highway leading from Littchett Church to the Becon on the west and East Marshe on the east, going towards the northeast.

[LM.183] George Trenchard, gentleman, holds freely one tenement called Newhowse with all the lands and meadow adjacent lying between the common river bank on the west, East Marshe to the east, abutting to the south over Wullverston lane and to the north over the Queen's highway near George Crosse, containing by estimation 62½ acres. [314-325, 328, 330-333]

[LM.184] Richard Geale holds by copy one tenement with garden and close adjacent between the river bank on the east, William Hillyard's land on the west, abutting to the south over Wullverston lane, containing altogether 3 acres, 2 roods, 38 perches. [357, 358]

[LM.185] William Hillyarde holds similarly by copy one tenement with adjacent garden, close and meadow between the aforesaid tenement on the east, the lands of diverse men on the west and abutting to the south over the Queen's highway, containing altogether 6 acres, 1 rood. [355, 356]

[LM.186] Richard Wolfrey holds freely near there of Sturmester Marshall one cottage with adjacent garden between his own tenement to the north, the Queen's highway to the south, abutting to the west over the way and to the north over William Hillyarde's meadow, containing 1 rood. [353]

[LM.187] He also holds freely of Newton Peverley one tenement near there, containing by estimation 1½ roods. [354]

[LM.188] He also holds similarly another tenement near there, containing by estimation 1½ roods. [352]

[LM.189] Item near there is the Rectory of Litchett which contains by estimation ½ acre. [351]

[LM.190] Richard Barnes son of John Barnes senior holds by copy one tenement with garden and croft adjacent between the Queen's highway on the west, William Hillyard's meadow to the east and abutting to the south over the Rectory, containing 1 acre, 2 roods, 22 perches. [349, 350]

[LM.191] He also holds by copy one pightle with adjacent meadow between the said way on the west, William Hillyard's land to the east and abutting to the north over the coppice and land of John Pennye, containing 2 acres. [343]

[LM.192] Richard Geale holds by copy near there one inclosure lying between his own land to the south, William Hyllyard's land on the south and north and abutting to the east over the common river bank, containing 4 acres, 2 roods. [342]

[LM.193] William Hillyard holds similarly by copy one inclosure near there between the said close on the south, John Pennye's land to the north and abutting to the east over the common river bank, containing 4 acres, 1 rood, 24 perches. [341]

[LM.194] John Pennye holds similarly by copy one tenement with garden and [arable] land, pasture, meadow and woodland lying together between the land of William Hyllyard and Richard Barnes on the south, the Queen's highway on the north, abutting to the west over the said way and to the east over the common river bank, containing by estimation 15 acres, 1 rood, 14 perches. [334-340]

*

The twelfth precinct containing all the lands and tenements lying between East Marshe on the west and Litchett Common on the east, going southwards.

[LM.195] George Trenchard holds certain lands freely called Eston Brookes on which the lord is building six cottages with diverse lands and woods adjacent between the Est Marshe on the west, Litchet Common on the east and abutting towards the south over Lilley Lane, containing 27 acres. [271-293]

[LM.196] Simon Chesmond holds by copy near there three inclosures with an adjacent pightle between Lilley Lane on the north, the land of John Mudge on the south, abutting to the west over Est Marshe and to the east over Litchett Common, containing 12 acres, 2 roods, 10 perches. [300,301,302]

[LM.197] John Mudge holds similarly by copy one tenement with diverse lands and parts lying together in diverse pieces between the land of Simon Chesmond on the north, a certain lane leading up to the Common on the south and abutting to the east over the Common, containing altogether 21 acres, 3 roods, 34 perches. [305, 306, 308, 309, 310, 311 + 295?]

[LM.198] Simone Henninge, widow, holds similarly by copy one cottage near there between the land of John Mudge on every part and abutting towards the south over the Queen's highway, containing 1 rood, 32 perches. [295?]

[LM.199] She also holds similarly by copy near there one pightle lying between the John Mudge's meadow on the east, the Queen's highway on the west and abutting to the south over the land of Christopher Antill, containing 2 roods. [part 311?]

[LM.200] Christopher Antill, esquire, holds freely one pightle lying near there, containing 1 acre, 11 perches. [312?]

[LM.201] Simone Henninge holds by copy one small area of ground lying opposite John Mudge's tenement between the Queen's highway on the north, John Barnes's land on the south and abutting to the west over Balsey Lane, containing 2 roods, 11 perches. [part 382?]

[LM.202] John Barnes holds by right of his wife one copyhold tenement with diverse lands adjacent lying between the said pightle and the Queen's highway on the north, the tenement and land of Simon Chesmond on the south, abutting to the west over Balsey Lane and to the east over Litchett Common, containing 11 acres, 3 roods, 2 perches.[384-5]

[LM.203] Simon Chesmond holds similarly by copy one tenement with certain land adjacent between the tenement and land of John Barnes on the north, Littchet Common to the south, abutting to the west over the Common and to the east over John Barnes's land, containing altogether 3 acres, 10 perches. [part 381, 382?]

[LM.204] John Barnes holds similarly by copy one pightle lying between Simon Chesmond's land on the north, Litchett Common on the south, abutting to the west over Simon Chesmond's land and to the east over the Common, containing 3 roods, 10 perches. [part 381-383?]

[LM.205] Simon Chesmonde holds similarly by copy one pightle near there lying between John Barnes's land on three sides and abutting to the east over Litchett Common, containing 3 roods, 24 perches. [part 381-383?]

[LM.206] Simone Henninge, widow, holds similarly by copy near the same two inclosures with one pightle adiacent called Salturne lying between the Common of Littchet on all parts and containing 6 acres, 1 rood, 27 perches. [part 384-386]

[LM.207] Memorandum: that there are certain lands called Rushe Grounde which belong to diverse tenements of this manor viz: to the tenements of Simon Chismond, John Barnes, John Mudge, Symay Henninge, Richard Geale, William Hillyard and Richard Sansome, containing by estimation 64 acres.

[LM.208] There is near there an island called Furgoore which belongs to diverse tenements of this manor viz: to the tenements of Simon Chismond, John Barnes, John Mudge and Simone Henning, containing by estimation 7 acres. [388?]

[LM.209] There is near there another island called Utter Hethe which belongs to diverse tenements of this manor viz: to the aforementioned tenants, containing 5 acres. [387].

[LM.210] There is another small island more to the east which is called Brakney Island containing by estimation ½ acre which belongs to the said tenements.

[LM.211] Memorandum: there are some cottages that have some Rushes belonging to them viz: two little pieces containing by estimation ½ acre.

*

Lands lying in Crayford [Crawford] within the parish of Spisberge [Spetisbury] parcel of the demeanes of the manor of Bere in Littchett.

The lord holds one meadow called Aldermedow now in the tenure of William Lockett lying next to Crayford Bridge on the north between the meadow of Boyar on the east, the river called the Stower on the west, abutting to the north over the meadow of Nicholas Wadham, gentleman, and over the bridge called Crayford Bridge to the south, containing 2 acres, 1 rood.

He also holds a piece of pasture in a croft called Parting Close between the land of [blank] Wells to the north, the land of Nicholas Wadham, gentleman, on the south, abutting to the east over Nicholas Wadham's land and to the west over the common way leading from Blandford to Poole, containing 1½ roods.

The meadow within the parish of Sturmester Marshall being divided amongst my master's copy holders of Lichett.

First of all Thomas Barnes holds	1 acre
Emma Hemming widow holds	2 acres
John Hemminge senior holds	½ acre
John Pennye holds	½ acre
Simon Chismond holds	½ acre
John Barne by right of his wife holds	½ acre
Simone Hemminge widow holds	½ acre
John Mudge holds	½ acre
Richard Geale holds	½ acre
William Hillyarde holds	½ acre
Julian Gould holds	½ acre
Nicholas Lucas holds	1 rood
Richard Lucas holds	1 rood
Eleanor Lucas widow holds	2 acres
Michael Hamper widow holds	½ acre
The ferme [farm] hathe there	½ acre
Total	1 1 acres

The freeholders of this manor havinge meadow in Sturmester aforesaid

Johes Sherman	1 acre
Richard Russell holds	½ acre

Days work belonging to Lichett farm also called Beare farm

Augustine Lawrence gentleman	4 days
Eleanor Lucas	3 days
Nicholas Lucas	2 days
Richard Lucas	2 days
Michael Hamper	3 days

A note to whom every freeholder in Lichett aforesaid pays rent and owes suit of court
Alice Sannson, widow, for a freehold court lying at Orgame owes suit and service to this manor.
John Warner holds a tenement and certain lands freely of this manor.
John Sherman holds a tenement and certain lands of this manor.
Agnes Russell, widow, holds likewise of this manor.
George Trenchard, gentleman, holds likewise of this manor.

The freesuitors to Newton Peverley in Litchett aforesaid:
Alice Sannson, widow, for one piece of land.
John Leake holds certain lands for 17d rent.
He also holds by the right of his wife certain lands of the manor of Camford [Canford] which is the Earl of Huntingtonn's and pays 6d a year.
He also holds certain land of the manor of Sturmester Marshall which is [occupied by] one Mr Gorgese and pays 18d a year.
Nicholas Medar hold likewise certain lands of the manor of Canndforde and pays 6d a year.
He also holds certain lands of the manor of Newton Peverley and pays 17d a year.
He also holds certain lands of the manor of Sturminster Marshall and pays 14d a year.
Alice Sannson holds certain lands of the manor of Camdford.
She also holds also certain lands of the manor of Sturmester Marshall.

SURVEY OF DURWESTON WITH KNIGHTON

Survey of the manor taken, made and examined by diligence, exact vision, perambulation, evidence and measuring by Thomas Wright surveyor of the lands of Sir Thomas Kitson, the lord of the manor by the oath of all the homage of the manor and of many of the tenants, that is to say: John Vallevine, John Stevens, Hugh Dashwood, Roger Reynolde, Thomas Lynsey, Richard Collins, John Rogers, John Standly, Richard Prower, John Howe, Edward Bennett, John Iles, John Shepherde, Robert Oliver, Nicholas Evered, Robert Hayter, John Fry, James Privet, Thomas Phelpes, Robert Segar, Robert Frampton, William Stone, Morgan Curlan, William Franklyn, John Pelly, Robert Skott, William Domine and of others. Begun in May 1583 and finished and confirmed at the court held 19 March 1585.

Knighton

[K1] The first precinct containing all the lands and tenements lying to the east of the common way leading from Shillingstone to Brenson [Bryanston] between the Stower to the east and the aforesaid way to the west beginning near the site of the manor of Durweston.

[K1.1] John Powlden holds by indenture in the manor of Knighton a building with garden and yard with appurtenances lying between the cemetery and Knighton Close on the south and the Queen's highway and the tenements of diverse tenants to the north abutting to the west over the Queen's highway leading from Shillingston to Brenson and to the east over the land of Emma Pelle, and containing 2 acres.

[K1.2] William Stone holds by copy one tenement with garden adjacent between the aforesaid site to the west and the pightle of John Howe to the east abutting to the south over the yard of the aforesaid site and to the north over the common way leading from the Stower to Ockford, and containing 1 rood, 32 perches.

[K1.3] John Howe holds one pightle between the aforesaid tenement to the west and the tenement held by Morgan Snell to the east, the ends abutting on all sides as above, and containing 1 rood.

[K1.4] Morgan Snell holds one tenement with garden adjacent between the tenement of William Franklyn abutting to the south over the aforesaid site and the land of

Emma Pelle, and to the north over the aforesaid Queen's highway leading from the Stower to Ockford containing 1 rood.

[K1.5] William Franklyn holds one tenement with garden adjacent between the aforesaid tenement to the west and the tenement of Christiana Loder to the east, abutting to the south over the lands of Emma Pelle and to the north over the aforesaid Queen's highway containing 1 rood.

[K1.6] Christiana Loder holds one tenement with garden adjacent between the aforesaid tenement to the west and the tenement of John Pelle to the east. abutting as above containing 1 rood.

[K1.7] John Pelley holds one tenement with garden adjacent between the aforesaid tenement to the west and the tenement of Emma Pelle to the east containing 1 rood, 32 perches.

[K1.8] Emma Pelley, widow, holds one tenement with garden and yard between the tenement of William Domine to the east and the tenement of John Pelley and her own lands to the west abutting to the south over the tenement of Christiana Loder and towards the north over the Queen's highway leading from the Stower to Ockford containing 2 roods, 30 perches.

[K1.9] William Domine holds one tenement with garden and croft adjacent between the aforesaid tenement to the west and the tenement of Robert Skotte to the east, with all sides abutting as above and containing 2 roods, 25 perches.

[K1.10] Robert Scott holds one tenement with garden and croft adjacent between the aforesaid tenement to the west and the land of Morgan Snell to the east with all sides abutting as above containing 2 roods, 25 perches.

[K1.11] Morgan Snell holds by copy one pightle between the aforesaid tenement to the west and the land of Thomas Lynsey to the east with all sides abutting as above containing 1 rood, 20 perches.

[K1.12] Thomas Lynsey holds near there one pightle between the aforesaid pightle to the west and the meadow of William Domine and the waste of the lord to the east abutting to the north over the common way leading from the Stower to Ockford containing 3 roods.

[K1.13] Emma Pellye, widow, holds one pightle between the lands of Christiana Loder to the south and the tenements of Diverford [sic should be 'diverse'] tenants to the north abutting her own yard to the east and to the west over the aforesaid site containing 1 acre, 3 roods.

[K1.14] Emma Pellye holds one inclosure called Knighton Close which contains 1 acre lying between the land of the Rector to the south and the aforesaid site to the north abutting towards the west over the tenement of Robert Frampton and the cemetery containing 4 acres, 38 perches.

*

[K2] *Stadium* to the west [this is clearly an error for 'east'] of the common way leading south from Shillingstone.

[K 2.1] Robert Frampton holds one tenement with garden and yard between the cemetery to the north, the lands of the Rector to the south, Knighton Close to the east and the common way to the west containing 2 roods, 10 perches.

[K2.2] The Rector of Durweston holds one inclosure called Ilandes between Knighton Close and Robert Frampton's tenement to the north, a drove leading to the land of John Powlden to the south, and Brenson Way to the west containing 4 acres, 3 roods, 32 perches.

[K2.3] John Powlden holds one separate drove leading to the tenement called Ilandes.

[K2.4] Robert Segar holds nearby one tenement with adjacent garden and croft between the aforesaid drove to the north, the land of Thomas Phillips to the south and Brenson Way to the west containing 1 acre.

[K2.5] William Stone holds nearby one pightle between the tenement of Thomas Phillips to the south and east and Brenson Way to the west containing 3 roods, 30 perches.

[K2.6] Thomas Phillips holds one tenement with adjacent garden and croft between the pightle and croft of Robert Segar to the north, the tenement of John Frye to the south and abutting Brenson Way to the west containing 1 acre, 2 roods, 20 perches.

*

[K3] *Stadium* abutting over Brenson Way to the west.

[K3.1] John Frye holds one tenement between the tenement of Thomas Phillips to the north, the tenement of Robert Hector to the south and abutting Brenson Way to the west containing 3 roods.

[K3.2] Robert Hector holds one tenement abutting to the east over the meadow of Nicholas Evered and to the west over the Brenson Way containing 1 acre, 1 rood.

[K3.3] John Frye holds one pightle nearby abutting as above containing 2 roods.

[K3.4] Nicholas Evered holds one tenement with garden and croft adjacent between the aforesaid pightle to the north and Watts Close to the south, abutting Brenson Way to the west containing 1 acre, 2 roods.

[K3.5] John Powlden holds by indenture one inclosure called Watts Close abutting to the east over Nicholas Evered's croft and Southmead and to the west over Brenson Way containing 1 acre, 1 rood.

[K3.6] The Rector of Durweston holds one inclosure nearby called Wythbeer abutting to the east over Southmead and to the west over Brenson Way containing 1 acre, 2 roods, 17 perches.

[K3.7] James Privett holds one garden nearby abutting on all sides as above containing 1 rood.

[K3.8] John Powlden holds one meadow adjacent lying in two pieces between the lands of Richard Rogers, knight, to the south and the Rector's garden and meadow, John Standley to the north, the meadow of John Frye, James Privet and the Stower to the east and to the west Brenson Way containing 10 acres, 26 perches.

[K3.9] John Frye holds one meadow between the aforesaid meadow on the west, the Stower to the east and the meadow of James Privet to the north containing 1 acre, 2 roods, 3 perches.

[K3.10] James Privet holds one meadow between the meadow of John Powlden to the west, the Stower towards the east and towards the south over the John Fry's meadow containing 1 acre, 8 perches.

*

[K4] *Stadium* called Southmeade abutting towards the west over the aforesaid tenement and towards the east over Brasmead going towards the north.

[K4.1] The Rector holds a piece of meadow containing 1 acre, 30 perches.

[K4.2] John Powlden holds another piece of meadow containing 2 acres, 1 rood.

[K4.3] Nicholas Evered holds another piece of meadow containing 2 acres. Northmeade.

[K4.4] Thomas Phelps holds one piece nearby containing 2 acres.

[K4.5] John Powlden holds one inclosure called Ilandes with a separate way leading to Brenson Way containing 9 acres, 1 rood, 28 perches.

[K4.6] Christiana Loder, widow, holds one inclosure between John Powlden's close to the south, the tenements and lands of diverse tenants to the north and abutting over Knighton Close towards the west containing 1 acre, 2 roods, 12 perches.

*

[K5] *Stadium* abutting over The Stower towards the east and over the aforesaid *Stadium* to the west going towards the south.

[K5.1] William Domine holds one piece of meadow called Gorehay abutting to the west over the land of Thomas Lynsey and to the east over the Stower containing ½ acre.

[K5.2] Edward Bennet holds ½ acre.

[K5.3] John Howe holds 2 acres.

[K5.4] Roger Ranew holds 1 acre, 1 rood.

[K5.5] John Henning holds 1 acre, 1 rood.

[K5.6] John Powlden holds by indenture one piece of meadow containing 3 acres, 2 roods, 20 perches.

[K5.7] William Domine holds to the western end of the aforesaid piece one piece of meadow containing 2 roods, 20 perches.

[K5.8] Thomas Lynsey holds to the northern end of the aforesaid meadow one piece of meadow containing 3 roods, 7 perches.

*

[K6] *Stadium* called Brasmeade abutting to the west over Southmead and Ilandes and over the Stower to the east going towards the south.

[K6.1] The Rector holds one piece of meadow abutting to the west over Ilandes and to the east over the Stower containing ½ acre.

[K6.2] Richard Collins holds one piece containing 1 acre.

[K6.3] Robert Hector holds 1 acre.

[K6.4] Richard Prower holds 1 acre.

[K6.5] John Stevens holds 1 acre.

[K6.6] John Rogers holds 1 acre.

[K6.7] Hugh Dashwood holds 1 acre.

[K6.8] John Howe holds 1 acre.

[K6.9] Robert Frampton holds one acre.

[K6.10] John Standley holds ½ acre.

*

[K7] *Stadium* abutting over Brenson Way to the east containing all those lands lying in Knighton beginning at the Rectory and going south.

[K7.1] William Domine holds one pightle between the Rectory of Durweston to the north, the tenement of Robert Skotte to the south and Brenson Way to the east containing 1½ acres.

[K7.2] Robert Skotte hold one pightle with Brenson Way towards the east containing 1 rood, 20 perches.

[K7.3] Robert Frampton holds one small piece of the meadow lying at the western end of the same with Brenson Way to the east containing ½ acre.

[K7.4] The Rector holds one inclosure beside North Haycome containing 3 acres.

[K7.5] Robert Skotte holds another inclosure called Haycombe between the aforesaid close to the east, the lands of William Franklyn to the west and abutting on all sides on the land of Robert Frampton containing 2½ acres.

[K7.6] Robert Hector holds one inclosure between the land of the Rector to the north, the lands of Robert Frampton to the south and Brenson Way to the east containing 2 acres, 2 roods.

[K7.7] Robert Frampton holds one inclosure abutting similarly over the aforesaid way to the east containing 1 acre.

[K7.8] Robert Frampton holds one inclosure lying at the western side of the aforesaid close between the land of Morgan Snell to the west, the aforesaid two closes to the east and abutting the land of William Stone to the south containing 2 acres, 3 roods, 16 perches.

[K7.9] William Stone holds nearby one inclosure lying lengthways along a drove leading to the Ridge to the south, the land of Robert Frampton to the north and abutting to the east over Brenson Way containing 3 acres.

*

[K8] *Stadium* lying adjacent to the western head of the aforesaid *Stadium.*

[K8.1] Morgan Snell holds one piece of land between the tenement of Robert Frampton to the east, the tenement of William Franklin to the west, Robert Seagar's tenement to the south and north the land of Robert Skotte to the north containing by estimation 1½ roods.

[K8.2] William Franklyn holds one piece of land abutting the headland to the south over the aforesaid land of Robert Segar and to the north over the land of Robert Frampton containing by estimation 3 acres.

[K8.3] Robert Frampton holds one piece formerly called the Stert descending to Brenson Way to the east and a headland to the west in part abutting over the land of Robert Segar containing by estimation 1 acre.

[K8.4] William Domine holds one inclosure between lands of Thomas Lynsey to the north, the aforesaid piece on the south and abutting his own land to the east containing 2 acres.

*

[K9] *Stadium* abutting on the aforesaid *Stadium* towards the east called Haycombe, going towards the south.

[K9.1] The Rector holds one piece abutting to the east over the land of William Domine and containing by estimation 2 acres.

[K9.2] Robert Segar holds 1 acre.

[K9.3] Morgan Snell holds 1 acre.

[K9.4] Robert Seygar holds 1 acre.

[K9.5] William Stone holds 1 acre.

[K9.6] Morgan Snell holds 1 acre.

[K9.7] William Domine holds 1 acre.

[K9.8] Christian Loder holds 1½ acres.

[K9.9] Robert Segar holds 1½ acres abutting towards the east over the close of Robert Frampton.

[K9.10] ~~John~~ James Privett holds one piece of land lying along the drove leading up to the Ridge containing ½ acre.

*

[K10] *Stadium* abutting over the aforesaid *Stadium* towards the east Hafehews going north

[K10.1] The Rector holds 3 acres.

[K10.2] Robert Seygar holds 1 acre.

[K10.3] James Privett holds 2 acres.

[K10.4] Robert Seygar holds 1 acre.

*

[K11] *Stadium* abutting over the aforesaid *Stadium* to the east lying over Challwells Cliffe going towards the south.

[K11.1] Robert Skotte holds 1 acre.

[K11.2] The Rector holds 1 acre.

[K11.3] Robert Frampton holds 1 acre.

[K11.4] Morgan Snell holds to the eastern head of the above one piece containing a half acre.

[K11.5] Morgan Snell holds one piece to the east of the headland and towards the north over the close of ~~Edward~~ Richard Prower containing 1 acre.

[K11.6] John Pelle holds 3 acres.

[K11.7] John Pelle holds 2 acres of land between the close of John Shepherd to the north, the land of William Domine to the south and over the land of Nicholas Everad towards the west.

*

[K12] The Land lying over Chalwell Cliffe.

[K12.1] William Domine holds 3 acres.

[K12.2] Nicholas Evered holds 1 acre.

[K12.3] William Domine holds 3 acres.

[K12.4] Robert Frampton holds 1 acre lying lengthways over the Cliffe.

[K12.5] Christiana Loder holds 1½ acres abutting to the west over the land of Morgan Snell and towards the east over the land of William Domine.

[K12.6] Nicholas Evered holds 1 acre lying lengthways along the boundary between Durweston and Knighton.

[K12.7] Morgan Snell holds at the eastern head of the aforesaid piece a piece containing 3 acres and a headland.

[K12.8] Morgan Snell holds at the northern head of the aforesaid piece another piece containing 2 acres lying by the division between Durweston and Knighton abutting to the north over Harway.

*

[K13] *Stadium* abutting over the aforesaid two pieces of Morgan Snell towards the east lying on every side against Harway going towards the south.

[K13.1] John Standley holds 1½ acres with the division between Durweston and Knighton to the north and Harway to the south.

[K13.2] John Standley holds at the western head of the aforesaid piece another piece containing 1 acre lying by the aforesaid division.

[K13.3] Thomas Philips holds ½ acre lying near Harway to the north of the previous entry.

[K13.4] Robert Hector holds 3 acres also lying to the south lengthways nearby.

[K13.5] The Rector holds 6 acres.

[K13.6] James Privet holds 1½ acres called Chalwell Cliffe.

[K13.7] William Domine holds 3 acres lying in the Bottom.

[K13.8] Robert Hector holds 1 acre abutting towards the west over the lands of Thomas Philips.

[K13.9] Robert Seyger holds 1 acre abutting similarly.

[K13.10] William Franklyn holds at the western end of the aforesaid two pieces, one piece containing ½ acre which is a headland.

[K13.11] Thomas Phillips holds one piece lying in Peckis Hole abutting to the north over the land of Robert Hector containing 1 acre.

[K13.12] Robert Hector holds one piece containing 1 acre lying next to Harway.

[K13.13] James Privet holds 1½ acres.

[K13.14] William Franklyn holds one piece containing 3 acres abutting towards the north over the land of James Privet and Harway.

[K13.15] Robert Frampton holds one piece of land containing 1½ acres to the east of the aforesaid piece.

*

[K14] *Stadium* of land lying under Cholwells Cliffe going towards the south.

[K14.1] Emma Pelley holds 1 acre.

[K14.2] Robert Hector holds 1 acre.

[K14.2] Emma Pelley holds 2 acres.

[K14.2] Robert Skott holds one piece of land lying by the way leading to the Drove and the headland to the aforesaid piece containing 3 acres.

*

[K15] *Stadium* abutting over the above.

[K15.1] Thomas Phillips holds 2 acres.

[K15.2] James Privett holds ½ acre.

*

[K16] *Stadium* abutting over the piece of land to the east going towards the north.

[K16.1] Nicholas Evered holds 1 acre.

[K16.2] William Domine holds 1 acre.

[K16.3] James Privett holds ½ acre.

[K16.4] James Privett holds another ½ acre.

[K16.5] Memorandum: there is also there one great piece called the Ridge containing 24 acres which is grazed only by the sheep of the tenants.

*

[K17] *Stadium* and land lying between Horshoe Way and the division between Kingston and Durweston.

[K17.1] Emma Pelley holds a piece lying lengthways along Horshoe Way containing 1 acre.

[K17.2] Robert Skott holds 2 acres lying lengthways near the division between Kingston and Durweston.

[K17.3] Thomas Phillips holds 2 acres.

[K17.4] Emma Pelley holds 2 acres.

[K17.5] Robert Skoot holds 2 acres.

[K17.6] Emma Pelley holds a piece containing 4 acres abutting towards the east over Horshoe Way.

*

[K18] *Stadium* abutting over Knighton Fore Downs towards the west and over the aforesaid *Stadium* towards the east.

[K18.1] Emma Pelley holds two inclosures lying together containing 10 acres.

[K18.2] Emma Pelley similarly one piece containing 3 acres, 1 rood.

[K18.3] Richard Prower holds one piece of a certain inclosure called Harthorne with appurtenances lying near the division between Durweston and Knighton, abutting towards the east over the land of Robert Skotte, containing 3 acres.

*

[K19] Land and closes lying to the south of a certain drove leading from the village to the Ridge.

[K19.1] James Privett holds one tenement with garden and croft adjacent between the aforesaid Drove to the north, the land of John Powlden and Thomas Phillips to the south, abutting over the land of the said Thomas towards the west and over Brenson Way towards the east, containing 1½ acres.

[K19.2] John Powlden holds near there one inclosure called Bugkes Close and certain cottages that have recently been built abutting towards the east over Brenson Way, containing 4 acres.

[K19.3] Thomas Phillips holds one inclosure, formerly in the Sterte, leading up to the aforesaid drove between the land of John Pelle and Nicholas Evered to the west, a certain small lane to the east and abutting towards the south over the land of James Privet, containing 2½ acres.

[K19.4] James Privet holds one inclosure near there with appurtenances lying in two squares between land of Robert Hector and John Powlden to the south, the land of diverse tenants to the north and abutting towards the west over the land of John Fry, containing 3 acres.

[K19.5] Robert Hector holds one inclosure abutting towards the east over Bugkes Close and towards the west over the aforesaid close, containing 1½ acres.

[K19.6] Christiana Loder holds one inclosure abutting on both sides as above and containing 3 acres.

*

[K20] *Stadium* lying at the western end of the aforesaid *Stadium* going towards the north.

[K20.1] John Frye holds one inclosure lying between the land of John Poulden to the south and the land of the same John Frye to the north containing 6 acres.

[K20.2] John Frye holds two inclosures lying together, formerly within the Sterte, leading to the aforesaid drove and between the land of the rector and Emma Pelle to the west and the land of diverse tenants to the east containing 15 acres.

[K20.3] John Pelle holds one inclosure lying between the land of Nicholas Evered to the north, the lands of John Frye to the south and abutting to the east over the land of John Frye, containing 3 acres.

[K20.4] Nicholas Evered holds two inclosures lying together between the aforesaid close to the south, the aforesaid drove to the north, abutting to the west over the land of John Frye and to the east over the land of Thomas Phillips, containing 6 acres.

*

[K21] *Stadium* containing closes to the west of the aforesaid *Stadium* going north.

[K21.1] Robert Hector holds one inclosure lying between the land of John Powlden to the south, the land of the rector to the north and abutting to the east over the tenement of John Frye, containing 2 acres.

[K21.2] The Rector holds one inclosure lying between land of John Frye to the east, the land of diverse tenements to the west and abutting over the aforesaid close to the south, containing 8 acres.

[K21.3] Emma Pelley, widow, holds near there two inclosures formerly the Stert leading to the said drove, containing 7 acres.

[K21.4] William Domine holds 3 acres of land abutting on the aforesaid closes.

*

[K22] *Stadium* lying lengthways to the south of the footpath leading up to the Ridge, going towards the south.

[K22.1] William Stone holds one piece of headland lying between the land of Emma Pelley to the east, the land of diverse tenants to the west and abutting to the north over the aforesaid tenements, containing 1 acre.

[K22.2] William Domine holds one piece of land lying lengthways by the said footpath abutting to the east over the land of William Stone containing 1 acre.

[K22.3] Emma Pelley, widow, holds 1 acre.

[K22.4] Nicholas Evered holds 1 acre, 1 rood.

[K22.5] Robert Hector holds 1 acre.

[K22.6] Emma Pelley holds 1 acre.

*

[K23] *Stadium* lying to the eastern end of the aforesaid *Stadium* called Stockum going towards the north.

[K23.1] Robert Segar holds one piece lying near the close of William Domine, abutting towards the east over the land of Emma Pelley, containing 1 acre.

[K23.2] Thomas Phillips holds 1 acre.

[K23.3] Nicholas Evered holds ½ rood.

*

[K24] *Stadium* lying at head of the aforesaid *Stadium* lying lengthways up to the said footpath, going towards the south.

[K24.1] Robert Frampton holds ½ acre lying lengthways near the footpath.

[K24.2] ~~Richard~~ Nicholas Evered holds 2 acres.

[K24.3] Morgan Snell holds 3 acres.

*

[K25] *Stadium* lying at the western end of the aforesaid *Stadium*, going towards the north.

[K25.1] Robert Hector holds 1 acre abutting towards the east over the land of Morgan Snell.

[K25.2] James Privet holds ½ acre.

[K25.3] Morgan Snell holds ½ acre lying lengthways near the footpath.

[K25.4] Thomas Phillips holds at the western head of the said piece one piece containing 2 acres with appurtenances lying lengthways near the footpath.

[K25.5] Thomas Phillips holds similarly at the western head of the said piece another piece containing 1 acre.

[K25.6] John Privet holds near there ½ acre lying to the south of the aforesaid two pieces.

[K25.7] Thomas Phillips holds, at the western head of the penultimate piece, one piece lying under the coppice of John Powlden called Wibsley, containing 2 acres.

[K25.8] Robert Seygar holds one pightle lying with the aforesaid coppice to the south, the Ridge to the north, abutting towards the east over the land of Thomas Phillips, containing 1 acre.

*

[K26] *Stadium* lying lengthways near the close of the Rector and Emma Pelle, abutting towards the south over the lands of William Domine, going towards the west.

[K26.1] Robert Seygar holds one piece near the aforesaid close containing 2 acres.

[K26.2] William Franklyn holds 1 acre.

[K26.3] Morgan Snell holds 1 acre.

[K26.4] James Privett holds ½ acre abutting towards the east over the aforesaid piece.

[K26.5] Memorandum there is there one piece of land which is called River Bache containing by estimation 13 acres.

*

[K27] *Stadium* abutting over the close of the Rector towards the east, going south.

[K27.1] William Domine holds 1 acre and a headland.

[K27.2] Robert Frampton holds 2 acres and a headland.

*

[K28] *Stadium* lying lengthways near the close of John Powlden, going towards the north.

[K28.1] Morgan Snell holds one piece containing 3 acres abutting towards the east over the land of the Rector and Robert Hector and towards the west over the land of Robert Hector containing [blank].

[K28.2] Nicholas Evered holds 2 acres.

[K28.3] The Rector holds 2 acres.

[K28.4] William Franklyn holds 3 acres with appurtenances lying near River Bache.

*

[K29] *Stadium* abutting over the aforesaid *Stadium* towards the east, going towards the south.

[K29.1] William Domine holds 2 acres lying lengthways by River Bache.

[K29.2] Robert Hector holds 1 acre.

[K29.3] John Pellye holds half a rood.

[K29.4] Morgan Snell holds 1 acre.

[K29.5] Robert Hector holds 3 acres lying lengthways near the land of John Powlden.

[K29.6] Robert Skott holds one piece containing 4 acres abutting towards the west over Wood Close.

[K29.7] Nicholas Evered holds 1 acre abutting towards west over Websley.

[K29.8] Thomas Phillips holds near there one inclosure called Wood Close between the land of John Powlden to the south and Websley to the north, abutting towards the west over the lands of Robert Frampton, containing 7 acres.

[K29.9] John Powlden holds by indenture one coppice called Websley containing 11 acres, 2 roods, 3 perches.

*

[K30] *Stadium* containing closes and land lying to the west of Websley and the Ridge, going towards the north.

[K30.1] First of all there is one acre lying lengthways over a close of Nicholas Evered called Tythingman's Acre and each tithingman has this acre for his use during his term of office.

[K30.2] Robert Frampton holds one inclosure near the land of John Powlden containing 8 acres.

[K30.3] Emma Pellye, widow, holds one inclosure containing 4 acres.

[K30.4] Nicholas Evered holds at the east end of the aforesaid close one pightle lying Between within Tythingman's Acre containing 2 acres.

[K30.5] James Privett holds one inclosure containing 4 acres.

[K30.6] Robert Hector holds 2 acres.

[K30.7] Robert Skotte holds 1 acre.

[K30.8] William Stone holds 6 acres.

[K30.9] Thomas Phillips holds 3 acres lying lengthways near Horshoe Way.

[K30.10] James Privett holds one piece of land lying at the eastern end of the aforesaid piece, it is a headland and contains 2 acres.

[K30.11] Thomas Phillips holds at the western end of the *Stadium* one piece containing 1 acre abutting towards the north over Horshoe Way.

*

[K31] *Stadium* abutting over Knighton Fore Downs, going west.

[K31.1] The Rector holds one piece of land containing 6 acres.

[K31.2] Robert Frampton holds 2 acres.

[K31.3] Thomas Phillips holds near there one inclosure containing 10 acres.

*

[K32] The closes lying between Knighton Cowpasture and Sheep Downe.

[K32.1] Nicholas Evered holds one inclosure which lies between Knighton Cowpasture to the north and the land of John Fry to the south, abutting towards the east over Knighton Fore Downe, containing 6 acres.

[K32.2] John Fry holds one close containing 4 acres.

[K32.3] Robert Frampton holds one inclosure near the Sheep Downe abutting similarly, as the aforesaid close, containing 4 acres.

[K32.4] William Domine holds one close near the land of John Pelle to the west and the aforesaid close to the east, abutting over Sheep Downe towards the south and over Cowpasture towards the north, containing 4 acres.

[K32.5] John Pellye holds one inclosure abutting on all sides as above and containing 2 acres.

[K32.6] Christiana Loder, widow, holds one inclosure containing 2½ acres.

[K32.7] William Stone holds one inclosure containing 2 acres.

[K32.8] Christiana Loder, widow, holds another inclosure containing 7 acres.

[K32.9] Robert Seygar holds one inclosure containing 2 acres.

[K32.10] Robert Hector holds one inclosure containing 6 acres.

[K32.11] James Privett holds one inclosure containing 3 acres.

[K32.12] The Rector of Durweston holds one inclosure containing 3 acres.

*

[K33.1] The Tithing of Knighton holds altogether one field called Knighton Cowpasture, lying between the aforesaid close to the south and Durweston Cowpasture to the north, containing 78 acres, 3 roods, 15 perches.

[K33.2] They hold similarly one pasture called Knighton Sheep Downe lying between the aforesaid close to the north and the land in the tenure of John Powlden called Firme Sheepe Downe, containing 79 acres, 1 rood, 24 perches.

[K33.3] They hold similarly one pasture called Knighton Fore Downe between the aforesaid close and pasture to the west and the land of diverse tenants to the east, containing 36 acres, 1 rood.

[K33.4] They hold similarly from the lord at farm one wood called Fillgrove now lying in two parts between the land of Francis Browne, gentleman, lying in the parish of [Winterborne] Stickland and the land lying in the parish of Turnworth on the west and the said close of pasture to the east, containing 39 acres, 17 perches.

[K33.5] John Powlden holds by an indenture his pasture called Firme Sheep Downe lying between Knighton Sheep Downe and Knighton Fore Downe to the north and the land of Richard Rogers, knight, lying in parish of Brenson [Bryanstone] and the land of Francis Browne, gentleman, lying in parish of [Winterborne] Stickland to the south, abutting to the west over the land of the said Francis, containing 88 acres, 1 rood, 24 perches.

[K33.6] John Powlden holds similarly one inclosure nearby between the close of Thomas Phillips to the north and the land of the said Richard Rogers, knight, to the south, abutting to the west over the Sheep Downe, containing 11 acres, 3 roods, 20 perches.

[K33.7] John Powlden holds near there two large inclosures lying together between the land of Richard Rogers, knight, to the south and the lands of Robert Frampton and Thomas Phillips called Wood Closse to the north, part abutting to the west over the other land held by John Powlden, containing 53 acres, 1 rood, 6 perches.

[K33.8] John Powlden holds similarly three large inclosures lying together between the land of the said Richard Rogers, knight, to the south and the land of diverse tenants to the north, abutting towards the west over the aforesaid two closes and containing altogether 71 acres, 1 rood, 34 perches.

[K33.9] John Powlden holds similarly four closes lying together between the land of the said Richard Rogers, knight, to the south and the lands of diverse tenants to the north, abutting towards the east over Brenson Way and towards the west over the said closes, containing altogether 23 acres, 1 rood, 4 perches.

THE SURVEY OF DURWESTON

Precinct containing all the lands and tenements lying within Durweston.

[D1] First Precinct contains all the lands and tenements lying between the fields of Knighton to the south and the the Queen's highway leading from Durweston to Ockford on the north beginning with the Rectory of Durweston and going towards the west.

[D1.1] First there is situated the Rectory of Durweston aforesaid with garden and croft adjacent between the aforesaid way leading from Durweston to Ockford on the north and the land of William Domine on the south abutting towards the east over Brenson Way and containing 1 acre, 3 roods, 24 perches.

[D1.2] Thomas Lynsey holds near there one inclosure lying lengthways near the aforesaid way leading to Ockford abutting towards the east over the Rectory aforesaid and containing 4 acres.

[D1.3] John Stevens holds similarly one inclosure near adjacent lying lengthways near the aforesaid way and containing 3 acres.

[D1.4] John Rogers holds similarly one inclosure similarly lying lengthways by the aforesaid way and containing 2½ acres.

[D1.5] Richard Prower holds similarly one inclosure lying similarly by the said way containing 3 acres.

[D1.6] John Shepherd holds similarly one inclosure lying lengthways by the aforesaid way and containing 4 acres.

*

[D2] *Stadium* abutting over the above close towards the east going towards the south.

[D2.1] John Stevens holds one inclosure lying lengthways by Harway abutting towards the west over the division between Durweston and Knighton and containing 3 acres.

[D2.2] Hugh Dashwood holds similarly one piece of land abutting as above and containing 2 acres.

[D2.3] Alice Dennis holds similarly one piece lying near the division between Durweston and Knighton to the south and containing 1 acre.

*

[D3] *Stadium* lying between Harway to the south and the way leading from Durweston to Ockford to the north, going towards the south.

[D3.1] John Howe holds one piece containing 1 acre lying lengthways along the aforesaid way leading from Durweston to Ockford.

[D3.2] John Rogers holds near there 2 acres.

[D3.3] John Howe holds 1 acre lying lengthways by Harway in part and the division between Durweston and Knighton.

*

[D4] *Stadium* called Sandpitts lying to the western head of the aforesaid *Stadium* going towards the north.

[D4.1] John Howe holds one piece of land lying lengthways by the aforesaid division and containing 2 acres.

[D4.2] John Standley holds similarly one piece of land near there containing 2 acres.

[D4.3] Roger Ranewe holds one piece of land near there containing 2 acres.

*

[D5] *Stadium* called Giddey Landes abutting towards the east over the aforesaid *Stadium* going towards the south.

[D5.1] John Iles holds 2½ acres.

[D5.2] John Henning holds 4 acres.

[D5.3] Thomas Lynsey holds one piece of land containing 3 acres 1 rood with the Stert at the east end of it.

[D5.4] Richard Prower holds at the west end of the aforesaid piece a piece of land containing half an acre.

*

[D6] *Stadium* abutting over Durweston Fore Downes going towards the west.

[D6.1] ~~John~~ Richard Prower holds one inclosure called Harethorne abutting over the Fore Downe towards the west and containing 8 acres.

[D6.2] John Stevens holds similarly one inclosure near adjacent abutting over Fore Downe aforesaid at the west end and containing 4 acres.

[D6.3] Richard Prower holds one inclosure near adjacent containing 3 acres.

[D6.4] Richard Prower holds near there one piece of land abutting towards the north over the way leading from Durweston to Ockford and containing 1½ acres.

*

[D7] Precinct containing all the lands and tenements lying between the way leading from Durweston to Shillingston to the west and the Stower to the east beginning at the mill.

[D7.1] Robert Oliver holds from the lord of this manor one water mill lying and situated near the Stower aforesaid.

[D7.2] The same holds similarly one meadow called Millhams with the Wythybed adjacent with appurtenances lying in the parish of Durweston to the east of the Stower and containing altogether 6 acres.

[D7.3] The same holds similarly one small island near there called Gasthams and containing 2 roods.

[D7.4] The same holds similarly to the south of the mill one small piece of land on which lately permission has been granted by the lord to build a tenement and containing 1 rood.

[D7.5] John Iles holds one tenement with croft adjacent called Court Close abutting towards the south over the Queen's highway and containing 2 acres, 4 perches.

[D7.6] Roger Ranew holds one inclosure called Court Close containing 1 acre, 2 roods, 10 perches.

[D7.7] Richard Prower holds similarly near there one inclosure similarly called Courte Close abutting towards the south over the tenement of Hugh Dashwood and containing 2 acres.

[D7.8] The Rector of Durweston holds one cottage called Chappell Hay with garden adjacent between the tenement of John Iles aforesaid to the east and the tenement of Roger Ranew to the west abutting towards the south over the the Queen's highway and towards the north over Court Close and containing 1 rood, 20 perches.

[D7.9] Roger Ranewe holds one tenement with half a garden adjacent abutting as above and containing 1 acre.

[D7.10] Hugh Dashwood holds similarly one tenement with garden adjacent with all sides abutting as above and containing 1 acre.

[D7.11] John Howe holds similarly one tenement with garden adjacent the southern end abutting as above and the northern end abutting over the garden of Edith Rogers and containing 1 rood, 10 perches.

[D7.12] John Vallevine holds one tenement near adjacent by the stone cross and containing half an acre.

[D7.13] John Shepherd holds similarly one tenement with garden adjacent containing 1 rood.

[D7.14] Edith Rogers holds near there one tenement with garden adjacent with the west end abutting over the Queen's highway leading from Durweston to Shillingston and containing 1 rood, 10 perches.

[D7.15] Richard Prower holds one pightle adjacent to the west end abutting as above and containing 1 rood, 10 perches.

[D7.16] Alice Dennis holds one tenement near adjacent abutting towards the west over the aforesaid way and towards the east over Courte Close and containing 2 roods, 30 perches.

[D7. 17] John Rogers holds one tenement near adjacent by the footpath leading to the mill the western end abutting as above and containing 1 acre.

[D7.18] John Iles holds at the eastern end of the aforesaid tenement one inclosure lying between Courte Closse aforesaid to the south and the close of Edward Bennet to the north abutting towards the east over the mill and containing 2 acres, 10 perches.

[D7.19] Edward Bennett holds similarly one inclosure with pightle adjacent abutting towards the west over the aforesaid way and towards the east over the Stower and containing altogether 2 acres, 3 roods.

[D7.20] John Vallevin holds near there one pightle abutting towards the west over the aforesaid way and towards the east over the above close and containing 1 rood, 20 perches.

[D7.21] John Standley holds similarly one inclosure abutting towards the west over the aforesaid way and towards the east over the Stower and containing 2 acres.

[D7.22] John Stevens holds similarly one pightle with the Stert leading to the way aforesaid and each end abutting as above and containing 1½ acres.

[D7.23] Richard Collyns holds one pightle near the western end abutting over the aforesaid way and containing 2 roods.

[D7.24] John Rogers holds one inclosure near adjacent the western end over the aforesaid way and the eastern end abutting over the Stower containing 3 acres.

[D7.25] Thomas Lynsey holds near there one inclosure each end abutting as above containing 4 acres.

[D7.26] Edith Rogers, widow, holds one inclosure near there and containing 2 acres.

[D7.27] Richard Prower holds one inclosure near there and containing 3 acres.

[D7.28] John Howe holds one inclosure near there containing 2 acres.

[D7.29] Hugh Dashwood holds similarly two inclosures together lying between the Stower to the east and the aforesaid way to the west containing altogether 4 acres.

[D7.30] The lord holds in his hands one coppice called Pressu' with appurtenances lying lengthways between the Stower and the aforesaid way and containing 4 acres, 3 roods.

[D7.31] Edward Bennett holds in the same lower part one meadow lying lengthways by the Stower and containing 1 acre.

[D7.32]And there is opposite the aforesaid meadow to the east of the Stower land called Wythbed belonging to the lord of this manor and within the precinct of the same now in the tenure of John Henning, Roger Ranew, John Iles and Edward Bennett and containing by estimation 1 rood.

*

[D8] Precinct containing all the lands and tenements lying to the west of the common way leading from Shillingston to Brenson, near the aforesaid way leading from Durweston to Ockford going towards the north.

[D.8.1]John Stevens holds one tenement lying between the tenement of William Coshe, clerk, to the east and the meadow called Twitchinge to the west abutting towards the south over the way leading from Durweston to Ockford and containing half an acre.

[D8.2] John Sheperd holds near there one tenement lying between the aforesaid tenement to the west and the way leading from Brenson W̶a̶y̶ to Shillingston to the east and the south end abutting as above and containing 1 rood.

[D8.3]John Standley holds near there one tenement with garden and croft adjacent to the aforesaid two tenements to the south and the tenement of Richard Prower to the north abutting towards the west over the meadow of the same John called Twitchinge and towards the east over the Queen's highway leading from Shillingston to Brenson and containing 1 acre, 2 roods, 15 perches.

[D8.4] The same holds similarly near there one meadow called Twitchinge lying between the lands of diverse men to the west and the aforesaid tenement and tenements of John Stevens to the east abutting towards the south over the way leading from Durweston to Ockford and containing 3 acres.

[D8.5] Richard Prower holds near there one tenement with garden and croft and pightle adjacent between the tenement and meadow of the aforesaid John Standley to the south and the tenement of John [sic] Lynsey to the north abutting towards the east over the Queen's highway leading from Shillingston to Brenson and containing altogether 2 acres.

[D8.6] Thomas Lynsey holds near there one tenement with garden, yard and pightle adjacent the east side abutting as above and containing 1 acre, 10 perches.

[D8.7] Richard Collyns holds near there one tenement with garden and croft adjacent and containing 1 acre, 30 perches.

[D8.8] John Rogers holds near there one pightle the end abutting as above and containing 2 roods, 10 perches.

*

[D9] A small *Stadium* abutting towards the east over the Queen's highway leading from Shillingston to Brenson going towards the north.

[D9.1] Hugh Dashwood holds half a rood.

[D9.2] John Vallevine holds half a rood.

[D9.3] Richard Collins holds 4 perches.

[D9.4] Edith Rogers holds 4 perches.

*

[D10] *Stadium* abutting towards the east over the aforesaid *Stadium* and aforesaid tenements going towards the south.

[D10.1] John Vallevine holds 1 acre.

[D10.2] Hugh Dashwood holds 1 acre.

[D10.3] John Howe holds half an acre.

[D10.4] John Vallevine holds half an acre.

[D10.5] Alice Dennis holds 1 acre.

[D10.6] John Rogers holds 1 acre.

[D10.7] Hugh Dashwoode holds 1 acre.

[D10.8] Thomas Lynsey holds 2 acres.

[D10.9] John Vallevine holds 1 acre.

[D10.10] John Stevens holds 1 acre.

[D10.11] John Howe holds 2 acres.

[D10.12] Hugh Dashwoode holds 1 acre.

[D10.13] Roger Ranew holds 1 acre 1 rood.

[D10.14] John Iles holds 1 acre 1 rood.

[D10.15] John Henninge holds one inclosure lying lengthways near the Queen's highway leading from Durweston to Ockford and containing 1 acre, 3 rood, 8 perches.

[D10.16] Richard Prower holds one inclosure near there lying lengthways over the said way and containing 2½ acres.

*

[D11] *Stadium* abutting towards the east over the aforesaid *stadium* going towards the ~~south~~ north.

[D11.1] John Howe holds one inclosure lying between the aforesaid way to the south and South Cliffe to the north abutting towards the east over the aforesaid close and containing 4 acres.

[D11.2] And there is next vacant land called The South Cliffe.

[D11.3] John Henning holds near there 1 acre.

[D11.4] The same holds near the same 1 acre.

[D11.5] John Iles holds 1 acre.

[D11.6] Hugh Dashwood holds 1 acre.

[D11.7] John Vallevine holds 3 acres.

[D11.8] And there is one piece of land containing half an acre called The Tything Man's Place which is allowed every year to him that is the tithingman.

[D11.9] John Stevens holds 1 acre.

[D11.10] John Sheperd holds 1 acre

[D11.11] John Rogers holds 2 acres.

[D11.12] Alice Dennis holds 2 acres.

[D11.12] John Rogers holds 1 acre.

[D11.13] Edith Rogers holds 1 acre.

[D11.14] Richard Prower holds 2 acres.

*

[D12] *Stadium* abutting towards the east over the aforesaid *Stadium* near the way leading from Durweston to Ockford and going towards the north.

[D12.1] Thomas Lynsey holds one inclosure between the close of John Howe to the east and the close of Hugh Dashwood to the west abutting towards the south over the aforesaid way and containing 4 acres.

[D12.2]And there is near there one pightle of empty land called The South Cliffe.

[D12.3] John Iles holds near there 1 acre, 1 rood.

[D12.4] The same holds similarly near there 1 acre, 1 rood.

[D12.5] John Henninge holds 1 acre, 1 rood.

[D12.6] And there is one piece of land vacant.

[D12.7] Richard Collyns holds near there half an acre.

[D12.8] John Standly holds 1 acre.

[D.12.9] John Vallevine holds half an acre.

[D12.10] John Shepherde holds 2 acres.

[D12.11] John Standley holds one inclosure with the Stert towards the west containing 2 acres.

[D12.12]Edith Rogers holds to the eastern end of the aforesaid close one piece of land containing 1 acre.

[D12.13] John Vallevine holds near there one inclosure lying between aforesaid piece of land and the aforesaid close to the south and a certain way leading to Norden to the north, to the west over the close of John How and towards the east over the land of Hugh Dashwood and containing 4 acres.

[D12.14] John Howe holds at the western end of the aforesaid piece one inclosure abutting towards the north over the aforesaid way and containing 4 acres.

*

[D13] *Stadium* abutting over the aforesaid *Stadium* towards the east beginning near the aforesaid way leading from Durweston to Ockford going towards the north.

[D13.1] Hugh Dashwoode holds one inclosure lying between the close of Thomas Linsey on the east and Cowards Drove on the west abutting towards the south over the aforesaid way and containing 6 acres.

[D13.2] And there is also some land vacant called the South Cliffe and containing 20 acres.

[D13.3] John Iles holds near there in the Bottom 1 acre.

[D13.4] John Henning holds near there 1 acre with appurtenances lying near Iping Grove.

*

[D14] *Stadium* abutting over the aforesaid *Stadium* towards the east going towards the north.

[D14.1] Hugh Dashwoode holds one inclosure lying lengthways near the way leading from Durweston to Ockford abutting towards the east over Cowards Drove and containing 3 acres.

[D14.2] And there is one piece of land vacant called South Cliffe.

[D14.3]John Henninge holds near the South Cliffe in Sutcome 3 roods.

[D14.4] The same holds near there 3 roods.

[D14.5] The same holds near there 3 roods.

[D14.6] The same holds near there half an acre.

*

[D15] *Stadium* abutting over the aforesaid *Stadium* towards the east going towards the north.

[D15.1] John Standley holds one inclosure lying lengthways near the said way and containing 3 acres.

[D15.2] And there is near there one piece of land vacant called South Cliffe.

[D15.3] John Henninge holds 1 acre called Wood Acre lying in Sutcome beside Iping Grove.

*

[D16] Closes lying lengthways near the way leading from Durweston to Ockford and near the coppice of the lord called Sutcome.

[D16.1] Roger Ranewe holds one inclosure with appurtenances lying between the aforesaid way on the south and the coppice of the lord called Sutcome and the South Cliffe on the north and containing 11 acres.

[D16.2] The lord holds in his hands one coppice called Sutcome and containing 18 acres, 3 roods.

[D16.3] The Rector of Durweston holds two inclosures together lying between the aforesaid coppice and containing together 7 acres, 5 perches.

[D16.4] John Rogers holds one pightle lying there between the aforesaid land of the Rector to the west and the aforesaid coppice of the lord called Sutcome to the east and containing 1 acre, 1 rood, 10 perches.

[D16.5] John Henninge holds one inclosure lying between the way leading from Durweston to Ockford on the south and the close of John Howe on the north abutting towards the west over Durweston Fore Downe and towards the east over the land of the Rector and containing 10 acres.

[D16.6] John Howe holds near there one inclosure all sides abutting as before and containing 6 acres, 1 rood.

*

[D17] Closes and lands lying to the north of Sutcome and Wulsley going towards the east.

[D17.1] John Henninge holds one inclosure lying near the drove on the south abutting towards the west over Durweston Fore Downes and containing 7 acres.

[D17.2] Roger Ranewe holds near there two inclosures together lying abutting towards the north over Inforde Combe and to the south over the said drove and containing altogether 10 acres.

[D17.3] John Iles holds near there one inclosure containing 10 acres all sides abutting as above.

*

[D18] *Stadium* abutting over Wulsley towards the south going towards the east.

[D18.1] Thomas Lynsey holds one piece of land abutting towards the south over Wulsley and containing 2 acres, 2 roods.

[D18.2] Richard Collyns holds near there 1½ acres.

[D18.3] John Stevens holds near there 5 acres.

[D18.4] John Rogers holds near there 2 acres.

[D18.5] Richard Collyns holds near there 1 acre.

[D18.6] Edith Rogers widow holds near there 2 acres lying lengthways near Norden.

*

[D19] *Stadium* abutting over Norden towards the east going towards the north.

[D19.1] Richard Collyns holds 1 acre called Broadacre and is abutting a headland towards the east over Norden.

[D19.2] Richard Prower holds near there 1 acre.

[D19.3] Hugh Dashwoode holds 2 acres called Timplin.

[D19.4] John Rogers holds 2½ acres called Timplin.

*

[D20] *Stadium* lying at the west end of the aforesaid *Stadium* abutting towards the north over Inforde Combe.

[D20.1] Alice Dennis holds 2 acres called Ryver and abutting a headland towards the north over Inford Combe.

[D20.2] John Stevens holds near there 1 acre.

[D20.3] John Standley holds near there 2 acres.

[D20.4] Hugh Dashwoode holds one inclosure with parcel of land adjacent abutting towards north over Inforde Combe and containing altogether 4 acres.

[D20.5] Thomas Lynsey holds near there one piece of land containing 2 acres the northern end abutting as above.

*

[D21] Closes and *Stadium* lying by the way from Shillingston to Brenson.

[D21.1] William Howsley holds one cottage situated and lying near the way leading from Shillingston to Brenson.

[D21.2] John Rogers holds one inclosure lying lengthways near the said way abutting to the north over the close of John Shephard and containing 2 acres.

[D21.3] Richard Prower holds near there to the west of the aforesaid close one piece of land with the Stert containing 5 acres.

[D21.4] Hugh Dashwoode holds near there 1 acre.

[D21.5] John Rogers holds 1 acre.

[D21.6] John Howe holds 1 acre.

[D21.7] Hugh Dashwoode holds 3 acres and is a headland.

*

[D22] *Stadium* abutting over aforesaid *Stadium* to the east going towards the north.

[D22.1] Hugh Dashwood holds 2 acres lying lengthways near the drove leading to Norden.

[D22.2] The same holds to the west end of the former piece one piece of land similarly lying lengthways near the said drove and containing 1 acre.

[D22.3] The Rector of Durweston holds there one piece containing 3½ acres.

*

[D23] *Stadium* abutting over the aforesaid *Stadium* towards the south going to the east.

[D23.1] The Rector of Durweston holds 5 acres lying near Norden.

[D23.2] Thomas Lynsey holds near there half an acre.

[D23.3] The Rector of Durweston holds near there 4½ acres.

[D23.4] John Stevens holds near there 1 acre.

[D23.5] John Vallevine holds 1 acre.

[D23.6] John Rogers holds near there 4 acres.

[D23.7] Richard Collyns holds near there one inclosure containing 4½ acres.

[D23.8] John Sheperde holds near there one inclosure lying lengthways near the said way leading from Shillingston to Brenson and containing 4 acres.

*

[D24] *Stadium* abutting over the above *stadium* towards the south going towards the west.

[D24.1] John Standley holds one piece containing 1 acre abutting towards the north over North Bache.

[D24.2] Alice Dennis holds one piece containing 2 acres the north side abutting as above.

[D24.3] John Henninge holds near there 4 acres.

[D24.4] John Iles holds near there 4½ acres.

D24.5] John Shepherd holds 1 acre.

*

[D25[*Stadium* abutting over North Batche towards the east going towards the north.

[D25.1] John Rogers holds 1 piece containing 2 acres abutting towards the east over the land of John Henninge.

[D25.2] John Howe holds 2 acres abutting towards the east over North Batche.

[D25.3] Richard Prower holds 3 acres.

[D25.4] Hugh Dashwoode holds 3 acres.

[D25.5] And there is there one piece of land vacant.

[D25.6] John Standley holds near there 2 acres.

[D25.7] Richard Collins holds near there one inclosure containing 4 acres.

[D25.8] And there is there at the eastern end of the aforesaid *Stadium* one piece of land called North Batche containing 4 acres. [Marginal annotation: leased for one year as common pasture for sheep and the next year for animals].

*

[D26] *Stadium* abutting over aforesaid *Stadium* towards the east going towards the south.

[D26.1] Edward Bennett holds one inclosure called Infordes Combe lying lengthways by the parish of Shillingston abutting towards the east over Inford way and containing 18 acres.

[D26.2] John Standley holds at the western end of the aforesaid close one inclosure with appurtenances lying near the aforesaid parish of Shillingston and containing 5 acres.

[D26.3] Thomas Lynsey holds one piece of land containing 3 acres abutting towards the east over the close of Richard Collins.

[D26.4] John Iles holds near there 3 acres.

[D26.5] John Vallevine holds 1 acre.

[D26.6] John Stevens holds 3 acres.

[D26.7] Alice Dennis holds 1 acre.

[D26.8] John Rogers holds 3 acres.

[D26.9] The same John holds there 1 acre.

[D26.10] Alice Dennis holds there 1 acre.

[D26. 11] John Standley holds there 2 acres lying lengthways by Norden.

*

[D27] *Stadium* abutting over the aforesaid *Stadium* towards the east going towards the south

[D27.1] Edward Bennett holds there one piece of land containing 10 acres.

[D27.2] John Shepherde holds there one piece of land containing 1½ acres lying lengthways by Norden.

[D27.3] Edith Rogers holds at the western end of the previous piece one piece of land containing one acre and a half with appurtenances lying lengthways by Northdon.

[D27.4] John Rogers holds at the eastern end of the aforesaid piece one piece of land lying lengthways near Norden aforesaid abutting to the west over Tymplin and containing 2 acres.

*

Memorandum: there is there one piece of land called Norden with Epingrout and Welsley with appurtenances lying between land of diverse tenements for each part and containing 73 acres, 1 rood, 33 perches.

[Marginal annotation: Norden is used from the eve of the feast of Pentecost up to the feast of All Saints as common meadow land, and from that feast until the Sunday from after the middle of the month of March for the sheep of the tenants and from that day it will lie fallow until the evening of the said Pentecost.]

There is also near there one great piece of land called Infordes Combe which extends to the west near the way leading to Bandsley Gate between the land of diverse tenements on the south and the land of Edward Bennett, John Standley and the land lying in the parish of Shillingston to the north and containing 138 acres, 2 roods and 20 perches.

[Marginal annotation: Common pasture for the sheep of the tenements of Durweston].

There is also one great pasture called Durweston Fore Downe, Durweston Sheepdowne lying together to the west of the aforesaid road leading from Durweston to Bandsley Gate and containing altogether 185 acres 1 rood and 22 perches.

[Marginal annotation: Common pasture for the sheep of the tenants of Durweston].

There is also there one great pasture called Durweston Cowpasture with appurtenances lying between Durweston sheep pasture to the north and Knighton cowpasture to the south abutting towards the west over land lying in the parish of Turnworth and containing 83 acres. 15 perches.

[Marginal annotation: Common for the sheep from the eve of the birth of Our Lord to the feast of the Purification of Holy Virgin Mary and from that day lying fallow until the Feast of the Holy Cross in the month of May and then is common land for the said also tenements until the first vigil.

Memorandum: there are 4 last pieces in the said fields of Durweston which similarly are newly used for sheep pasture by the tenants of the said manor on which each tenant can take care of his sheep according to the proportion and quantity of their tenancy. At Christmas eve annually or at the feast of purification of the Holy Mary, etc.

[Marginal annotation, presumably referring to a contemporary rental: this varies according to what is given in the margin].

*

The tenants' days work due to the farm:

William Domine 3 days	)	
Morgan Snell 3 days	)	This means
William Franklyn 3 days	)	1 day at weeding
John Pelley 3 days	)	1 day at harvesting
William Stone 3 days	)	The third at reaping
Nicholas Evered 3 days	)	
James Provitt 3 days	)	

Memorandum: that all these which do those days works are tenants within the tithing of Knighton.

Memorandum That the tenants of Knighton aforesaid in the respect of the said days' work do challenge one customary dinner at Christmas. [ie. The tenants contend that they should receive one dinner at Christmas as an estover]

*

Out Rents:

Firstly all the Law Days of the lord's court at Pimperne   10s 4d.

Memorandum: this court is the one half the Queen's the other half Sir Richard Rogers Knight.

No freeholders within the manor save only the Rectory.

And the said Thomas Kitson, knight, is the only lord of the said manor and the undoubted patron of the parish church of Durweston aforesaid and this is worth now per annum [blank].

And by me Thomas Wright.

APPENDIX A

Calendar of the abstract of copyholds taken at Okeford Fitzpaine in 1582.
S.R.O. HA 528/ 27

The numbers at the beginning of each paragraph refers to the text of the 1584 survey. The first name given is that of the person who presented their copies of court roll and indenture in May 1562.

[Several of the entries are said to be estimated others are most likely to have been roughly measured by pacing, but it is thought that none of the areas were measured properly until Wright came to Dorset in 1583.]

[English]
An abstract of the copies of the said manor taken the 26th May 1582

[4] **Henry Reynolds** showed forth a copy bearing date 14 April 1462 by which it appears he and Roger his brother took the reversion of a tenement and 46 acres of land, meadow and pasture by estimation and paid for fine of that grant £50. Rent £1 9*s*..

[4] **The same Henry** showed forth another copy dated 22 April 1568, by which it appears that John Reynolds, son of the aid Henry, took the reversion of the premises and paid the fine £8. Rent 4*d*.. Two lives remaining.

[35] **William Forde** showed copy bearing the day and date abovesaid, by which it appears that he and John Berryman took up for term of their lives and the life of the longer liver one tenement, with appurtenances, containing by estimation 13 acres of arable land, 6 closes containing by estimation 21 acres and 1½ acres of meadow. Fine £50. Rent 18*s*.. Two lives remaining.

[44] **Jasper Kene** son of Hugh Kene showed a copy dated 8 June 1564 by which it appears that the said Jasper and Agnes Kene, his sister, took up the reversion of one tenement and 34 acres of land, meadow and pasture. Fine £26 13*s*. 4*d*.. Rent £1 3*s*.. Two lives remaining.

[30] **John Whyte**, son of William Whyte, showed a copy 8 June 1564, by which it

appears that the said John Whyte and Edward his brother took up the reversion of one tenement with appurtenances containing by estimation 10 acres of land lying in two fields, five closes of pasture containing 50 acres and 1 acre of meadow. Fine £60. Rent £3 1*s*. 10*d*.. Three lives remaining.

[Heading] 14 April 1562

[7] William Whyte showed a copy dated the said day and year by which it appears that the said William and Walter Whyte, sons of John Whyte, took up the reversion of one tenement with appurtenances containing seven acres of arable land, lying in two fields, three closes of land and pasture containing by estimation 11 acres and 1 acre of meadow. Fine £16. Rent 2*s*. 10*d*.. Two lives remaining.

[3] Henry Wakeforde showed forth a copy, dated as before, by which it appears that the said Henry and Elene his daughter took one tenement which it appears contained, by estimation, 24 acres of arable and pasture and one rood of meadow. Fine £30. Rent 14*s*. 2*d*.. Two lives remaining.

[47] David Byles and William, his son, took by a copy, dated as before, one tenement built in West Street containing by estimation 9½ acres of inclosed land and pasture formerly held by John Norman. Fine £24. Rent 10*s*. 1*d*.. Two lives remaining: Alice Byles, widow of David, holds in her widowhood.

[39] Alice Lyndsey showed a copy dated as before by which it appears that Roger Lyndesey and Robert Lyndesey, sons of William Lyndesey took up the reversion of two tenements which contain 34 acres and 1 rood of inclosed land, diverse pieces and 1 acre of meadow. Fine £33. Rent 17*s*. 10*d*.. Two lives remaining: Alice holds during her widowhood.

[36] Agnes Whyte showed a copy dated 14 April 1521 by which it appears that Richard Whyte took up a reversion of one tenement containing 4 acres of land lying in two fields, 4 closes of land and pasture containing 20 acres and 1 acre of meadow, by which copy she claims her widow's estate. Rent £1 17*s*. 8*d*.. Three lives remaining: John and Robert in reversion.

[36] Agnes Whyte , widow of Richard, showed forth a copy dated 8 June 1564 by which it appears that Robert Whyte and Margery Whyte, children of Richard Whyte, took the reversion of one tenement containing by estimation 12 acres of land and meadow. Fine £8. Rent 5*s*. 11*d*.. Three lives remaining (sic.): Agnes in her own right, Richard, Robert and Margery in reversion.

[5] John Howe son of William Howe brought forth a copy dated as before by which he and William took a cottage with appurtenances containing by estimation 9 acres of land and pasture and one acre of meadow in a close. Fine £18. Rent 7*s.*. Two lives remaining: Christian in her widowhood and John Howe.

[5] **John Howe** showed a copy dated 22 April 1577 he and Alexander took up the reversion of one tenement in Whytestrete containing 11 acres of land lying in a close called Orber, 1 close of pasture called Casles containing 8 acres, two closes of pasture adjacent containing 4 acres, 1 close of meadow called Yemeade containing 5 acres, 1 close of pasture containing 2 acres called Lysworth and 6 closes of land and pasture called South Ley containing 40 acres. Fine £40. Rent £2 12*s.* 9*d.*. Three lives remaining: Edward in possession and John and Alexander in reversion.

[51] **John Frampton** showed a copy dated 8 June 1564 by which he and Joseph his brother took up the reversion of 1 tenement in Okeford containing by estimation 27 acres of land, meadow and pasture. Fine £16. Rent 10*s.* 2*d.*. Two lives remaining: Lawrence Frampton in possession and John Frampton in reversion.

[34] **John Saye and Richard Saye** his brother showed a copy dated 4 September 1571 by which they took the reversion on 1 tenement containing 10 acres of land lying in two fields, 6 closes of land and pasture containing 20 acres and 3 acres of meadow. Fine £60. Rent £1 7*s.*. Three lives remaining: Elizabeth Saye, widow, and John and Richard in reversion.

 [33] **Robert Hyne** brought a copy dated 8 June 1564 by which he and Walter Tucker took 1 tenement containing 20 acres of land and meadow. Fine £24. Rent 17s. 1d.. Two lives remaining: Robert Hyne and Walter Tucker.

[36] **John White,** mercer, and Robert Whyte, his brother, showed a copy dated 14 April 1562 by which they took the reversion of 1 tenement, with appurtenances, containing 1 orchard and 7 closes of land and pasture, containing by estimation 30 acres, and 1 acre of meadow. Fine £26. Rent £1 8*s.* 4*d.*. Three lives remaining: Agnes Whyte in her widowhood and John and Robert in reversion.

[?] **The same John Whyte** showed a copy dated 1 December 1572 by which he and John, his son, took up one cottage containing 1 acre of land and 3 closes of pasture containing 8 acres and 1 paroke of meadow containing 3 roods, which were surrendered by John Ramsbut and William and Edward his sons. Fine £6. Rent [blank]. Two lives remaining: John in possession and John his son.

[29] **Margery Mullett and Helen** her sister showed a copy dated 15 May 1580 by which she took the reversion of 1 cottage with appurtenances and 7½ acres of land and pasture and 2 acres of meadow in the tenure of Edward Williams. Fine £12 6*s.* 8*d.*. Three lives remaining: Edward Williams in possession and Margery and Helen Mullett. [Marginal annotation: This copy not entered in the court rolls. Remember

to seke the court rolls].

[50] Morgan Bythewood brought forth a copy dated 30 October 1564 by which he and William his brother took the reversion of one tenement, with appurtenances, called Strowde, containing 6 closes of land and pasture, containing by estimation 20 acres, and 6 acres of meadow. Fine £20. Rent 10*s*. 3½*d*.. Two lives remaining: John Bythewood and Morgan his son in reversion.

[8] Richard Prower, son of Roger Prower, and Alice Henning showed a copy dated 4 September 1571 by which they took up the reversion of two tenements, containing by estimation 47 acres of inclosed land and pasture, and 3 acres of meadow. Fine £76. Rent 18*s*. 9*d*.. Two lives remaining: Richard and Alice.

[58] Thomas Snowke showed a copy dated 8 June 1564 by which he and Thomas, his son, took the reversion of 1 tenement, with appurtenances, containing by estimation 18 acres of land and 3 acres of meadow. Fine £36 13*s*. 4*d*.. Rent 18*s*. 8*d*.. Two lives remaining: Thomas and Thomas.

[27] Robert Skott, son of Robert Skott, showed a copy dated 8 June 1564 by which he took reversion of one tenement containing 20 acres of land and meadow called Churchewaye, one cottage containing 2 acres of land, 1 close called Fylgrove containing 4½ acres, 1½ acres called Langstone, 1 grain water mill, 1 close called Greate Gardyn containing by estimation 8 acres, 1 stable with a close of land containing 1½ acres called Courte Close and Fysheponds, 1 close of pasture called Batiehalle containing 4 acres, 1 close of arable called new close containing 5 acres, 1 cottage containing 4 closes of land and pasture containing 10 acres, and 2 acres of meadow. Fine £60. Rent £2 14*s*. 4½*d*.. Two lives remaining: Morgan Scott, widow, and Robert Scott.

[31] John Osmond and Richard Osmond his brother showed a copy dated 3 November 1574 by which they took the reversion of two tenements and their appurtenances containing by estimation 39 acres of land and pasture, 3 acres of meadow, a parcel of land called Haycrofte containing 10 acres, 1 close of pasture called Culverhouse containing 1 acre – except for a dovehouse in Culverhouse. Fine 4s. [Marginal annotation: "it appears that this fine was but for changing of a name]. Rent £1 16*s*. 8*d*.. Three lives remaining: Joan Osmond, widow, Richard and John.

The same John Osmond showed a copy dated 14 June 1580 by which he and Edward, his son, took the dovehouse surrendered by John Henning. Fine 5*s*.. Rent 1*d*..
Two lives remaining: John and Edward. [Note at side says this dove house pulled down without licence as it does appear]

[60] Edward Scotte, son of John Skotte showed a copy dated 8 June 1564 by which he and Robert, his brother, took reversion of one tenement containing by estimation

21½ acres of land, meadow and pasture. Fine £26 13s. 4d.. Rent 18s. 8d.. Three lives remaining: Chura[?] Scott, widow, Edward Scott and John Scott.

[13] William Chepman showed a copy dated 14 April 1562 by which he and Laurence, his son, took one tenement and 18 acres of inclosed land and pasture. Fine £40. Rent 16s. 2d.. Two lives remaining.

[11] Henry Forde showed a copy dated 13 August 1574 by which he and Henry and Walter, his sons, took the reversion of one tenement and 40 acres of land and pasture and 2 acres of meadow inclosed in diverse inclosures. Also another tenement containing 5 acres of land and pasture. Fine £50. Rent £2 3s. 3d.. Three lives remaining: Henry, Henry and Walter.

[6] William Mayowe showed a copy dated [blank] by which he took the reversion of 1 tenement with 23½ acres of inclosed land and pasture. Fine £30. Rent 19s. 2d.. Two lives remaining: Agnes Mayowe, widow, and William Mayowe.

[38] Roger Whyte showed a copy dated 14 April 1562 by which he and William Whyte, his father, took 1 cottage containing by estimation 9 acres of inclosed land and pasture. Fine £22. Rent 3s. 8d.. Two lives: the widow of William and Roger.

[55] John Mayhoo and Agnes wife showed a copy dated 14 November 1567 by which they took on one tenement in Fyttleforde containing, by estimation, 18 acres of inclosed pasture and 3½ acres of meadow surrendered by Walter Apowle and Joan his wife. Fine 4s. 4d.. Rent 18s. 4d.. Two lives remaining.

[14] Robert Pope showed a copy dated 14 June 1580 by which he and Morgan Pope took the reversion of one tenement containing, by estimation 27 acres of inclosed arable and pasture. Fine £26 13s. 4d.. Rent £1 6s. 0½d.. Two lives remaining: Robert and Morgan.

[15] Emma Russell, widow, holds by copy 1 tenement containing 16 acres of of land, meadow and pasture. Fine £16. Rent 11s. 10d.. Three lives remaining: Emma Russell, John Russell and John Norman.

[Latin]

[43] Henry Shottow, son of John Shottow, by a copy dated 14 April 1562 took the reversion of 1 tenement 28 acres of pasture and 2 acres of meadow. Fine £33. Rent 20s. 11d.. Lives remaining: John & Henry.

[?] Hugh Howchins by a copy dated 22 April 1577 took, for himself and William Maio junior, one messuage with tenement containing 24 acres of land and meadow. Fine

£30. Rent £1 0s. 6d.. Two lives remaining; Agnes Maio, widow, and reversion to Hugh Howchyns.

[48] **Richard Foote** by a copy dated 8 June 1565 took, for himself and Mathew, son of William Foote, reversion of 1 tenement and 48 acres of land, meadow and pasture. Fine £26 13s. 4d.. Rent 26s.7d.. Two lives remaining: Mathew Strowd and Richard Strowd (sic.).

[?] **John Philips** and John Phillips by a copy dated 23 March in the reign of Henry VIII took one tenement in West Strete and another tenement called Strowde, 6 acres of land lying in two fields, 7 closes of land and pasture containing an estimated 22 acres and 4 acres of meadow. Fine £50. Rent £1 10s. 3½d.. One life remaining: John Philips junior.

[1] **Edward Eyles** and Alice Eyles, in a copy dated 8 June 1564, took the reversion of 1 tenement containing by estimation 48 acres of land, meadow and pasture. Fine: £35. Rent £1 16s. 1d.. Three lives remaining: John Eyles, Edward Eyles and Alice Eyles.

[2] **William Pelly** and Thomas Pelle, in a copy dated 8 June 1564, took reversion of 1 cottage and 3 closes containing by estimation 8 acres of pasture and meadow Fine £613s. 4d. Rent 6s. 8d.. Two lives remaining: William and Thomas.

[10] **John Newton** and Robert Newton in a copy dated 8 June 1564 took reversion of a cottage containing by estimation 8 acres of meadow and pasture. Fine £6 13s. 4d.. Rent 5s. 10d.. Two lives remaining: John and Robert.

[12] **Thomas Harrys** and William Harrys in a copy dated 14 April 1562 took 2 tenements containing by estimation 42 acres of land and pasture and 4 acres of meadow. Fine £70. Rent £1 14s. 3d.. Two lives remaining: William Harris and Alice Harrys, widow.

[21] **Joseph Harrys** and Barsabe his sister, by a copy dated 14 March 1580 took 1 cottage near the cemetery of Okeford and 1 waste plot with garden, 1 parcel of land, 1½ acres called Mawrydge. Fine 10s.. Rent 2s.. Two lives remaining: Joseph and Barsabe.

[45] **Richard Goby** and Henry Goby in a copy dated 3 October 1575 took 11 acres of land, meadow and pasture surrendered by John Sevior. Fine £4. Rent 10s. 10½d.. Two lives remaining: Richard and Henry.

[57] **Henry Brigg and Joseph Brigg in a copy dated 22 April** 1577 took a vacant plot of land in the south part of Fiddleford measuring 7 rods in breadth by 4 rods in breadth (sic.). Fine nothing. Rent 2s.. Two lives remaining: Henry and Joseph.

APPENDIX B

Suggested references for the abbreviations shown on the Okeford Fitzpaine map of 1782.

The cartographer used abbreviations of surnames to differentiate the tenements shown on the map. There is no surviving, contemporary survey so the following suggestions have been made with reference to later documents. Where the same surname is given for different letter combinations, this is either referring different members of the same family, or different tenements. If no suggestion can be given the reference has been omitted.

A	Alport	Fr	Ford	R	Ridout
B	Bennett	Fu	Furnell	Ra	Raynolds
Ba	Baldwin	G	Gawler	Rb	Robens?
Bd	Bridge	Ga	Galton	Ro?	Robens?
Bi	Bird	H	Hardy?	Ru	Reynolds
Bk	Blake	Ha	Hallett? Haskell?	Ry	Reynolds
Bl	Butler?		Hayward?	S	Seymour
Br	Bridge, Thomas?	J	Jeans? James?	Sc	Score?
Bs	Bastard	K	Kerley	S.t	St. Lo
Bt	Bartlett	Ka	Kaines	T	Twynihoe or
Bu	Bunter	La	Lambert		Templeman
Bv	Bennett?	M	Mundy	Th	Thornhill?
Bw	Brown	Me	Melmouth	Thv	Thornhill?
Bwr	Brown	Mi	Mitchell	Tz	Tizard
C	Chapman?	Pa	Pope?	Wa	Watts
Ca	Carter	Pd	Pope	Wh	White? Whiffen?
Cl	Clench	Ph	Phelps		Woolridge?
Cr	Crew?	Pi	Pope	Y	Young
D	Downe	Pl	Pleydell	Ya	Yeatman
Da	Dawson	Po	Pope	V	Vater
E	Etheridge	Pp	Pope	W	Williams?
F	Feltham	Pr	Prower		

INDEX